Book of the Heart

STUDIES
IN IMAGINATION

A series edited in collaboration with
The Institute for the Study of Imagination

•

The Planets Within, Thomas Moore
Facing the World with Soul, Robert Sardello
Archetypal Imagination, Noel Cobb

Book of the Heart

The Poetics, Letters, and Life of John Keats

Andrés Rodríguez

Lindisfarne Press

Published in the United States by Lindisfarne Press,
R.R. 4, Box 94 A-1, Hudson, New York 12534

LIBRARY OF CONGRESS CATALOGING-IN-PUBLICATION DATA

Rodríguez, Andrés, 1955–
Book of the heart : the poetics, letters, and life of John Keats / Andrés Rodríguez.
—(Studies in imagination)
Includes bibliographical references and index.
ISBN 0-940262-57-6 (paper)
1. Keats, John, 1795–1821. 2. Poets, English—19th century—Correspondence. 3. Poets, English—19th century—Biography. 4. English letters—History and criticism. I. Title. II. Series.
PR4836.R52 1993
821'.7—dc20 92-44895
[B] CIP
r92

Cover painting of John Keats by William Hilton after Joseph Severn, original 1819. Oil on canvas, 76.2 x 63.5 cm. Courtesy of the National Portrait Gallery, London.

Cover design: Barbara Richey

10 9 8 7 6 5 4 3 2 1

Printed in the United States of America

CONTENTS

In memory of my mother

I have no child, I have nothing but a book,
Nothing but that to prove your blood and mine.

Preface

John Keats was born of humble origin in London on October 31, 1795, and died of tuberculosis in Rome on February 23, 1821. He wrote some 150 poems and stands, as he had hoped, "among the English Poets" for all time. From the first publication of Keats's letters, up to the present, readers have been impressed with both the character of the young poet and the expression of his mind in what has become a unique legacy. Writing a book on Keats, the man and the poet, is unthinkable without the letters. Yet the letters themselves are the proper subject of a book, a legacy equally as precious as the poems. This book treats Keats's letters as works of art and autobiography, focussing on the threads of genius and fresh human wisdom that runs through all of them.

The texts of the letters used in this study are taken from *The Letters of John Keats 1814-1821*, edited by Hyder Edward Rollins, in two volumes, published by Harvard University Press in 1958. Letters are referred to by the dates assigned by Rollins in his authoritative edition. The texts of the poems are taken from *The Poems of John Keats*, edited by Jack Stillinger, published by the Belknap Press of Harvard University in 1978, except in those cases where the poems appear in Keats's letters. All letters and poems are reproduced in keeping with the printed versions collated in these two scholarly works. Readers may wish to consult earlier editions of Keats's letters for their commentaries and annotations (see the selected bibliography at the end of this work). All other letters, such as those of the Keats circle of family and friends, are cited in the notes. The etymologies of words from Keats's poems and letters are taken from *The Oxford Dictionary of English Etymology*, edited by C.T. Onions, published by the Clarendon Press at Oxford in 1966.

I am indebted to the great scholarship on Keats, and most obviously to Keats biographers, in particular Walter Jackson Bate, Aileen Ward, and Robert Gittings. Without their works this book could not have been written. I am grateful to former teachers for their advice and criticism: Professors Gabriel Berns, Michael H. Cowan, and Thomas A. Vogler, who read the manuscript in its beginnings. I am grateful as well to Professor Norman O. Brown for his words in conversations and letters. Needless to say, none of these persons are in any way responsible for the conclusions presented. I owe special thanks to two poets and former teachers who have helped and guided and encouraged me in very different but equally special ways: W.S. Di Piero and Duncan McNaughton. Whatever is worthwhile here has been derived from their influence and is a tribute to them.

Finally, I dedicate this book to the memory of my mother. With her solicitude always present, she has taken me into Keats, and now takes me further toward what she could not before—a new relation which turns grief inside out forever.

INTRODUCTION

A Noisy, Savage Genius

There are many illuminating approaches to the study of the poetical works of John Keats. All are valuable and gain for the reader, scholar, or poet material and modalities of real practical use. In a great English author like Keats, one has readily available a vast treasure of critical insights, all of which deal with, at some point, what Keats says in his own letters about himself, about his views of poetry, and about the relations between the two. "And the more one studies Keats's letters the more, I believe, one becomes convinced that the critics who are not too proud to accept Keats's self-analysis are wiser than those who, prompted by a serene vanity and a misplaced confidence in their own analytical powers, present us with a Keats in their own image."[1] So wrote M.R. Ridley fifty-nine years ago. In the following study, I attempt to apply Ridley's conviction to Keats's letters as a whole and profit from them. For it is not enough, I believe, only to read Keats's poems in the light of his letters. The *Letters* alone contain a vast poetics.

Poetics itself is at issue here, and poetics needs not in the least be confined to the poem. The range of poetics matches the action of making a poem insofar as each may claim or know or propose to include anything germane, necessary, and possible to its continuity and fixity. For the poetics of a Romantic like Keats, possibility and process and redefinition are themselves idealizations, registering the encounter between the external

---

1. M.R. Ridley, *Keats' Craftsmanship* (Oxford: Clarendon Press, 1933), 4. Hereafter cited as Ridley.

and interior worlds. One central question of the study here is: Are Keats's letters apt to be, on the whole, more advanced as poetics than his poems? What liberty of mind, what spaciousness of thought, may be more available to Keats in the *Letters* than in the composition of his poems? The crux is poetics itself, not as a *meta-* anything but as in fact the driving occupation of a poet such that his or her poems are evidences of the same driving occupation and contain the markers pointing to its grasp and interpretation; but also that any evidence of the man or woman (letters, remarks, known deeds) testifies to poetics, since poetics is not limited finally to the making of poems but involves life itself in the largest possible sense.

What is a poetics? How do you make one? Where does it come from? Poetics is everything most beautiful or important to a poet whereby the connections are arrived at (to adopt Keats's phrase) by "a regular stepping of the Imagination." It comes first and foremost from the real world, the world that matters, that of men and women and things, "the world apprehended by the senses and feelings, where the imagination has its unfettered scope."[2] Poetics comes from being, and its truth or beauty is proved upon our pulses. "Man lives by pulses," Emerson wrote. He was speaking of experience. And our chief experiences, he believed, were casual and have been casualties. Who cannot accept the realism of such an extreme picture of life? But Emerson also recognized a "mid-world," between the extremes of good and bad, which we may climb into and find there "the equator of life, of thought, of spirit, of poetry—a narrow belt."[3] This "narrow belt" is by no means the only place where a poet can or should reside. Keats not only flew to this middle zone "on the viewless wings of Poesy." He returned from his flights there to test or prove what was beautiful and true (and a truth was gained by a clear perception of its beauty) upon those extremes constituting our experience. This journey

---

2. Ridley, 6.

3. "Experience," *Essays: Second Series* (Boston: Houghton Mifflin, 1903-1904), 62. Hereafter cited as Emerson.

was not so much a constant shuttling between equator and the poles of life as it was an advance, an ordered progress, not "that of the reasoner; but the steps of the progress are those of imagination."[4]

Experience certainly has a great deal to do with poetics. But a poetics must be made. Poetics can be given to one so long as one makes the connections between all that is there and not there. That of course depends on imagination. Though some may dispute the veracity, even the reality, of the imagination (a stupid or empty skepticism to me), Keats knew it to be real when he was writing both letters and poems. As he felt it, the imagination was an act of desire—a desire for reality transfigured into a more perfect image of the real. His experience of the real was essentially religious. But for Keats, and for Emerson, the key to the meaning of experience lay in the very motions of organic life, in its change, motion, and rhythm. It also lay in the experience of the heroes of the past, whether they were real or imaginary like Hamlet. As the historian of myth and science Giorgio de Santillana notes, such heroes are all equally present in the realm of "true existence." What has interested me most in writing about Keats's *Letters* is this living reality as it helped him to form a poetics of art and truths of self-restoration.

For me the most important element in Keats's *Letters* is the demand of writing itself, intensely accepted, urgent and honest. Keats writes as if everything is at stake. So much of anything he writes is under this demand: that it may as well be the last page. So too Emily Dickinson in her letters writes with that same urgency or heat. This is also true of Antonio Gramsci's "letters from prison," which are totally inspiring works of his life, circumstance, and desire to achieve real usefulness. For the matter is not literary or what letters can be said to reveal about the character of the author vis-à-vis his or her work; rather, Keats's *Letters* are primary *as* work. They are work, equal at their best to the best of the poems, and essential to the greater term of poetics.

---

4. Ridley, 5.

Keats's sincerity, like that of Emily Dickinson or Robert Burns, is the ground of one's attraction to and affection for him. But instead of taking that sincerity as a charm of naive personality, we must take it as *formal* evidence testifying to a more and more complex intelligence and *its* needs. I do not think Keats's letters are designed to do anything more than his poems do. The question is, What *do* they do, and how? Keats wrote letters because he could and had to; and since he was still understandably caught in the inherited suppositions of verse and prosody, his poems on the whole remain conventional in that respect, albeit warm and exact in their words. But there is overflow apart from those conventions, and it would have expression in the *Letters.* That overflow, unencumbered by formal supposition, has seemed to provide some liberation of form allowing Keats's mind to move ahead, or deeper, into what the prosodic inheritance of "frame" allowed.

Such flow and liberation is what I take to be, at the outset of this study, Keats's "life of allegory." Allegory, which Keats called "figurative" in his letter to America (February 19, 1819), is the poesis or *making* one needs to live in a universe that binds all things, human and natural, in mystery. For Keats, "Mystery" (a recurrent term in the *Letters*) is intimately related to a "life of any worth." It is not a determination but rather the best of all possible time. That is, mystery is its own action that frees humanity from the world of circumstance and from the worn-out frame of self-centeredness. (And there is, along with this, an implied struggle between the "Man of Achievement" and the "Man of Power.") Keats did not mean that we act out a kind of fable or myth to replace what is antithetical to the "figurative," namely circumstance or harsh reality. His allegory is the advocacy of tapping into a ground which had not existed in the two centuries of science and satire since Shakespeare. The result was that allegory became a kind of "romance," a spiritual adventure. This creativity in the biography is what I track and explore, convinced that there is a weaving in the *Letters* of "allegory," "mystery," "beauty," "truth," "salvation," and so on. This weave is the poet's greatest action in time, and the construction Keats performs, in the writing of his letters, is at the very least a middle zone where fact and inspiration are (however unevenly) fused.

The response to Keats's *Letters* has ranged from admiration to outright hostility and disgust. In the period immediately following his death, the detractors were many and the language of vituperation incredibly cruel. I do not know how many English poets were part of the attack, but among them were Algernon Swinburne, Matthew Arnold (to an extent), and Coventry Patmore. The harshest criticism was reserved for Keats's letters to his fiancée Fanny Brawne, which were deemed shocking examples of Keats's "lustful" indulgence and "Cockney vulgarity."[5] I feel this says more about the Victorians' sexual obsession than it does about Keats's love letters. Amid all the hostility, Gerard Manley Hopkins alone saw something compelling in Keats's letters. In a letter to Patmore on the subject of Keats's "life of Sensations rather than of Thoughts," Hopkins wrote: "I feel and see in him the beginning of something opposite this, of an interest in higher things, and of powerful and active thoughts."[6] Such testimony not only shows one poet's interest in the creativity of another; it also measures the genius of Keats's art, a genius that concerns the true uses of thought in poetry.

The twentieth century has shown a much needed appreciation of Keats's *Letters*, a new or more real attempt to communicate the truth of his other poetic work. In an essay titled "Shelley and Keats" (1933), T.S. Eliot found Keats's letters "attractive" and admired "the general brilliance and profundity of the observations" scattered throughout them. "Their merit," Eliot stated, is as "models of correspondence."[7] W.H. Auden

5. See Hyder E. Rollins, ed., *The Letters of John Keats*, vol. I (Cambridge: Harvard University Press, 1958), 6-7. Hereafter cited as Rollins.

6. See Claude Colleer Abbott, ed., *Further Letters of Gerard Manley Hopkins* (London: Oxford University Press, 1956), 386.

7. T.S. Eliot, "Shelley and Keats," *The Use of Poetry and the Use of Criticism* (London: Faber and Faber, 1933), 101.

praised the letters for their Shakespearean vigor and spoke of the day when they might be more widely read than the poems.[8] And Charles Olson, one of the most thought-provoking of all readers of Keats's *Letters,* wondered how Keats could write such excellent letters while the poems remained so poor.[9] I share the enthusiasm but not the kind of praise all three authors have bestowed. Keats had to write letters before he could embody their truths in poems. Yet his letters stand on their own as testaments to poetic truth. Keats's letters, like his poems, release a flow that no other form can contain, and such flow is not by any means simply an emotional torrent. He brings energies into half-conscious play in and through words. All this came about as a development over time which the letters faithfully track.

To write of the *Letters* is necessarily to tell Keats's story. It's not a long one. It begins with his birth in 1795 to Thomas Keats and Frances Jennings. He was the oldest of four children: his brothers were George and Tom, his sister Frances Mary ("Fanny"). Their father, who had worked as a livery-stable keeper in the northern outskirts of London, died in 1804 as a result of being thrown from his horse. That same year the Keats children went to live with their maternal grandparents, John and Alice Jennings, in the village of Edmonton. In 1810 Keats's mother died of consumption after a sudden decline, and Mrs. Jennings was appointed guardian for the Keats children. She in turn placed their estate in the charge of two trustees, one of whom was Richard Abbey, a dishonest, unfeeling businessman of some prominence. It was Abbey who removed Keats from school and apprenticed him to a surgeon. In 1814 he began to write his first poems. A year later he entered Guy's Hospital in London as a student, and continued to write verse. In 1816 he passed his examination and became eligible to practice as an

---

8. See Rollins, I, 8

9. Olson's remark, related to me by poet Kenneth Irby, overstates his own opinion of the facts.

apothecary. Keats never did practice medicine, for this was the year in which he began his career as a poet.[10]

This was also the time when Keats began writing letters. By the early nineteenth century, letters-as-literature were a definite tradition. One thinks of the letters of Lady Mary Wortley Montague, Thomas Gray, Horace Walpole, and John Wilmot, Earl of Rochester, to name a few of the most well-known eighteenth-century letter writers in England. Such letters apparently reflect a mode of expression as common as conversation itself. And yet what is anything but common is the style—highly sophisticated and cultivated, retaining a seventeenth-century aristocratic bias. "Wit" distinguishes letter-writing of this period, just as it marks the literature, a literature addressed to readers who admired intellectual prose.

In *The Converse of the Pen* (1986), Bruce Redford argues that the eighteenth-century familiar-letter writer was "committed to [in Samuel Johnson's phrase]'prattling on paper'." Since conversation depends on "presence," Redford contends, the letter writer must "find satisfactory equivalents to the resources of an actor: the ironic intonation, the raised eyebrow, the rueful smile, the sudden whisper, the emphatic change of posture, the meaningful glance across the room."[11] This practice—a raid upon "the public forms of drama and satire"—turns the familiar letter into a form of "*repraesentatio,* an exercise in 'making present' like the performance of a play." The eighteenth-century familiar letter, he claims, both *creates* and *reflects* a context at once. Redford's study is thorough and helpful. But I feel he is impatient to leave the familiar letter unfixed to a critical apparatus. He wishes to formulate "appropriate aesthetic

10. Keats's first known poem, "Imitation of Spenser," was written early in 1814. His friend Charles Brown reported that it was Spenser's *Faerie Queen* which awakened Keats's genius: "In Spenser's fairy land he was enchanted...till, enamoured of the [Spenserian] stanza he attempted to imitate it, and succeeded." See Hyder E. Rollins, ed., *The Keats Circle: Letters and Papers 1816-1879*, vol. 2 (Cambridge: Harvard University Press, 1948), 55. Hereafter cited as *The Keats Circle*.

11. Bruce Redford, *The Converse of the Pen* (Chicago: University of Chicago Press, 1986), 5-6.

criteria" in discussing this subject. To me, what is more appropriate and important than aesthetic criteria, especially in studying the letters of Keats, is seeking to answer the questions about the life of poetry that, for one reason or another, demand some response.

But was Keats consciously aware of being in a tradition concerning his letters to family and friends? It would be hard to argue that he was, that his letters are self-conscious, rhetorical acts within an epistolary tradition containing a whole set of conventions and strategies. The less well-educated population in Europe was becoming increasingly literate by the second half of the eighteenth century, and by the early nineteenth century people wrote letters as normally as we talk on the telephone, and for much the same reasons. The fact that Keats writes penetrating things in his letters means that his was a poetic intelligence that never ceased to look at the world with faith, understanding, and love. And the fact that he wrote to friends who he knew would keep his letters only proves the deep, abiding feeling shared by these people. We should feel grateful that such friends as Charles Brown and Richard Woodhouse kept his letters, for us, after his death.

Keats shares with the eighteenth-century letter writers an interest in pure ideas and social intimacy. But the more I read his letters, the more I am led to conclude that the familiar letter with Keats is really different from the model Redford proposes. It is closer to the idea that Susan J. Wolfson proposes in an essay "Keats the Letter-Writer: Epistolary Poetics" (1982). Calling Keats's letters "creative events in their own right," Wolfson argues that they enact "processes of mind" as well as possess a "performative character."[12] She distinguishes between two kinds of epistolary staging in the *Letters*: "that of society and business," and (Keats's "favored"), that of "the theatre of his own mind, wherein the mind's various actions and attitudes

---

12. Susan J. Wolfson, "Keats the Letter-Writer: Epistolary Poetics," *Romanticism Past and Present* 6, 2 (1982), 43-61.

can be framed as performances to be studied for their plays of error or energy. Epistolary occasions are often such performances for Keats, complete with greetings, entertainments, and a bow." I find common ground with Wolfson, whose work on Keats's letters I was not aware of while writing this book. However, the way I look at Keats informs me that, contrary to Wolfson's view that the *Letters* demonstrate one category of poetics (epistolation) and the poems another, there is only one poetics. Keats's life and art has a remarkable wholeness that is everywhere evident in all he did and wrote.

For Keats, the poet and the letter writer are the same; his words embody a poetics that is meant for real use. By "use" I mean the opposite of aesthetics, which does not mean there is no beauty involved in Keats's poetics. On the contrary, the beauty there is breathtaking. But more than verbal artifact, certainly much more than conversation, even more than performance or presence (though that is no small thing), the letters of John Keats involve noetic vision.[13] In the *Letters* one finds a poet's interpretation of the universe, a vivid account of the nature of the whole of life, along with a portrait of a young man whose mode of awareness was at once erotic and self-critical: erotic in the desire to fly "on the viewless wings of Poesy" and to share this flight with others; self-critical in the sense of continually falling short of definitiveness and having to adjust and begin again with greater nerve and strength. This running together, this pushing and pulling, of Keats's philosophical interests and his sensualism, is very interesting and conforms to my sense of the artist. This is the real story, amid biographical or historical facts, to follow: Keats's thought and feeling.

In telling Keats's story through his letters, I have tried to apply my own imagination while making use of all literature and knowledge as I now know them absolutely to be at the heart of

---

13. With regard to fundamental forms of consciousness, I have found the relation of *need* and *eros* illumined in Harry Berger, Jr., "Naive Consciousness and Culture Change," *Second World and Green World* (Berkeley: University of California Press, 1988), 98-101. Hereafter cited as Berger.

Keats. Keats is my theory, and I proceed by the proposition that Keats's work will, if read hard, if listened to closely and without prejudice of prior assumption, show one how to read him.[14] All the markers are there in his work. All the details are what anyone has to work with. The discipline of such work over time is the discipline which does all in its power to permit every element of Keats to come forward. There is a great deal of patience involved, and a sort of necessary arrogance, and even an extraordinary *maya* of embarrassment that must be endured, humored, ignored. But one must be responsible to everything, no matter what. One must be willing to always stand on the truth of the fact of one's immense responsibility to the poem and poetics. Neither vanity nor pride has anything to do with this effort, as Ridley recognized so long ago. There is only dead sober work.

The strength of any scholarly or interpretive work on the *Letters* must be to grasp, in whatever way is particular to oneself, the propositional core of Keats's thinking and to apply that core right back to the work at hand. In other words, one's method must be Keats's method filtered through one's own critical *and* creative imagination. Anything else is ancillary to what Keats's texts suggest. History, theory, and so forth, are only what anyone ought to feel welcome to use. But what is

14. I have found it necessary to give more attention to poetics than to any one of a number of topics in epistolary genre and theory. Without doubt, Keats is a great stylist of the familiar letter. Simply put, he is a great stylist of the written word. He evidently studied the letters of Robert Burns and Jean Jacques Rousseau, for instance, as several references in his letters show. Although issues of epistolation are discussed in Chapter 1, for the most part I take up the *Letters* without feeling obliged to make accommodation to theory or any other assumption of what scholarship is. I certainly do not feel one must in any way rewrite Keats to some prior assumption of satisfaction. Nor do I believe that in needing to know what Keats is doing in the *Letters* one necessarily becomes absorbed into or dominated by Romantic ideology, as Jerome McGann argues in *The Romantic Ideology* (Chicago: University of Chicago Press, 1983). McGann calls for a historical criticism that takes into account how ideologies are embedded in Romantic poetry and theory. The "ground thesis" of his study is that "the scholarship and criticism of Romanticism and its works are dominated by a Romantic ideology, by an uncritical absorption in Romanticism's own self-representations." What I'm attempting to do is plunge into the very thing McGann implicitly resists or denies, the so-called idealizations of Romanticism, which to me are formal recognitions of reality. Yet I do so without *analysis* as a critical "weapon."

primary is to go from Keats outward and then back to him. What is essential is to explain what the *Letters* explain.

The eight chapters of this book pursue themes of personal urgency rather than constitute a disinterested systemization. My intention was to answer certain needs that had for some time been building in my life. I wanted to make adequate formal response in language to these needs. I was instinctively drawn back to Keats because his sense of life and his questions about poetry mattered very much to me. At a time when I was groping for a foundation poetics of my own, I recaptured my original experience of Keats's *Letters*, which in turn made available all manner of contexts for concentrating on the issue of poetics. I do not claim to have connected my inmost motivations with my conscious meditations here. But these are the seeds of my thought and experience which make up a structure best explained by such thought and experience themselves. My first response was to "The Penetralium of Mystery," the first essay to be written.

Living and excavating in the terms of Keats's *Letters* and poetics became a way for me to map what is finally mine, not his. Keats is simply a great guide and friend, one who has given so much to those who can respond to and use what is initially beyond comprehension. What one must do, what any good, rigorous critic does, is to make a web or nest in which to live. Everything that feels pertinent, everything of one's own faith in what is going on in life and literature, everything one can find out, is the midden heap that exists for one to compose as best as one can, and according to what it directs as composition. As one awakens to the fact that a web has been spun which one finds oneself caught in, one then commences to spin one's own web, to counter the first, at least to equal it. Finally, the first seems not to have been determinative and, slightly rewoven, is incorporated into one's own greater web. This is one meaning, value, and practical use of what Keats is doing in the *Letters*.

Everything of course is not in this book. Keats wrote so many letters that we have an almost day-by-day account of his life, and no less than three hundred letters from a seven-year period are known to have survived in either transcript or original form. It would be impossible to account for them all. Certainly not all of Keats's letters deliver the kind of treasure I mine in this book. But more than enough contain treasure, allowing me to attempt an interpretation of poetics. Since I could not really discuss poetics without including the issues and influences in my education, literature of the modern period appears here and there. I see William Carlos Williams and Federico García Lorca, for instance, as two modern poets who were not so much followers of Keats as ones who responded to his heart and sweetness. There are others I could have included—Wallace Stevens and F. Scott Fitzgerald to name a couple more authors—but it was not my aim to write a study of Keats's influence or legacy among artists and intellectuals.

Although it was written midway through the composition of this book, the essay on the theoretical side of Keats's letters appears first because the later essays, which discuss specific letters, must be shown within the broader context of poetics. The rest of the essays engage the growth of Keats's poetics as it is recorded and illumined in select letters from 1817 to 1820. My selection tries to make clear that the imaginative sympathy of Keats's Romanticism is a rich source of knowledge, and it is one of the supports of the advance of creation. Certainly the early letters show Keats intent upon a life of sensation rather than of thought. But even then in his "speculations," as he called the ardent matter of his letters, he was able to take aim and perceive his target with brilliant results."Keats was hungry," W.S. Di Piero writes. He was hungry and attentive and possessed all of the faculties which made for "a finely articulated moral being and certainly a different kind of artist." The subject of these letters is always nothing less than life and literature in all their reflections upon "a noisy, savage, rude genius."[15]

---

15. W.S. Di Piero, "Something of Self," *Memory and Enthusiasm* (Princeton: Princeton University Press, 1989), 168. Hereafter cited as Di Piero.

Di Piero distinguishes between the letters of Keats and Byron, finding the latter the mark of an aristocratic gentleman. Only in the Turkish and Greek letters, Di Piero says, does Byron exhibit the desire and need to become "a different kind of artist," that is, one more like Keats.

Keats's Letters and the Complex Mind

It has been said that the Character of a Man
may be known by his hand writing—
if the Character of the age may be known
by the average goodness of said,
what a slovenly age we live in.... Look at
Milton's hand—I cant say a word for shakespeare.

—John Keats to C.W. Dilke
March 4, 1820

. I .

IN A LETTER to his family in America, John Keats once described himself in the act of writing to them as "sitting with my back to [the fire] with one foot rather askew upon the rug and the other with the heel a little elevated from the carpet—I am writing this on the Maid's tragedy which I have read since tea with Great Pleasure—Beside this volume of Beaumont & Fletcher—there are on the tabl[e] two volumes of Chaucer and a new work of Tom Moores." It's a quaint picture of leisure—Keats the idle artist, surrounded by his beloved books—the kind of scene his painter friends Benjamin Robert Haydon or Joseph Severn might have rendered on canvas. But the nuance of a couple of details modifies this impression of ease. The book Keats has previously been reading is a tragedy, the subject of his life and art. And the raised, tensed heel upon the carpet gives the sure sign of the body's share in the intellect's work, the dance while sitting down that is writing. These things comprise a salient motif for readers of Keats's *Letters*, and Keats himself is conscious of the realism which helps to produce any work of art:

> I require nothing so much of you as that you will give me a like description of yourselves, however it may be when you are writing to me—Could I see the same thing done of any great Man long since dead it would be a great delight: as to know in what position Shakspeare sat when he began "To be or not to be"—such thing[s] become interesting from distance of time or place.
>
> (March 12, 1819)

They surely do, and not only because it is Keats who is writing but because "such things," the details that complete a picture of an artist at work, bridge the distance between Keats's time and our own, and bring us to that place where, as Walter Benjamin said, a work of art really happens to be.[1]

Keats and Benjamin both speak for the greatness of art interpenetrated by circumstance, which adds to our knowledge of reality: the past moment that becomes present to us when we read a writer's words. To read Keats's *Letters* is to enter both moments (*then* and *now*) when the word, the very letter, is immediate. When we read Keats's autograph letters, we sense the immediacy of the act, both literal and literary, of Keats in the word. He writes in a clear, elegant hand, with loops and curls and few words crossed out. He capitalizes certain words that for him not only indicate formal values but also contain mythic presences. Hyder E. Rollins attributes the many misspellings in the *Letters* to the belief that Keats "dashed off sentences, ignoring unity and coherence, seldom rereading what he had written."[2] But I wonder if Keats may instead have been slightly dyslexic, since his numerous misspellings are phonemically consistent. Above all, I find it hard to accept that Keats ignored any matter in what he wrote. As one discovers, the etymologies of words in Keats's poems and letters can explode into a terrain vast enough to occupy one interminably. It's what Keats himself is doing all the time with Shakespeare: tracking into every word, plumbing it to its deepest resonances and suggestions, without violating it, and then putting it back together according to his need. He kept the word primary to himself in the heat of knowing.

For the greatest poets, the action of language is of a piece: poems and letters, art and life, far from being polar opposites, constitute a poetic mode or exist on a poetic continuum. The forms and genres of language are all coterminous by virtue of

---

1. Walter Benjamin, *Illuminations: Essays and Reflections* (New York: Schocken Books, 1969), 220.

2. Rollins, I, 220.

providing a model of what writing can be: possibility and speculation-in-the-making.[3] From the distance of time and place, Keats's *Letters* deliver a kind of treasure, a vision of reality in words, that is beautiful and profound. In each and every letter that same mind is present, absolutely centered on and blazing with the light of imagination. All experience for Keats, when he wrote, achieved the form of poetry. From the instructive discovery of Negative Capability in December 1817 to the necessary condition of suffering as stated in letters throughout 1818, the light of Keats's imagination grew brighter with its beautifully dark incandescence, illuminating his growth as a poet and as a human being.

The genesis of Keats's poetics is almost always in the *Letters,* though certainly the sheer number of poems that have no explicit source in the *Letters* make it clear that Keats often enough formulated poetics away from or outside the frame of the letter. The point to emphasize here is that the occasion of poetics for a poet like Keats, once his letters can be seen on a plane equal to that of his poems, is whenever he is in the word, whether written, spoken, or contemplated. Although one cannot say why Keats was *given* to write letters, one can at least try to say, as best as one can, what action his letters do perform. Such action includes or depends upon the very "fingerings and gropings" of Keats's imagination that exist in the *Letters*. Knowing this is no less important than knowing the order of poems as Keats published them in three separate volumes, an order Keats's editors have often disregarded in favor of the order of composition.[4] That is one order of unity; the *Letters* are another. If Keats, like Shakespeare, led a life of allegory, then his works, all of them, are the commentary on it and ought to be restored to their original contexts. Thus Keats's letters *as* letters reveal both poetics and the form of expression of such poetics. And it is in the epistolary form itself

3. Di Piero, 69.

4. See Stillinger, "The Order of Poems in Keats's First Volume," *The Hoodwinking of Madeline* (Urbana: University of Illinois Press, 1971), 1-13.

that we might find more beneficial details of Keats's poetic ambition.

Recent scholarship has examined the bases of classical epistolary theory in the literary and nonliterary works of English authors.[5] What informs these studies, even if their emphases are elsewhere, is the foundation of an organizing poetics vis-à-vis the genre conventions of the letter. In this context, poetics is the literary and oratorical heritages of the Bible, Cicero, Seneca, and Plutarch, with their injunctions and practices of writing and discourse. These and later authorities categorize the "familiar" letter and the "special" or topical letter. The familiar letter is that which passes between friends for the purpose of gossip or reflection. This form later developed as a mode of philosophical speculation and character depiction, the tradition which gave us the essay and epistolary novel.[6] Familiar letters have been viewed as "a rich mixture of contrivance and intimacy" based on strategies and idioms derived from both rhetorical theory and poetry.[7]

First and foremost, the familiar letter is the preeminent form of individuality and intimacy; it involves both one's own voice and that other whom one knows well enough to feel free or open with. The familiar letter evinces a symbolic freedom conferred on friends who share the writer's confidence. Such freedom implies or provides an outlet for expressing spontaneity. There is always an element of spontaneity present in Keats's letters, and it should not be mistaken for an "effect."[8] That such

5. See, e.g., Frank Whigham, "The Rhetoric of Elizabethan Suitors' Letters," *PMLA* 96, 5 (October 1981), 864-882; Margaret Maurer, "The Poetical Familiarity of John Donne's Letters," *Genre* 15, 2-3 (Spring-Summer 1982), 183-202; C.A. Patrides, "The Epistolary Art of the Renaissance: The Biblical Premises," *Philological Quarterly* 60, 3 (Summer 1981), 357-367; and Susan Wright, "Private Language Made Public: The Language of Letters as Literature," *Poetics* 18, 6 (December 1989), 549-578.

6. Whigham, "The Rhetoric of Elizabethan Suitors' Letters," 879.

7. Maurer, "The Poetical Familiarity of John Donne's Letters," 184.

8. There are some who argue that "sincerity" is an effect in Keats's letters, that is, an artistic-rhetorical contrivance. I do not deny the self-conscious *work* the letters are or admit. But Keats's sincerity arises not separately from situations, or from Keats in such situations. It springs from the remarkable wholeness of his life.

spontaneity is, in its deepest, most primary source of human conduct and understanding, an alliance or bonding through formal engagement becomes evident when one looks to the etymology of the word, which derives from the same Latin word as does "sponsion": *spondere,* "to promise solemnly," which itself is related to the Greek *spéndein,* "to pour a libation, promise." It's odd how this word has come to mean "impulsive" and "unconstrained," the very opposite of its original meaning. But something of the root sense of ritual promise making is retained in the willful character of the letter. Of one's own accord one engages another in the word. When one's writing becomes a dialogue (correspondence), it has coherence and threads of thought and response that are conspicuously one's own. Writing itself becomes part of the act of discovering what it is one feels and thinks and promises to tell.

Like the journal or diary, the familiar letter restores habits of thought that are closer to and more in accord with the self. If one could call poetry the practice of craft, then the letter would be the practice of self. It is an introspective mode that exists between writing to oneself and writing to the world, a looking inward for the sake of turning outward, from one person to another. Its method is a simple but true one: to detail a life by starting at the inside of things. From the standpoint of a historian, much of forgotten life can be reclaimed in the letter, perhaps the nine-tenths of one's life that is forgotten in the living of it. But what emerges in letters is nonetheless the self, that is, when one gives oneself in the word. As William Carlos Williams wrote to his editor on the impending publication of his letters, "You must let the letters speak for themselves [rather

---

Keats's sincerity often seems to elicit a "problematic" for some critics. Paul de Man, for example, imputes to Keats a dread, avoidance of, and escape from self-knowledge, asserting that "authentic" self-discovery is lacking. His view of Keats is questionable because authentic selfhood here means the presence of "feelings of guilt and dread as well as sudden moments of transparent clarity," which sounds balanced but misses or negates the import of the radical nature of Keats's "self," one whose annihilation is a condition of mystery. De Man sees this mystery as "a darkening, growing opacity of the consciousness." It is simply too "poetic" for him. See his "The Negative Road," in *John Keats,* ed. Harold Bloom (New York: Chelsea House, 1985), 29-48.

than prefacing them with second hand information] or you will kill them entirely." For the text of the letters was "a creation and a contribution to the lore of the written word."[9] That lore always concerns the self, or some essential part of it, in relation to another. While it is true that Williams's letters are a kind of portrait gallery of his friends—friends such as Ezra Pound, Marianne Moore, Gertrude Stein, Marsden Hartley, and Alfred Stieglitz, among many—nevertheless those letters to his friends were often written to enlarge his mind and spirit. "He was no Gray or Walpole," his editor writes, "carefully phrasing each letter with publication in mind."[10] Williams's epistolary style varies, registering the pressures of an extremely busy life as a doctor. Thus his letters take the form that fits his thought at the time they were written, which is probably true of any letter writer. If that way of thinking is indeed often enough forgotten, perhaps it's because it arises from the buried self, which in letters or poems is brought to life with an intensity all its own, different from those experiences or extremities we remember all too easily.

Keats too was no Gray or Walpole. These eighteenth-century men of sensibility (one a poet, the other an earl) wrote in an age that made letter writing an art among the literate and educated class in England. For them the familiar letter was a highly conspicuous form of expressing wit and restrained emotion, and of displaying a wide breadth of learning and intellectual interests. In contrast, Keats's letters negate the kind of impersonality and artificiality which was characteristic of the mid-eighteenth century. Or rather, the dividing line between Keats and men like Gray and Walpole is the assumed persona of the "man of letters" and not the work of writing itself, whether poetry, criticism, or familiar letters. Keats does not assume a persona. His letters are "open" but no less perspectival than the letters of any other age. Indeed, they reveal one of the

---

9. John C. Thirwall, ed., *The Selected Letters of William Carlos Williams* (New York: McDowell, Obolensky, 1957), xvii. Hereafter cited as Thirwall.

10. Thirwall, xviii.

most astute, discriminating judgments of all time. More significantly, Keats responds to the pressures and joys of a real preoccupation with spiritual wholeness. This dimension takes the *Letters* beyond the tradition of the plain bourgeois style as well as the older Renaissance and medieval modes of elaborate rhetoric. Put another way, it includes them and liberates what has been exiled inside both, namely a third possibility of soul that served both artistic and practical purposes for Keats.

In the second part of his *Autobiographies,* W.B. Yeats refers to Keats as one of the "great lesser writers." For Yeats, Keats's greatness lay in his passionate love of the physical world and in the sensuous music he created out of its beauties and processes. He was among the lesser poets because his ability to penetrate the metaphysical was not equal to his desire to evoke the actual world. Yeats's comment turns on his knowledge that "genius is a crisis that joins [the] buried self for certain moments to our trivial daily mind." Crisis is spiritual possibility, the confrontation of obstacles without despair. Such "masters" as Dante and Villon, Yeats claims, have suffered and understood the immense spiritual changes which brought them to their supreme creative power. We gaze at them in awe since we are gazing at a new kind of human being. "They and their sort alone earn contemplation, for it is only when the intellect has wrought the whole of life to drama, to crisis, that we may live for contemplation and yet keep our intensity."[11] That is Yeats's preoccupation, and his famous image of Keats in "Ego Dominus Tuus," as a schoolboy with his "face and nose pressed to a sweetshop window," is followed by this judgment:

---

11. W.B. Yeats, *Autobiographies* (New York: Macmillan, 1927), 183-184. Yeats argues that in Landor and Keats, "we are shown that Image and that Mask as something set apart," whereas Dante and Villon "turn all to Mask and Image, and so be phantoms in their own eyes.... The two halves of their nature are so completely joined that they seem to labor for their objects, and yet to desire whatever happens, being at the same instant predestinate and free, creation's very self." What Yeats denies Keats in his complicated doctrine of personality is precisely what I find in the letters, especially in Negative Capability, a quality of imaginative response, a paradoxical experience.

For certainly he sank into his grave
His senses and his heart unsatisfied,
And made—being poor, ailing and ignorant,
Shut out from all the luxury of the world,
The coarse-bred son of a livery-stable keeper—
Luxuriant song.[12]

One must allow for all the dimensions of artistic life, for both success and failure. But I suspect that Yeats's judgment is based solely, and unfairly, on Keats's poems. Where are the great poems in Yeats's judgment, major poems such as the "Ode to a Nightingale" and the two *Hyperion* poems, which are patient and fully impassioned calibrations of states of *being,* more than simply states of *feeling* or "luxuriant song"? A major lyric poet like Keats or Yeats does not confine himself to the poem as the only site of exploration of actual and metaphysical reality. In Keats's *Letters* one finds as intense a creative relationship with the world as Yeats had; in them one finds that melding point of crisis in which the buried self and the waking mind join or become one.

On the face of it, Keats seems often to be writing only a letter. But often he is following or dovetailing something, and brings up some form not unlike what Yeats calls the "Image," which is brought into the world in men and women by "personifying spirits we had best call but Gates and Gate-keepers."[13] By a curious paradox, this work of dovetailing for an object happens when one desires whatever may happen, when one is "creation's very self." This is like the process of Negative Capability which envisages not only man's art but the poetics of his recreation through that art. It is not that daily labor which is akin, in its form and result, to digging. The image of digging in the work of Irish poet Seamus Heaney, for instance, conveys the particular truth of digging with the pen, of "excavating, unearthing histories of families, country, and self."[14] But in

12. *The Collected Poems of W.B. Yeats* (New York: Macmillan, 1933), 159.
13. W.B. Yeats, *Autobiographies,* 183.
14. Di Piero, 109.

Keats's dovetailing, the process results in an upthrust or rift that is quite unique.

Rift ordinarily means a fissure in a rock, a break or split that opens the earth. Or as Keats himself uses the word in a letter to Shelley, "'load every rift' of your subject with ore" (August 16, 1820). But I'm using *rift* as a metaphor not for what's buried and unseen in the earth but for what is thrown up, into the air, like the mountain or volcano created from the earth's material. Rift is both the formation and the mass that appear from below, or rather, from within. For it seems to me that with the convergence or dovetailing of whatever is presented to the mind, momentum carries such stuff into the world as an Image.[15] The fact that the Image comes from *within* and yet bears the form of something from *without* suggests several things. One at least is that the world "out there" has moved inside, and that the rift is an *evagination,* a turning inside out.[16] Whether it be the Penetralium of Mystery, the Chamber of Maiden Thought, From Feathers to Iron, or some other Image from among many, it seems to me that Keats is talking about and building upon, from letter to letter, a terrain or region that is interior to another it resembles, as a church dome recalls that other interior roofed by stars. For Keats, this eversion bodied forth every mote of the richest, most indispensable living he had ever lived. But greater than his own individual existence, it was Life itself that flowed out of him like words read in a book. Keats knew this, and knowing it gave him a vista to his own life of a vast starry mental depth.

I characterize Keats's interior vista as "starry" because of the endless preoccupation in his letters and poems with stars, both

15. Cf. Mario D'Avanzo, *Keats's Metaphors for the Poetic Imagination* (Durham: Duke University Press, 1967), ix-xii. D'Avanzo calls all uses of a particular image or metaphor in Keats's poetry "collation," and characterizes Keats's letters as an "extratextual reservoir." No matter how "important" he finds such a reservoir, I don't agree that Keats's remarks on poetry in the *Letters* are in any way "offhand." D'Avanzo's approach, essentially, is to explain the poems through the letters since the latter are "more prosy."

16. This is a term Charles Olson gave to his students at Connecticut to help them learn "to put the inside outside." See *Charles Olson at Mansfield: Last Lectures* (Boston: Northeastern University Press, 1978), 9-11.

in their luminous appearance and in their effect upon nature. The stars concentrate the impulse of piety toward them. They are divine. In his letters especially, Keats deems them "ethereal" and "real" by virtue of imagination and passion. The stars are intensities of fire corresponding to his "ardour" (which comes from Latin, *ardere,* "to burn," and which is related to Greek, *aithos,* "fire," from whence "ether" and "ethereal"). The reality of these things in Keats's poetics has a wholeness, a holiness which he feels as intimately, as primally, as the warmth of love. As he wrote to his family in America in the autumn of 1818:

> The roaring of the wind is my wife and the Stars through the window pane are my Children. The mighty abstract Idea I have of Beauty in all things stifles the more divided and minute domestic happiness—an amiable wife and sweet Children I contemplate as a part of that Beauty. but I must have a thousand of those beautiful particles to fill up my heart. I feel more and more every day, as my imagination strengthens, that I do not live in this world alone but in a thousand worlds.
>
> (October 24, 1818)

This is no mere way to pretty up his refusal to marry, which Keats equated with abandoning or compromising his vocation and solitude. The wind and stars as Keats's wife and children—forms of light and beauty—represent his true family as it were, his feeling of kinship with the transcendent or sacred, and the drivenness of his art is due to the conviction of other worlds, of the form of things unknown, felt in the heart. Here and elsewhere in his letters, the testimony he gives of his life and art reveals that a cosmic romance, one of great velocity and stillness, like that of his sonnet "Bright Star," was ever beginning, ever enacting itself in his life.

The complex structures in Keats's *Letters* (which is to say, the reality he imagines) are not themselves an explanation of how the passions create beauty, but rather an exemplification involving the life of the imagination, a life grounded in the senses and complex chains of association. This thought-work is a power that is achieved not as any authority or triumph, but as the fullness of content of Keats's own consciousness. It's a fullness, moreover, that in the ardor of composition struck him with astonishment and seemed the result of another person's effort. Keats's friend Richard Woodhouse, reporting on the poet's method of composition, called this sensation of astonishment and pleasure "*curiosa felicitas,*" a feeling attached to an idea the excellence of which the writer is unaware until he or she comes to read it over.[17] I think this same ardor of composition is to be found in Keats's letters, which yield, as he put it to his friend Benjamin Bailey, the "rewards" of imagination:

> The simple imaginative Mind may have its rewards in the repeti[t]ion of its own silent Working coming continually on the spirit with a fine suddenness—to compare great things with small.... [S]ure this cannot be exactly the case with a complex Mind—one that is imaginative and at the same time careful of its fruits—who would exist partly on sensation partly on thought—to whom it is necessary that years should bring the philosophic Mind.
>
> (November 22, 1817)

The rift in the letters, rather than simply being matter for literary use, is this "fine suddenness." It's the Image that comes of erotic attractions, of stirring unions, of high romance. With both images and sensations, Keats makes answers to the questions of poetry and reality—answers "referable ultimately to sensation," but nevertheless "not unphilosophical."[18]

---

17. Woodhouse's account is quoted in full and discussed by Ridley, 13-15, 291-292.

18. See James R. Caldwell, *John Keats' Fancy* (New York: Octagon Books, 1972), 158, where Caldwell argues that this complex process of association, involving "a life solidly grounded in bygone events of eye, ear, palate, etc.,. . .is precisely what the simple imaginative mind always gives. Its mighty abstract ideas are modes of operation—frankly conveyed—in the 'halo or penumbra that surrounds and escorts' the subject. They evolve as the poems evolve from the free work of the associative principle. The striking thing is that Keats dares allow them to stand alone, that he dares 'think' as well as 'dream' with his imagination." Caldwell calls this thinking-dreaming an "enrichment."

One cannot forget that the eruptions of powerful and active thought in the *Letters* are evidence "of the process of poetry as approaching truth with no guise other than itself."[19] For Keats, truth was eminently that predicament of humanity pursuing imagination at the limits of language, life, and death. In two brief years from 1816 to 1818, he had come a long way toward fulfilling the promise he made to himself in "Sleep and Poetry" to bid farewell to the joys of nymphs and nature, and "pass them for a nobler life / Where I may find the agonies, the strife / Of human hearts."[20] In his letters as in his poems, Keats turned out "Shapes of delight, of mystery and fear," from his mind's own silent working, and he did so with great speed and in bold relief. His development in poetics encompassed both poems and letters; and in letters especially, he located the power of imagination that, without having many years in which to grow, brought him the "complex Mind" he had contrasted with his own "simple" one. He worked *toward* wisdom and understanding, toward a new life that would account for suffering as if he knew all along he was going to die. Indeed he did know, as we all do and often neurotically try to deny, that death is inevitable.

"Keats's letters are, in their own way, a classic work of English literature," Robin Mayhead has written. Yet "work," he claims, is "technically incorrect." He argues that work connotes the outcome of conscious application, of something "worked at," while Keats's letters "were simply written *as* letters, not as works of art."[21] This is not mindful of the dual nature of the poet's office: he or she is a *tekton*, a builder, framer, form-giver, and a *poietes*, an imaginal maker. "Work" *is* technically accurate here, for such poetry as that found in Keats's letters does not surrender its complex and elusive thought-character, which is finally what makes it the most human of the arts. "The work of poetry," W.S. Di Piero writes, "is most human when it is like

---

19. Charles Olson, *Poetry and Truth* (San Francisco: Four Seasons Foundation, 1971), 15.

20. Stillinger, 72, lines 124-128.

21. Robin Mayhead, *John Keats* (Cambridge: Cambridge University Press, 1967), 112.

the work of philosophizing, less so when it is like knit-craft."[22] Mayhead concedes that to go through Keats's letters is "to experience a sense of extraordinary unity in what may at first seem to be quite heterogeneous material." Thus he conjectures that this sense of unity has its origin in Keats's distinctive personality. Such unity for me has less to do with personality than with the complex mind and with the steps Keats took to explore and develop his art. That this deepening or maturation is one of both personality and intelligence is proven by the distance Keats traveled from the first to the last poems. That is, a distance not so much recorded as illumined in both poems and letters. Put another way, the proof of Keats's urgent striving toward maturity, as an artist and a human being, is in the letters as much as it is in the poems. More so in the letters, finally, I believe. Coming out of the organic, associationist model of nineteenth-century literature and thought, Keats's activity in all his writings was to make "a thing of beauty," not to produce a beautifully functioning thing. This may be the most compelling sort of work there is, the soul's work. That is why his letters, and his poems equally, exist on a plane of imaginative composition, actual work. Indeed, the terms of creation in the *Letters* are those of imagination, which takes with it, time after time, the formal feeling and pattern of all previous experiences in the configuration of a poetics and of a world. It is not familiarity with correspondents which dictates or influences the terms of creating this world in words. It is the drive of imagination. This is what one finds so rarely in the letters of English authors—the creation of a palace of words that are never limited to intellect but are words of passion, a passion that answers the world "out there" by its dutiful, life-sustaining work.

I have heard Keats spoken of as "feminine," which is perhaps a way of identifying his sensuous lapse into landscape, into an original sense of maternal amplitude of evocation. Many of the poems derive their power from precisely such evocation. Yet

22. Di Piero, 253.

as the sonnets, odes, and two *Hyperion* poems show, Keats's creative imagination tests his own concentrated power of expression against an acute vision of life. Likewise his letters are not sheer acts of divination, words in a feminine mode functioning more as evocation than as address, command, or labor of shaping. The architectonic is there too. It is the conscious half of the dynamic quality of the letters, words put together easily and quickly, it seems, but which on closer inspection support the creation of a world of ethereal beauty as solidly and weightily as bricks.

For one who spoke so much about climbing "the Cliffs of Poetry" or about mounting "on the viewless wings of Poesy," it may seem odd to think of Keats as earthbound, rooted, and watering the ground—the gesture and activity of husbandry and one of ancient Greek poetry's associations with itself. Yet as these lines from Blake's "The Human Abstract" remind us,

> He sits down with holy fears,
> And waters the ground with tears:
> Then Humility takes its root
> Underneath his foot[23]

This position concerns a humility achieved through the fact of "holy fears" and tears shed as goodness or grace for the decencies and import of words. Moist with his own tears, Keats's words are always the means by which Heart moves all forward. What matters most in reading the letters and the poems is that which exists between Keats and anyone: the great modulation of all his texts by the quiet ardor of his faith. This is neither a question of gullibility nor an issue of leaving Keats's meaning arguable. It is a matter of honoring that depth of feeling in Keats's words.

---

23. David V. Erdman, ed., *The Complete Poetry and Prose of William Blake* (Los Angeles: University of California Press, 1982), 27, lines 9-12. Hereafter cited as Erdman.

The Penetralium of Mystery

The artist is the servant of need.

—William Carlos Williams
"Against the Weather"

Both truth and beauty on my love depends.

—William Shakespeare
Sonnet CI

What Keats proposes as Negative Capability
is the readmission of the familiar. He says,
I mean, when a man is capable of uncertainties,
mysteries, doubts, without any reaching after
fact and reason. In other words, the condition
itself is the penetralium (the innermost secret).

—Charles Olson
The Special View of History

· II ·

I HAVE HAD two very pleasant evenings with Dilke yesterday & today; & am at this moment just come from him & feel in the humor to go on with this, began in the morning, & from which he came to fetch me. I spent Friday evening with Wells & went the next morning to see *Death on the Pale horse.* It is a wonderful picture, when West's age is considered; But there is nothing to be intense upon; no women one feels mad to kiss; no face swelling into reality. the excellence of every Art is its intensity, capable of making all disagreeables evaporate, from their being in close relationship with Beauty & Truth—Examine King Lear & you will find this examplified throughout; but in this picture we have unpleasantness without any momentous depth of speculation excited, in which to bury its repulsiveness—I dined with Haydon the sunday after you left, & had a very pleasant day, I dined too (for I have been out much lately) with Horace Smith & met his two Brothers with Hill & Kingston & one Du Bois, they only served to convince me, how superior humour is to wit in respect to enjoyment—These men say things which makes one start, without making one feel, they are all alike; their manners are alike; they all know fashionables; they have a mannerism in their very eating & drinking, in their mere handling a Decanter—They talked of Kean & his low company—Would I were with that company instead of yours said I to myself! I know such like acquaintance will never do for me & yet I am going to Reynolds, on wednesday—Brown & Dilke walked with me & back from the Christmas pantomime. I had not a dispute but a disquisition with Dilke, on various subjects; several things dovetailed in my mind, & at once it struck me, what quality went to form a Man of Achievement especially in Literature & which Shakspeare posessed so enormously—I mean *Negative*

> *Capability,* that is when man is capable of being in uncertainties, Mysteries, doubts, without any irritable reaching after fact & reason—Coleridge, for instance, would let go by a fine isolated verisimilitude caught from the Penetralium of mystery, from being incapable of remaining content with half knowledge. This pursued through Volumes would perhaps take us no farther than this, that with a great poet the sense of beauty overcomes every other consideration, or rather obliterates all consideration.
>
> (December 21, 27? 1817)

There were many things on Keats's mind when he wrote to his brothers between December 21 and 28 in 1817: Edmund Kean's return to the stage in *Richard II,* Christmas gambols and pastimes, Benjamin West's painting *Death on the Pale Horse,* Shakespeare's *King Lear,* the Christmas pantomime *Harlequin's Vision,* all of which swelled into reality or dovetailed in his mind as *Negative Capability.* This famous phrase has been the subject of much discussion ("pursued through Volumes") but it is still not taken altogether with Keats's letters as part of the greater terms of his poetics. The Negative Capability letter, I believe, has its great and singular importance in the fact that the twofold unity of imagination, Beauty and Truth, yielded the discovery of "the Penetralium of Mystery," a less famous phrase that nonetheless manifests Keats's depth and complexity of desire.

The first draft of his early major poem *Endymion* had been finished only a month before his letter to his brothers. In the interval, he had returned from Burford Bridge in Surrey, where he completed *Endymion* and read William Shakespeare's *Sonnets* both amid a landscape and solitude of great beauty. He had dined with the artist Benjamin Robert Haydon, whom Keats practically worshipped for a time. He had seen Kean, the greatest Shakespearean actor of the time, perform in *Richard II* and in Sir James Bland Burges's play *Riches,* an adaptation of Philip Massinger's *City Madam.* He had met William Wordsworth in Haydon's studio at a small dinner in honor of the elder poet. He had been invited to dine at the home of Horace Smith, a stockbroker and parodist of the time. He dropped in at Wentworth Place (now the Keats House) in Hampstead almost every day during December to see Charles Dilke and his wife—their house a veritable home for the Keats brothers—or occasionally to call on Dilke's neighbor and former schoolfellow Charles Brown, with whom he made his famous walking tour of northern England and Scotland a year later. He had entertained, with the painter Joseph Severn, his brother Tom's old friend Charles Wells. And he had evidently spent Christmas Day at the home of John Reynolds, one of his dearest friends. George and Tom Keats had since left Hampstead (probably in early December) for Teignmouth, Devonshire, a coastal town in the south of England. The brothers had hoped the change of climate would improve Tom's health. But tuberculosis would kill him a year hence. It would kill Keats, too, as a result of nursing his dying brother, three years from this time. Keats was twenty-two.

What Keats tells George and Tom in his letter is what he feels as well as his impressions during the course of several days. The arresting and, to some, puzzling part of the letter is where he refers to Negative Capability, that quality which forms a "Man of Achievement" and by which "man is capable of being in uncertainties, Mysteries, doubts, without any irritable reaching after fact & reason." Much ink has been spilled over just this one sentence. Walter Jackson Bate has written an entire book on Keats's remark.[1] Unfortunately, Negative Capability has become a literary cult object these past several years, or a monumental object of inquiry, encased within scholastic objectivity, that obscures the center of Negative Capability and travesties the poetic intelligence which located that center within the context of a life. To deal with what this term, and what the letter as a whole, is pointing to, one ought to begin with what the words themselves disclose. They point the way to a center of imaginative insight, however narrow that sight, however small that center.

1. Walter Jackson Bate, *Negative Capability: The Intuitive Approach in Keats* (Cambridge: Harvard University Press, 1939).

The first inkling comes with the final value Keats himself discovered in his long poem *Endymion, A Poetic Romance* (1818). *Endymion* is based on the Greek myth of the king of Ellis with whom Selene, goddess of the Moon, fell in love. According to one story, Zeus gave Endymion the opportunity to choose his own fate, and he chose to sleep forever, never growing old. Keats took this fable and composed a story in verse about the love of a mortal for the ideal. But when he had set himself the task in April 1817 of writing an ambitious poem four thousand lines in length, and to be completed in four or five months, he did not even have a subject, only the search for a large theme. He had traveled from Hampstead to Southampton, and thence to the Isle of Wight, trying to repeat the experience that had yielded two sizable poems the year before at Margate. As Keats began writing, he was reading Shakespeare's plays and sonnets very seriously, especially *King Lear*. Keats was haunted by *Lear*. His sonnet "On the Sea" was copied in a letter to Reynolds on April 8, 1817, in which he quotes from *Lear*, IV.vi.4: "Do you not hear the Sea?" The atmosphere of Shakespeare's world-plays, as well as Spenser's *Faerie Queen*, filled him with the presence and need to write "eternal poetry."

Writing *Endymion*, like reading Shakespeare and Spenser, schooled Keats as a poet during months of intoxication and depression. It taught him not what to write but how. The long poem in particular is itself an exercise in courage and in understanding the spirit that moves a poet to write for the future. As Keats wrote to Bailey, in whose rooms at Magdalen Hall, Oxford, Keats had written the third book of *Endymion* between September 3 and 26, both courage and fame inspired him to write his long poem. Inserting an extract from a letter to his brother George (now lost), Keats explains:

> As to what you say about my being a Poet, I can retu[r]n no answer but by saying that the high Idea I have of poetical fame makes me think I see it towering to high above me. At any rate I have no right to talk until Endymion is finished—it will be a test, a trial of my Powers of Imagination and chiefly of my invention

> which is a rare thing indeed—by which I must make 4000 Lines of one bare circumstance and fill them with Poetry; and when I consider that this is a great task, and that when done it will take me but a dozen paces toward the Temple of Fame—it makes me say—God forbid that I should be without such a task! I have heard Hunt say and may be asked—why endeavour after a long Poem? To which I should answer—Do not the Lovers of Poetry like to have a little Region to wander in where they may pick and choose, and in which the images are so numerous that many are forgotten and found new in a second Reading: which may be food for a Week's stroll in the Summer? Do not they like this better than what they can read through before Mrs Williams comes down stairs? a Morning work at most. Besides a long Poem is a test of Invention which I take to be the Polar Star of Poetry, as Fancy is the Sails, and Imagination the Rudder. Did our great Poets ever write short Pieces? I mean in the shape of Tales—This same invention seems indeed of late Years to have been forgotten as a Poetical excellence. But enough of this, I put on no Laurels till I shall have finished Endymion....
>
> (October 8, 1817)

By "invention," Keats meant something like Shakespearean imagination, which is capable of creating "a little Region to wander in." That is, Keats saw the long poem as a site where "the fruit of Experience" (a phrase from a letter to Haydon just the week before) nourished the human spirit. Indeed, Keats speaks of "reading" as "food"; both are not only equal but identical in giving sustenance and health to the human soul. Keats especially thought of *King Lear* as a text, a symbolic space in which the power of imagination was unfettered. There is no question that Keats associated his "being a Poet" with "the high Idea...of poetical fame." However, the fact remains that *Endymion* represented "a poetic romance," that is, a work which has little or nothing to do with the accidents of this world, such as fame and individual valorization. Romance in fact marks a rupture with the plane of everyday existence and posits a horizon of a radically new consciousness of being.

Romance is, first of all, adventure, especially spiritual adventure, as the oldest tales in both verse and prose show. It's often a quest, which presupposes that the form of the adventure is chronologically linear. This is shown in the Homeric poems, especially the *Odyssey,* which can be seen as a romance in that the reconstitution of society at Ithaca denotes a completed time and condition of things, both spiritual and historical. Odysseus becomes "human" again after having lost his humanity during the years of destruction at Troy, and his passage from symbolic nonbeing to restored human being is the entire figuration of the poem. So much of Western literature—from the *Epic of Gilgamesh,* to the *Odyssey,* the *Aeneid,* the *Divine Comedy,* and on—is based on a pattern of spirituality which, in all its phases, and despite genre differences, has resonance with romance because of the extravagant qualities of these works, bearing in mind the root sense of extravagance (from Latin, *extra,* "outside," and *vagari,* "to wander"). It is the human spirit that goes outside the confines of profane or everyday reality to encounter sacred reality or the dimension of the soul. This going outside (wandering or exodus) best expresses our time of being, that which endures and moves from experience to experience. And the telling of this movement does not imply the poet speaking at one remove from experience. For the experience, whether written or unwritten, is inseparable from the system of metaphor imagined for the romance.

I find the scholarly works of Henry Corbin on Islam, especially that version known as Sufism, extremely illuminating on romance. In Sufi usage romance is a "recital" of spiritual initiation into the reality of transcendent being.[2] Rather than calling it "story" or "allegory," Corbin deliberately uses the term "recital" because it more accurately conveys the truth of inner transformation such as one finds, for example, in the recitals of the eleventh-century Persian philosopher-mystic

2. See, e.g., *Avicenna and the Visionary Recital* (Princeton: Princeton University Press, 1960); *Creative Imagination in the Sufism of Ibn 'Arabi* (Princeton: Princeton University Press, 1969); and *Temple and Contemplation* (London: Islamic Publications, 1980).

Avicenna.[3] This spiritual romance re-cites, that is, "again puts into the present," a fundamental meaning or direction that situates human existence as a spiritual adventure. It is spiritual autobiography that teaches us who we are, where we come from, and where we are going. The adventure related is of personal experience, but one revealing the soul's triumphant passage beyond the forces of the world that hold it prisoner. The recital above all is a vision of a totality in the form of symbols that must be interpreted by the spiritual imagination. The Active Imagination is the "organ" or chief means of perceiving this totality in the fullest sense. It visualizes "persons" and presences that the soul experiences on its journey from successive stages of imprisonment to gnosis or knowledge. Such persons are Guides, archetypal figures of the cosmic drama or visionary recital itself.

Although *Endymion* was probably inspired by the English (and likely Italian) tradition of romance, the personal experience entrusted to his "poetic romance" reveals a situation with which the visionary recital has something in common. This is vividly seen in November 1817, when Keats took up residence in Burford Bridge in Surrey to complete his long poem. While there, Keats was able to compose *Endymion* into the thing he needed it to be. Although he had been tired of it since the end of September—when he wrote to Haydon,

> My Ideas with respect to it I assure you are very low—and I would write the subject thoroughly again. but I am tired of it and think the time would be better spent in writing a new Romance....
>
> (September 28, 1817)

—he nevertheless recognized that *Endymion* was indeed a test, a trial from which he emerged with far greater powers of insight than he might have thought possible. This is precisely the discovery attested by the "Cave of Quietude" passage written

3. See Corbin, *Avicenna and the Visionary Recital*, 3-4.

on his first day at Burford Bridge, a passage in which Endymion falls into a dreamless sleep and awakens mysteriously renewed. This discovery represented "a whole new dimension of experience," Aileen Ward writes, "to be grasped only by surrendering to the wayward and endless richness of the immediate moment."[4]

Surrendering to the richness of the immediate moment has at least two suggestive angles. From the Western humanistic perspective, one is surrendering oneself to an idea of freedom from sin, without having to pay for it. Lucretius was one of the first great proponents of this philosophy which was originally intended to console the heart of man and liberate his soul from the terrifying fear of an afterlife hell.[5] This of course led to *carpe diem* in the West, an attitude more assertive than surrender perhaps, but one nonetheless motivated by a fear of the nothingness of death. From another perspective, that of Islam, surrender is love, devotion to a creative center which Keats perceived through Shakespeare's solicitude and all of poetry's beneficence. Love is the heart's experience, and the heart is a center of "mystic physiology," as Sufis call it, known as an "eye" whose supreme vision is of the divine form. In short, the power of the heart, its love, is a secret force or energy which perceives and knows purely; in its unveiled state the heart is like a mirror in which the divine is reflected.[6] This power is called *himma* by Sufis, *enthymesis* by Gnostics, and *Negative Capability* by Keats, as we shall see.

Now all this was made possible by an extraordinary letter Keats wrote to Bailey on the day he arrived at Burford Bridge, before he composed the "Cave of Quietude" passage. This letter is eloquent of the latencies and stirrings of the "new Romance" *Endymion* was pointing to, of the new revelation Keats's soul

---

4. Aileen Ward, *John Keats: The Making of a Poet* (New York: Farrar, Straus and Giroux, 1986), 137. Hereafter cited as Ward.

5. See *De rerum natura*, especially Book III. Lucretius, for all his courage in the face of superstitious evil, never once acknowledges the sort of thing Keats does, namely our fundamental attachment to life.

6. Corbin, *Creative Imagination*, 221-222.

had awakened to. It tells of apprehensions of a world coming into its own particularity, and is an example of what Robert Duncan has aptly called "a dream of poetry."[7] The letter to Bailey anticipates Endymion's awakening to a world full of blessings, realizing at last that the goddess Cynthia is the love of his visions. The love Endymion feels as "the chief intensity," as the most "self-destroying" of entanglements, brought him (and Keats himself) to an actual means of love whose beauty and truth are most vividly seen in Negative Capability.

Keats begins his November 22 letter to Bailey by speaking of "the World's Quarrels," a remark apparently occasioned by a rude letter Bailey had lately received from Haydon, whose temperament Keats rightly understood as "imperious." He then writes:

> I wish you knew all that I think about Genius and the Heart—and yet I think you are thoroughly acquainted with my innermost breast in that respect or you could not have known me even thus long and still hold me worthy to be your dear friend. In passing however I must say of one thing that has pressed upon me lately and encreased my Humility and capability of submission and that is this truth—Men of Genius are great as certain ethereal Chemicals operating on the Mass of neutral intellect—by they have not any individuality, any determined Character. I would call the top and head of those who have a proper self Men of Power—

Whether or not Keats is telling Bailey that Haydon is possibly a man of genius or a man of power is uncertain. What is certain is that an inner change has occurred—Keats calls it an "encrease" in humility and "capability" of submission—allowing him to perceive the "truth" that *genius* has a chemical-like quality, and that "Men of Genius" lack *individuality* or a fixed

7. Robert Duncan, "Why 'Poetics?" an introductory note to the course offerings catalogue, *Program in Poetics: 1981-1982,* New College of San Francisco. Kenneth Irby informs me that Duncan derived the notion of poetics as a dream of poetry from Igor Stravinsky's Charles Eliot Norton lectures for 1939-1940; see *The Poetics of Music* (Cambridge: Harvard University Press, 1942).

nature. Where did such increase and capability come from? I think that the "Cave of Quietude" passage was already somehow in his head, informing him of his own situation, which was that same mysterious awakening anticipated here without yet fully knowing it. Certainly it's true that Keats perceived a vast difference between men who have genius by virtue of having no "self," and those whose "Power" comes by virtue of having "a proper self." Such a difference seems to have been a guide to the humility and submission he speaks of and which will recur in the Negative Capability letter as part of poetics.

Keats wants Bailey to be as convinced as he—which is an act of the heart, not of the mind—"about the authenticity of the Imagination." Bailey had recently been "started" by it, Keats mentions in this letter, surprised or alarmed by something Keats had told him, a version perhaps of what he now speculates on:

> I am certain of nothing but of the holiness of the Heart's affections and the truth of Imagination—What the imagination seizes as Beauty must be truth—whether it existed before or not—for I have the same Idea of all our Passions as of Love they are all in their sublime, creative of essential Beauty.

One is reminded here of the ending of "Ode on a Grecian Urn": "'Beauty is truth, truth beauty,'—that is all / Ye know on earth, and all ye need to know." Though the composition of the great odes lay over a year ahead, beauty and truth were now (in 1817) immediate, needed and desired.

Creativity is born out of the stimulus of exigence, Lionel Trilling argues, and it is "a right quality of life."[8] It is right, fitting, and proper because creativity is a way of delivering ourselves from that which gives rise to it, necessity. Hence what is created (a poem or painting for instance) is "essential" to the soul which desires to live fully and freely in the world. The

8. Lionel Trilling, *Sincerity and Authenticity* (Cambridge: Harvard University Press, 1971), 166.

beneficence of life as necessity is that we can create and feel an intensity of our lives as human beings. It's a certitude ("I am certain of nothing but of the holiness of the Heart's affections") which for Keats involves poetry and the poem. It's also a future idea, a promise the soul exacts of us, that there will in truth be beauty to achieve, touch, or *seize.* Beauty and truth are twin brothers; they exist, implicitly, to rescue us from what is unhappiness on earth. But beauty and truth are, more profoundly, a twofold unity that helps keep romance alive and in action. Such action, above all, is creative and essential to the heart because without it there can be no movement. Life means movement and progression. For Keats, progression begins with the recognition of this necessary double, Beauty and Truth. It's the first step toward Negative Capability, though all the essentials are contained in it: holiness, heart, imagination, passion, and love.

Keats accepts the passions as sublime or lofty, and the imagination as a concrete "representation," as he continues to Bailey:

> In a Word, you may know my favorite Speculation by my first Book and the little song I sent in my last—which is a representation from the fancy of the probable mode of operating in these Matters—The Imagination may be compared to Adam's dream—he awoke and found it truth.

Keats's comparison of the imagination to Adam's dream represents or locates the imagination as a bestowal of grace within the encounter of the divine and human such as that in *Paradise Lost.* Milton's epic poem, it seems, was also in his head, especially the lines wherein Eve is dreamed and created at once:

> Under his forming hands a Creature grew,
> Manlike, but different sex, so lovely fair,
> That what seem'd fair in all the World, seem'd now
> Mean, or in her summ'd up, in her contain'd

And in her looks, which from that time infus'd
Sweetness into my heart, unfelt before,
And into all things from her Air inspir'd
The spirit of love and amorous delight.
She disappear'd, and left me dark, I wak'd
To find her, or for ever to deplore
Her loss, and other pleasures all abjure:
When out of hope, behold her, not far off,
Such as I saw her in my dream, adorn'd
With what all Earth or Heaven could bestow.[9]

Adam's dream is of the creation of Eve, who infuses love into the heart of Man at the moment he beholds her. Eve's creation out of Adam's dream breathes life and love into everything present or known to him. With Keats, Adam's dream is also creative; it is an unveiling of the heart whose "touch" creates that which exists outside itself.

Adam's dream is a "dream" precisely because the workings of imagination yield their truth not by "consequitive reasoning" (logic or analysis) but by that which is creative. "That which is creative must create itself," Keats will write to his publisher John Hessey a year from now, when he begins to work out for himself the "salvation" of poetry. In other words, a new matter, exactly like Adam's dream, comes into the commonality out of the individual. How this is possible is seen in the fact that Love, a sublime Passion, is also a secret or mystic modality of being. This is not merely a premise or assumption. In countless works of poetry and theosophy throughout the ages, in the ordinary experience of men and women in fact, we find examples of the heart's creative power which Keats, like so many before him, had come to know through an intense desire engendering his humility, submission, and receptivity. This desire of the heart makes possible a vision in the form of the divine, and it does so only by means of Imagination.

---

9. Merritt Y. Hughes, ed., *John Milton: Complete Poems and Major Prose* (Indianapolis: Odyssey Press, 1957), 373-374. From Book VIII, 470-483.

In the hermeneutics of Sufism such as that found in the thirteenth-century Arab theosopher Ibn 'Arabi, what is called Active Imagination (*quwat al-khayal*) serves the heart or *himma* by its capability of creating objects in the world "out there." But a paradox of Active Imagination, as Corbin explains, is that what it creates already exists in the heart and thus projects what is reflected in the heart, what it mirrors, "and the object on which [the gnostic] thus concentrates his creative power, his imaginative meditation, becomes the *apparition* of an outward, extra-psychic reality."[10] Without Active Imagination, the ability to perceive transcendent reality is not possible.

What all of this means for Keats's letter to Bailey becomes evident in the experience he goes on to relate, an experience of *seeing* not some figment of his own imagination, as we commonly say, but rather "a Vision in the form of Youth a Shadow of reality to come." But first he must speak of what normally discredits imagination and its power:

> I have never yet been able to perceive how any thing can be known for truth by consequitive reasoning—and yet it must be—Can it be that even the greatest Philosopher ever arrived at his goal without putting aside numerous objections—However it may be, O for a Life of Sensations rather than of Thoughts!

Although Keats cannot perceive how truth can be known by analysis or reason (since truth for him is a *making* of the imagination), he questions "that even the greatest Philosopher" (Socrates or Plato perhaps) ever arrived at his goal without argument, debate, reason. It "must be" possible, he grants, and by granting it he is capable of understanding another modality

---

10. Corbin, *Creative Imagination*, 223. This paradox is not unlike that of the poet creating images which are original yet representative of preexisting things; or the divine primordial act of creating the world through that which exists in the Creator's imagination. This is not true of course in the Genesis story, where the Creator simply *says* creation; there is not attribution of imagination there. But man imagining God, as God imagines him, are only two phases of one and the same eternal process: the creative passage from darkness to illumination.

or function of man's existence, namely the creative imagination. And so he puts the question aside and inclines toward "a Life of Sensations rather than of Thoughts!"

The word "sensations" was an addition to Keats's vocabulary taken from the great English literary critic of his time, William Hazlitt, who used it in the traditional empirical sense as the concrete experience of the five senses.[11] Its appearance in Keats's letter has likely several meanings. But the most compelling one is that only by sensations does the poet create.[12] Poets see or hear or otherwise sense the physical world, as all men do, in all its sweet or cranky forms of accident. But then they surrender to the absorption of sense into a verbal music, which is the expression of a vision of reality. The work of imagination is to realize experience in the whole image or metaphor that a poem comprises. It is to take experience into an intenser realization of what is real. This is of course done in a nondiscursive, subjective way, though it is only so to those "Men of Power" whom Keats will return to in the Negative Capability letter. I think the reason Keats here opposes a life of "Sensations" to a life of "Thoughts" has to do with the fact that the first is primarily phantasmagoria, the second stated knowledge, and Keats, a young master of bodily excitement, rightly knows that poetry and imagination are essentially acts of desire—a desire for reality, to meet it, answer it, remake and intensify it. For to do this is to seek the transcendent. While it's certainly true that even the greatest philosopher has desire (*eros*) to ascend realities and achieve Ultimate Knowledge, such desire, as in Plato's *Republic,* is put to uses which make that Ultimate Knowledge misanthropic and morally bankrupt.[13]

---

11. W.J. Bate, *John Keats* (Cambridge: Harvard University Press, 1963), 239. Hereafter cited as Bate.

12. Emerson links the sense of seeing especially with the poet whose creativity is the soul's desire to live in the world. See "The Poet," *Essays: First Series,* 20-21.

13. Whether or not this is the point of the Platonic dialogues has been interestingly debated; see, e.g., Harry Berger, Jr., "Plato's Flying Philosopher," *The Philosophical Forum* XIII, 4 (Summer 1982), 385-407; and James O 'Rourke, "Mythos and Logos in the *Republic,*" *Clio* 16, 4 (1987), 381-396.

Keats opposes sensation to thought because he wants a "life," that is, a life "time," of sensations, of that which fuels his desire for Life. And such a life, he claims, yields or is

> 'a Vision in the form of Youth' a Shadow of reality to come—and this consideration has further conv[i]nced me for it has come as auxiliary to another favorite Speculation of mine, that we shall enjoy ourselves here after by having what we called happiness on Earth repeated in a finer tone and so repeated—And yet such a fate can only befall those who delight in sensation rather than hunger as you do after Truth—Adam's dream will do here and seems to be a conviction that Imagination and its empyreal reflection is the same as human Life and its spiritual repetition.

I think Keats's "finer tone" is not a supposition of heavenly joy since his entire letter concerns consciousness and knowledge adequate to the telling of our human existence. Only those who "delight in sensation" shall possess a sort of *repetition,* the meaning of which Keats unveils by referring to imagination once again. The imagination reflects an ardor, a fire which corresponds to "empyreal" in its Greek root *empúrios,* "in fire." The fire comes from the element or abode of the divine, the Heaven of heavens, which is the meaning of "empyreal" as Milton uses it in *Paradise Lost.* How this is the same as "human Life and its spiritual repetition" is borne out now in Keats's example to Bailey, which is that of another kind of Eve seen by Adam:

> But as I was saying—the simple imaginative Mind may have its rewards in the repeti[t]ion of its own silent Working coming continually on the spirit with a fine suddenness—to compare great things with small—have you never by being surprised with an old Melody—in a delicious place—by a delicious voice, fe[l]t over again your very speculations and surmises at the time it first operated on your soul—do you not remember forming to yourself the singer's face more beautiful that it was possible and yet with the elevation of the Moment you did not think so—even then you were mounted on the Wings of Imagination so

> high—that the Prototype must be here after—that delicious face you will see—What a time!

This is the fiery activity of possibility, process, and redefinition. It is re-visioning, hot and luminous as fire. It is divine possibility, which is discredited by the world's "consequitive reasoning." Keats not only talks about repetition, he represents it by "repeating" himself. Remembering, too, in this passage is a kind of repeating.

In spiritual terms, the moment evoked here is a recital / romance of the soul, an initiation into the meaning of "a delicious place" and "that delicious face you will see" hereafter. The initiation is a journey, the soul's journey "mounted on the Wings of Imagination." The visitation of the song and singer is an Image present to the soul from the beginning which becomes "felt over again," re-actualized to a knowing subject who, like Endymion, awakens to a new consciousness of reality. The "old Melody" is not necessarily normalized reality, accident, mere fact. It is a catalyst or a true report of the real. It may even be the mask of transcendence itself. For its value lies in the fact that it volatizes visionary feeling, or is itself volatized by visionary feeling. Hence Keats's flight in this letter, which returns him to his own devices as a poet: urgent, self-reflexive techniques of consciousness. The visionary feeling becomes part of him and offers him access to a "happiness on Earth repeated in a finer tone." This moment—whether of Adam's awakening or of ordinary human life—is not a symbolic harking back to Eden, the "loss" of which Milton justified, but an actual recovery, without effort and without tears, of that which is most intimately familiar. It is not unlike Blake's "Moment" in his poem *Milton*:

> There is a Moment in each Day that Satan cannot find
> Nor can his Watch fiends find it, but the Industrious find
> This Moment & it multiply. & when it once is found
> It renovates every Moment of the Day if rightly placed.[14]

14. Erdman, 136. From Book Two, 42-45, plate 35.

This moment indeed appears without effort and without tears. Yet it is no small achievement to come to this state or capability of recovery whose truth, as Blake saw, is a result of the effort of the industrious. One must work to get at truth. And the truth was leading Keats to a new romance, an inner pilgrimage or journey of the heart.

Near the end of Keats's letter there appears a most fascinating passage suggestive of the spiritual possibility of imagination as it is later realized in Negative Capability. After contrasting the "complex Mind—one that is imaginative and at the same time careful of its fruits—who would exist partly on sensation partly on thought"—with his own "simple" mind, Keats returns to the subject of "Worldly happiness," again occasioned by his friend's disposition, and writes:

> I scarcely remember counting upon any Happiness—I look not for it if it be not in the present hour—nothing startles me beyond the Moment. The setting sun will always set me to rights—or if a Sparrow come before my Window I take part in its existince and pick about the Gravel. The first thing that strikes me on hea[r]ing a Misfortune having befalled another is this. 'Well it cannot be helped.—he will have the pleasure of trying the resources of his spirit, and I beg now my dear Bailey that hereafter should you observe any thing cold in me not to but it to the account of heartlessness but abstraction.

At first glance it may seem that Keats is capable of nothing so much as outright indifference to human suffering while revelling in nature's matter-of-factness. But it would be a mistake to believe in this appearance. It would be a further mistake to believe that Keats's desired world, while it may be occupied at this point with things that excite the senses, remains a place without a human element or personality. When Keats says that a person befallen with misfortune "will have the pleasure of trying the resources of his spirit," he believes that humanity works out its destiny in time, and derives its meaning in the world from the soul's immortality. This meaning for Keats has much to do with the imagination's longed-for ease among the ordinary, which he singles out here in the sparrow's presence before his window. It's neither mythic nor symbolic, but a perfect unselfconscious example of a more human response to delighted contemplation with everything in the world, especially that which appears in the felt shape of the immediate "moment."

Keats's letter to Bailey becomes the intimation of a poetics, of a dream of poetry, that not only resulted from his toil on *Endymion* and all the early poetry, but was also coeval with the sudden fresh ending of his poetic romance. That ending was precisely a beginning. The letter to Bailey announces the terms of Keats's new start, and as such it stands as an emergent matrix of poetics which the Negative Capability letter will articulate. Negative Capability becomes a proliferating form of Keats's faith in and conviction of "Beauty" and "Truth."

If Beauty and Truth are all ye need to know, as the basis of the heart's method, then it must be that they yield time. In poetry, beauty and truth deliver us from the crush of necessity. Yet we are never without the time and memory of the poem, even if we write a poetry of sheer improvisation. Time is the undetected basis for that flowing reality of beauty and truth which adds its own felt weight to the twofold, making it a threefold. In Keats's life and art, time is the tragic. This "drama," as Bate explains, is the one in which "the resolutions are precarious, and the preciousness of the attainment ultimately crossed by tragedy."[15]

The tragic first shows its face, less than a month after the letter to Bailey, in the response Keats makes after seeing the painting *Death on the Pale Horse* by Benjamin West (1738-1820). With Charles Wells, Keats went to the Royal Academy exhibition on December 20, 1817. West, an American, was nearly eighty when Keats saw his work, a fact which is remarkable both for West's longevity and Keats's interest in so aged an artist. "It is a wonderful painting," Keats exclaims, "when West's age is

---

15. Bate, 242.

considered." Yet despite its title and subject, the painting lacks for Keats genuine tragic feeling:

> there is nothing to be intense upon; no women one feels mad to kiss; no face swelling into reality. the excellence of every Art is its intensity capable of making all disagreeables evaporate, from their being in close relationship with Beauty & Truth.
>
> (December 21, 1817)

In the context of Keats's use of "intensity" here, one hears a method or process or demand relating to the "holiness of the Heart's affections" and to "passion" in the root sense of suffering (from Greek *pati,* "to suffer").

More than a reaction, "intensity" (from Latin *intendere,* "to direct, intend, promote") suggests the phenomenology of an experience whereby an object "swelling into reality" is simultaneous with imagination greeting that object. Time is a given, and as such it makes that *sympathia* ("feeling with") subject to tragedy. The pathos of sympathy is that time enforces an end to it. That ruin brings the torment of memory or the intolerably burdened sense of distrusting or lusting after all moments of intensity. Certainly time causes the dissolution of the process and the object. It incapacitates the knowing subject who experiences and exclaims, "What a time!"

One of the means or methods by which Keats could begin to equal, even exceed, the inevitable fact of decay and the equally universal and central image of the web of life, was not to *wish away* the first and *imitate* the second, but to try to make himself capable of meeting, withstanding the force of, and transforming the given of a human being's circumstance. Hence the proposition, "What the Imagination seizes as Beauty must be truth." This imaginative action of seizing is precisely a means or capability of life-giving motion and direction, permitting humanity to discover the value of beauty and truth, instead of losing them to the onslaught of time.

Intensity is also the work of art itself, and the art of the work itself. "Art is not, at its best, the mirror—which is far too ready a symbol," William Carlos William asserts. "It is the life—but transmuted to another tighter form."[16] Imagination is the transmuter, the changer to another tighter form. As Keats spoke of the long poem as somewhere he could "wander in," so in any poem the poet must *stretch* and show his or her powers, which is an action that accords with another root sense of intensity (*intensus,* "to stretch"). One must take intensity, in all its etymological and conceptual senses, as formal evidence testifying to the needs of a more and more complex, enlarging intelligence. Hence the immediate correspondence Keats perceives with *King Lear,* his epitome of tragedy.

Having brought forward the dynamic of Beauty and Truth, it was all-important that Keats enter the tragic in order to expose it. The surprise is that he did this so quickly, in a month's time. Keats's letter to his brothers now turns from his two statements on intensity to a third, which completes the two, thus paraphrased: Examine *King Lear* and you will find this intensity exemplified. In the case of *Lear,* the tragedy of mortality engenders the old king's worth at the conclusion of the play. For "tragic" is a situation that brings out the cost, in human terms, of something brilliant. Played out in terms of mortal love, as in the tragic situation of *Lear,* the dynamic intensity of beauty and truth is the recognition for Keats of sensual reality. For what is sensual is tangible; it is intensity and touch. Tragedy hurts, pain is real. Thus the ending of *Lear,* when the king expires, exemplifies the insight that "all disagreeables evaporate from their being in close relationship with Beauty & Truth." For the horror we feel at the mask of death ("Is this the promised end?" Kent asks, "Or image of that horror?" Edgar replies) is vaporized like Lear's lifebreath at the moment he sees the mask of transcendence on Cordelia's lips: "Look on her! Look her lips, / Look there, look there—" (V.iii. 311-312). The ending is pure, not as of abstract thought but felt-thought, and love. The sudden joy that lets Lear die in a state of bliss is

16. William Carlos Williams, "Against the Weather: A Study of the Artist," *Selected Essays* (New York: New Directions, 1959), 198.

love. And we, experiencing it, are one with its form-feeling that evaporates, burns up, whatever is not agreeable or in harmony with the work of art itself, including the human. That intensity in life is a kind of foreshadowing of the intensity of death. What remains is that "depth of speculation" Keats mentions, which was a qualification of his subject and scale to come.[17]

Keats's discovery must certainly have had manifold causes. But his letter to his brothers makes it clear that the "Man of Achievement," whose quality of being he called Negative Capability, was utmost in his mind. Shakespeare was his presiding spirit, as he had written to Haydon in a letter of May 1817. And as Shakespeare's challenger, Keats discovered that imaginative sympathy gave him sight of a particular embodiment of method which he characterized as *Negative Capability*. Negative Capability, with its quality of "being in uncertainties, Mysteries, doubts," is contrary to the human bid for timelessness. This "negative" context is relevant to the ancient artists of Crete, who also disregarded the immortalization of proud human deeds.

I draw heavily upon C. Kerényi's study, *Dionysos: Archetypal Image of Indestructible Life*. In this discussion of human experience reflected in a totality of religion and art, we learn of an attitude which existed among the Minoan artists toward the visionary capacity and which is shared by Keats. Like them, Keats does not seek a refuge in abstraction. "Abstraction," in the letter to Bailey, is a defense of a life of sensation. A strange word to use in this context, perhaps. Nevertheless, abstraction for Keats involves nothing less than the "resources" of the human spirit. Life, to Keats, as to those artists of Greek antiquity, "means movement, and the beauty of movement was woven in

---

17. See discussion of "intensity" by David Perkins, *The Quest for Permanence* (Cambridge: Harvard University Press, 1969), 210. Perkins asserts that "intensity" can be defined as a "sympathetic participation so massive that it obliterates consciousness not only of self but also of anything other than the object focussed upon." However, intensity is not an "escape," nor does it offer one, as Perkins argues. His view of Keats's art as "escapist," however permanent or significant he finds that art, simply fails to elucidate the deepest sense of Keats's sympathetic imagination. For the imagination was not desired to be used in an escapist way and matched by a rudimentary aesthetic theory to justify it.

the intricate web of living forms which we call 'scenes of nature'; was revealed in human bodies acting their serious games, inspired by a transcendent presence, acting in freedom and restraint, unpurposeful as cyclic time."[18] Kerényi proposes that archaic man was always on the edge of an epiphany of the spirit. (Since that time man has increasingly lost the capacity of vision, though never completely as yet). He was always alive, awaiting "an intimation of the godhead [which] could be manifested....in a human gesture, and it could in turn determine man's gestures."[19] Keats's "negative" characterization of this capacity for knowing—negative from the standpoint of man as the center, as the vehicle of his own historical and nonhistorical glory (according to Kerényi) but not from the standpoint of spiritual life—is a *gesture* representing man's decentered position, which demands an "opposite" and can be understood only as an "opposite."

Gesture figures in Keats's intimation of mystery, not only in the meaning of attitude, posture, and movement, but also in that archaic sense of "story" (Latin *gesta*, "actions, exploits") embedded in the word; the story then being one of inspiration from and always having contact with Mystery. In the Negative Capability letter, Keats is face-to-face with mystery. Moreover, he is witnessing something, making use of what is the positive experience of mystics in all times, and the negative experience of non-mystics. This witness brings to mind that lovely passage in *A Midsummer Night's Dream*, V.i.4-17:

> Lovers and madmen has such seething brains,
> Such shaping fantasies, that apprehend
> More than cool reason ever comprehends.
> The lunatic, the lover, and the poet
> Are of imagination all compact.
> One sees more devils than vast hell can hold:
> That is the madman. The lover, all as frantic,

---

18. C. Kerényi, *Dionysos: Archetypal Image of Indestructible Life* (Princeton: Princeton University Press, 1976), 10. Hereafter cited as Kerényi.

19. Kerényi, 11.

Sees Helen's beauty in a brow of Egypt.
The poet's eye, in a fine frenzy rolling,
Doth glance from heaven to earth, from earth to heaven;
And as imagination bodies forth
The form of things unknown, the poet's pen
Turns them to shapes, and gives to airy nothing
A local habitation and a name.

Kerényi's insight bears further elaboration: "Our thinking in this matter ordinarily revolves around these two extremes [mysticism and non-mysticism]....We find little explicit testimony concerning what lies between the two extremes, although without such intermediate phenomena—the light, hovering visions of persons of moderate visionary endowment—a religion possessed of a living mythology would be unthinkable."[20] Precisely between these two extremes lies the intermediate world of imagination, which has for centuries been virtually a lost continent except to the lovers, madmen, and poets. It is the world situated midway between the world of purely intelligible realities (the transcendental) and the world of sense perception (the quotidian). In Sufism it is called the *imaginal* world, but it is not to be confused with what is commonly designated imaginary, nonexistent.[21] The

---

20. Kerényi, 15.

21. Corbin, *Temple and Contemplation*, 265-266. The imagination itself possesses a twofold aspect and fulfills a twofold function, according to the metaphysics of imagination in the Arab theosopher Suhrawardi's *Ishaqiyun*, of which Corbin writes: "On the one hand there is a passive imagination, the imagination that 'represents' or 're-produces' (*khayal*). As such the imagination is, quite simply, the storehouse that garners all the images perceived by the *sensorium*, this latter being the mirror in which all the perceptions of the external senses converge. On the other hand there is the active Imagination (*mutakhayyilah*). This active Imagination is caught between two fires. It can submit docilely to the injunctions of the estimatory faculty (*wahmiyah*), in which case it is the *rational animal* that assesses things in a way related to that of animals. The rational animal can and in fact does fall prey to all the deliriums and monstrous inventions of the imaginary, obstinately rejecting the judgment of the intellect. Yet the active Imagination can, on the contrary, put itself exclusively at the service of the intellect—of, that is to say, the *intellectus sanctus* as this functions in both philosophers and prophets. In such a case, Imagination is called cogitative or meditative (*mufakkira*; it should be noted that this is another name for the active Imagination, the productive Imagination)."

whole task for men and women who would achieve Negative Capability consists of purifying and liberating their inner being so that the intelligible realities perceived on the imaginal level may be *reflected empyreally*, as Keats says, in the world of sense perception. It's something like Blake's song:

> To see a World in a grain of Sand
> And a Heaven in a Wild Flower
> Hold Infinity in the palm of your hand
> And Eternity in an hour.[22]

Or like Adam's dream: "he awoke and found it truth." Or like that delicious face in a delicious place. These things are the understanding or translation of visionary experience, the spiritual revolution or cycle of human life.

One could substitute the terms *The Real* and *The Actual* for these two extremes. But these are extremes only when the human mind shuts its eyes and chills the heart; when the faculty of the soul is never born. That's the burden of extremes; they pinch the middle region more and more as one lives life with loose and imperfect perception. That's why Kerényi says "ordinarily" with regard to our thinking about mystery. These two extremes are fused by the power of imagination in Keats's remark; even the phrase "Negative Capability" combines the two extremes as a single thing, which sounds contradictory but actually means the ability to hold mystery (Latin *capere*, "to take," and Greek *ne-*, as in "nepenthe"). Hence the image of the face and the place, both "delicious," do not emerge from the negativity of the unconscious but from the positively differentiated centrality of *supra-consciousness*. The heightened awareness developed by or granted to Keats resulted from his soul's search for a vision of the world in both his life and his art. Negative Capability is one such stage, following that of the work on *Endymion*, of coming

22. Erdman, 490. "Auguries of Innocence," 1-4.

into possession of a living mythology or liberating forms of being.[23]

Keats certainly did not possess an orthodox religion, and his "ideas about Religion," as he later wrote to Bailey, were certainly not such that he thought himself "more in the right than other people" (March 13, 1818). Nor did he ever deem the poetic imagination as the sole means of arriving at truth. Keats did share a sense of the sacred virtually equivalent to the concrete experience that both Corbin and Kerényi describe. Negative Capability testifies to a situation not solely of man and his fellow man, but "something other, something outside himself, caught up in an atmosphere of festival as in an enchanted world."[24]

It was the day after Christmas as Keats and his two friends, Brown and Dilke, walked back from the Christmas pantomime, Keats having "not a dispute but a disquisition with Dilke, on various subjects." His very pleasant evenings with Dilke, the viewing of West's exhibition, and the Drury Lane and Covent Garden performances, serve as much as anything to evoke what can only be called an atmosphere of festival as in an enchanted world. The importance of the calendar is undeniable here. The year as a unit of time for Keats is pervasive in the poems and letters, and not just the calendar year but the seasons, as shown in *Endymion*:

> Many and many a verse I hope to write,
> Before the daisies, vermeil-rimmed and white,
> Hide in deep herbage; and ere yet the bees

23. Cf. Stuart Sperry, *Keats the Poet* (Princeton: Princeton University Press, 1970), 62. I agree with Sperry that Negative Capability is "heuristic," i.e. "a way of outlining a position with the end of clarifying it." I disagree that there is any "irony" here in the way "it qualifies itself in the uncertainty it affirms." My reasons center on the Penetralium of Mystery, a term, which Sperry does not explore, of vital importance to what Keats is saying in this letter.

As for a living mythology, see Ward, 144: "Keats was the first English poet to sense the possibility of a human meaning implicit in the [classical] myths themselves, rather than to fit them into preconceived allegorical patterns, as in general the Elizabethans did, or merely use them for decorative effect, like the eighteenth century poets."

24. Kerényi, 12.

Hum about globes of clover and sweet peas,
I must be near the middle of my story.
O may no wintry season, bare and hoary,
See it half finished; but let Autumn bold,
With universal tinge of sober gold,
Be all about me when I make an end.[25]

Robert Gittings shows how the atmosphere of winter added to the vision of "The Eve of St. Agnes." Keats, in the composition of that poem, had been thinking of lines from Spenser's *The Faerie Queen* quoted by Leigh Hunt, author and editor of the *Examiner* in which Keats's early work was first published. Apropos Hunt's essay on the month of January, Gittings writes: "Here is form and matter for the opening of the poem: the Spenserian stanza, and the personified figure of January."[26] And indeed, the legend itself, that on St. Agnes's Eve (January 20) a girl could dream of her husband-to-be, becomes a visionary point where one can see how the poem is going to end. There is a dimension to the seasons which is no mere accoutrement or backdrop; it is an influence, and one that penetrated to the core of Keats's mind.

Truly there was a festive peace as Keats walked and talked and discovered Negative Capability; and it was still with him as he wrote to his brothers about it all just two days after Christmas. That occasion, of course, wasn't wholly determinative of what Keats was called to and to which he harkened. He was also coming off the first step, Beauty and Truth. I think it is not incorrect to hear Keats this way, so that the great joy of intellect in the discovery and confirmation of Negative Capability in his

---

25. Stillinger, 104. Book I, 49-62. Not only do these lines convey the import of the seasons for Keats, but they are also prophetic of the poetic harvest that was to come with his great ode "To Autumn" in the fall of 1819, a year before his end.

26. Robert Gittings, *John Keats: The Living Year* (Cambridge: Harvard University Press, 1954), 67-68. Hereafter cited as Gittings. Apart from the seasons and literary influences, Gittings states that there is an additional source for the poem in the engravings of the Campo Santo at Pisa by Carlo Lasinio which Haydon had shown Keats, and in the Georgian city of Chichester itself, where Keats composed "The Eve of St. Agnes" on January 21, 1819.

letter was part of a celebratory time. For a moment, the tragic of time yielded to the greater pattern of time as the romance of the soul, and Keats found a way to express this reality by means of what was all around him. While it is usually the case that a host of things spurred Keats to his dreams, discoveries, and activities, the seasons, as much as the world of heart, mind, and circumstance combined, stand in advance of his poetics and equal to his struggle to understand himself both as a poet and a human being. After the winter of "The Eve of St. Agnes" will come that marvelous spring in which the odes were composed while Keats was writing his journal-letter to his brother George and sister-in-law Georgiana, then living in Kentucky, America.

Of the odes, that to Psyche "is the first product and the happiest in mood of this interval of peace."[27] Keats was then at Wentworth Place. The very site was enchanted by all that spring there encompassed: Keats's reading of William Adlington's translation of Apuleius's *The Golden Asse*; the garden outside his window; the pair of nightingales whose music flooded the garden; and Keats's love of a beautiful woman, Fanny Brawne. This world, as well as that exemplified in the "Ode to Psyche," was a "temple of delight" into which Keats had fallen sixteen months before in the Negative Capability letter.[28] To be more precise, a door or gate had opened in December 1817 onto all of what else existed for him.

Keats called this place which the door of Negative Capability opened onto "the Penetralium of mystery." It's a place from which, he says, "Coleridge, for instance, would let go by a fine isolated verisimilitude caught" there as a result of "being incapable of remaining content with half knowledge." The term "Penetralium" has the strong suggestion of an innermost room

---

27. Ward, 279.

28. Ward, 278-287, makes the illuminating observation that "it is not so much [the odes] which cast light on Keats's life this spring, as all of Keats's life that illuminates the odes. For these few weeks he stood at a point of perfect balance, confident in his ability to meet the future, able to contemplate his past with calm, and rejoicing in the beauty of the season, the joy of an answered love, the delight of a mastered craft—the theme of the odes as well as his incentives to writing them."

with the prominent position of center. The Latin plural, *penetralia* means "innermost parts," especially of a building, such as the sanctuary of a temple. Other forms of this word (*penetrare, penitus,* and *penes*) all contain the related meanings of "to enter within," "deeply, into the inmost recesses," and "within, in the power of." In this localization, as in myth and in all tales that embody myth, vision and language are equally fundamental. They speak for the imagination aroused by the mystery harbored in the Penetralium. One possible correspondence or resonance brings us to the enclosure of a feminine sanctuary. The Penetralium bears some resemblance to the palace of Cupid and Psyche, to the darkness and depth in that story of Apuleius with which Keats was to close his "Ode to Psyche," first copied in his letter to America (April 30, 1819):

> And there shall be for thee all soft delight
> That shadowy thought can win;
> A bright torch, and a casement ope at night,
> To let the warm Love in—

"Out of the meeting of these two lovers," Ward writes, "in the dark palace, Keats has evoked a lighted window seen from a garden outside—no part of Apuleius's story—and his own longing to enter it. For a brief moment the joys of reality and imagination strike a balance."[29]

But it's possible that Keats is speaking already from inside this temple of delight. For as one searches out the etymologies of the terms in the close of the "Ode to Psyche," one finds that *shadowy* means "dark" more than "vague, indistinct, or dim." Thus with *torch* one has the darkest brightness, the blackest light. This is an inkling of the mind's perception from within the Penetralium. For with *casement,* not only is there a lighted window through which the warm Love enters, but the "dwelling" itself (from Latin *casamentum*). It is the place where Love really came from and where one is obliged to go in order to

29. Ward, 280.

stay with it. Love dwells in this Home and leads Soul home. And as the close of the "Ode to Psyche" suggests, that homecoming is a ritualization of the wedding of Love (Eros) and Soul (Psyche) within the Penetralium, all three "persons" constituting a triumvirate.[30]

This same temple of delight should be compared with the *Imago Templi,* the Image of the Temple, because the Soul of this place invokes a romance of spiritual initiation similar to that in the story of Cupid and Psyche.[31] This Soul or Person or Place is one of many hypostases of history. Hidden beneath history, even farther, below the veil of what is called myth or legend, is such power that forestalls all empirical perception. It is known only by the imagination. "The *Imago Templi,*" Corbin writes, "is the form assumed by a transcendent reality in order for this reality to be reflected in the soul [that is, at the level of the imaginal world or imagination]. Without such a form, this reality would be ungraspable. However, the *Imago Templi* is not allegorical but 'tautegorical'; that is to say, it should not be understood as concealing the Other whose form it is. It is to be understood in its identity with that Other, and as being itself the thing which it expresses."[32] To *grasp* this reality is to *achieve* it, not with fact and reason but with humility and initiation. The initiation consists in that angel-like presence, that "delicious" face, showing the initiate how to go into the Temple to which the angel (Greek *ággelos,* "messenger") belongs and to which the initiate belongs. Outside the Temple, he or she is merely an exile. Keats saw this Temple with the eyes of imagination, the eyes of inner vision. That is the meaning of his visionary recital: to go outside himself in order to enter the Temple.

---

30. The Penetralium is a "person" because it possesses a soul—but a soul unlike that of man who succumbs to the delirium of the senses. It should be thought of as a Person in the same sense as any one of García Lorca's trio, *Duende, Angel, Muse.* See his "Play and Theory of the Duende," *Deep Song and Other Prose* (New York: New Directions, 1980), 42-53. Hereafter cited as Lorca.

31. See Erich Neumann, *Amor and Psyche* (Princeton: Princeton University Press, 1971).

32. Corbin, *Temple and Contemplation,* 267.

The soul of the *Imago Templi* is represented as Wisdom, *Sophia,* a hypostasis common in wisdom literature.[33] The suggestion of her in Keats's proposition of the Penetralium of Mystery, where "man is capable of being in uncertainties," brings and keeps us to a lore or tradition of knowledge which is not "Muse" from classical literary usage. The *Sophia* implied here is a virtual Presence that leads or allows Keats to penetrate to the heart of that which he was seeking, which is that same Presence; leads him to an experience not of any negativity but of a positive, sacred nature. There is an anima inside Keats whom he loves deeply, and she is no stranger but ever near, nearer than can be estimated. With her the language of conversation is the language of love and the language of poetry. This *Sophia* is not to be found in the biographical record. The phenomenon I am considering is the temple of the soul which is activated by grace (real life) and in which the angel-like presence of *Sophia* has already been building her temple. *Sophia* is identical with the Word, the *Logos,* and thus is described in certain theosophies as a high priestess celebrating her liturgy in the temple.[34] The Penetralium, in effect, is both *where* Keats was given, and *who* gave him, poetry.

Like other visionaries and interpreters, Keats discovered an Other (identified with the Penetralium of Mystery) that instructed him in the vital perception of Negative Capability. When he declared himself a poet, he began a preparation of mind to welcome all of what else would then be possible, developing that reflectiveness which would become a style in the odes. Keats's reflectiveness—intensely self-corrective, self-adjusting—speaks for the remarkable wholeness of his life. It is one with the formalizing power of his best poems. When Keats wrote the Negative Capability letter, he was testing the faculty of imagination or fancy. Discovering the capability of divesting one's mind of all but one's trust in mystery, he surrendered to an unconditional term of possibility. Men of "consequitive

33. Corbin, *Temple and Contemplation,* 293.

34. Corbin, *Temple and Contemplation,* 306.

reasoning," in contrast, promoted the grab at truth with the counsel of fact, not the principle of fact.[35] Keats apparently met the radical philosopher and novelist William Godwin on Christmas Day, a fact which has resonance with his "disquisition with Dilke," whose character he equated with that "irritable reaching after fact & reason." In his letters he calls Dilke "a Godwin perfectibility man" and a "Godwin-methodist" for having made up his mind about everything. Even Coleridge, who possessed a mental quality similar to Keats, was not capable of absolute surrender to uncertainty, perhaps because he was so scrupulously philosophical. He would not be willing or able to achieve "a fine isolated verisimilitude" except in poems like "Frost At Midnight," "This Lime Tree Bower," and "Dejection: An Ode," poems that test the ways of the mind's knowing. Keats intuited the heart of the problem (which wasn't so much truth as it was power) by taking a stance toward uncertainty as opposed to willfully setting in motion events related to the power of the self. He rejoiced in the "Mysteries," who were or could be guides with feminine-female resonance.

According to Ward, Psyche's meaning for the modern world is that of a tutelary goddess. She teaches how the Soul is formed by submitting to the trials of the world. Ward argues that the sacred grove in which Psyche is worshipped is in fact the poet's own "working brain."[36] Why then did the Psyche story attract Keats when it appears from the poem that Keats is more concerned with the shifts of self-consciousness than with the meaning of the announced object of his meditation, the

---

35. This is the contribution Charles Olson makes in his challenging reading of Keats's Negative Capability letter, *The Special View of History* (Berkeley: Oyez, 1970), 15-16. He writes: "Keats more than Goethe or Melville, faced with the Man of Power, got to the heart of it. He took the old humanism by its right front. It wasn't the demonism of Genius he saw was the hooker (almost nobody yet has caught up with Keats on the same subject—he was almost the only man who has yet seen the subjective tragedy as no longer so interesting), but the very opposite, the Sublime in the Egotistical, the very character of Genius, its productive power.... The stance which yields the possibility of acts which are allowably historic, in other words produce, have to be negatively capable in Keats' sense that they have to be, they have to be uncertain."

36. Ward, 280.

goddess herself? Who is the goddess that he should address her halfway through the poem in a strained voice: "But who wast thou, O happy, happy dove?" Ward spies a deeper meaning in the close of the "Ode to Psyche" when she says that it is "no part of Apuleius's story." For the ending vaporizes all residual traces of the story and formulates something all for the poet himself, namely "the form-giving impulse of Mind, suffused with possibility generated by Imagination, [which] is the fullest and most accurate preparation for the transforming integration of Soul and Love."[37]

This sacred region of the poet's mind, this temple of delight and intellection, is the Penetralium. The Penetralium of Mystery is a *place,* and a difficult one at that to map. Keats doesn't have a map, he is *making* one. But a paradox of that making is that what is made, or is to be made, does already preexist elsewhere, so that the mapping is a recovery of that which in its disclosure is felt to be the most intimately familiar thing of one's own being. We all know that experience very well. Keats is *working* it. In the phenomenology of this mapping and recovery, the reorientation of "self" constitutes its annihilation, and hence the annihilation of the split of self-consciousness into "here" and "there." It is this annihilation to which the Negative Capability letter alludes, whereby felt-thought replaces (without deposing) the self-centered reaching after fact and reason. Certainly the mystery is dependent on an "I," but an "I" that becomes the center of mystery, an "I" other than the self-identity ordinarily proposed.

Keats's struggle wasn't that of having to choose between one of two dualistic opposites, as if beauty and truth or sensation and knowledge were separated by an unbridgeable chasm. Nor was he merely stating postulates, which were never more than "speculation," a guess or shot in the dark that would play a minor role in his life. Once Keats chose imagination, possibility was returned, the spell of dualism broken. What then

---

37. Di Piero, 154.

appeared was the ground of Keats's life, that hugely populated heart-abode which prospects a soul's true home.

Some have used Negative Capability as a justification of ignorance. In a published section from one of his notebooks, poet-scholar W.S. Di Piero writes about this spurious use of Keats's faith:

> Embrace doubt and uncertainty, the current wisdom has it, for it will do you good. Indeed, it will ennoble you. I suppose it's easy to heroize one's fearlessness in the presence of uncertainty. We travesty Keats's inquiring, sensuous intelligence, however, if we cite him as an endorsement of the unwillingness to pass judgment, to evaluate, to assert or deny. Negative Capability is no counsel for failed nerve. Keats was advising himself to be patient in the quest for definitiveness. It is the counsel of patience of the imagination.[38]

As a step in the direction of definitiveness, Negative Capability cleared the ground of suppositions about truth and poetry, offering a perfect "negative" to the dry, intellectual mode of fact and reason. It also opened a door to the soul.

Keats was a young master of felt-thought, as the poems and letters show. He was one who showed daily acts of love and devotion to family and friends in gifts of money, books, and a wealth of letters. He also embraced the physical senses, equally precious gifts, which have all too often been denied from the earliest inheritance of joy by man's soulless assertion of self-will, that bitterly gloomy thing Keats recognized as the "egotistical sublime" (October 27, 1818). He refused the travesty of human nature and thereby allowed himself to discover what the soul actually desires. But he was young, and such things as his brother Tom's suffering and death kept the tears always flowing from his eyes. It was too quick for him. On the other hand, some large portion of those tears were the other sort, the great joy of intellect (Blake said a tear is an intellectual thing),

---

38. Di Piero, 73-74.

the soul's joy in the discovery and confirmation of what exceeds all the assumptions of good and evil, heaven and hell, life and death.

The Light of Supreme Darkness

O Maker of sweet poets, dear delight
Of this fair world, and all its gentle livers;
Spangler of clouds, halo of crystal rivers,
Mingler with leaves, and dew and tumbling streams,
Closer of lovely eyes to lovely dreams,
Lover of loneliness, and wandering,
Of upcast eye, and tender pondering!
Thee must I praise above all other glories
That smile us on to tell delightful stories.
For what has made the sage or poet write
But the fair paradise of Nature's light?
In the calm grandeur of a sober line,
We see the waving of the mountain pine;
And when a tale is beautifully staid,
We feel the safety of a hawthorn glade:
When it is moving on luxurious wings,
The soul is lost in pleasant smotherings:

—John Keats
"I Stood Tip-Toe Upon A Little Hill"

· III ·

DURING the last ten years of his life, years of great physical and mental suffering in prison, Antonio Gramsci produced the *Prison Notebooks*, an original prose work that contains the famous "letters from prison" which situate "the great vast world" as that from which Gramsci was shut away forever, while "liberty grew possible only for the inner life."[1] Only at the end of his life did Gramsci thus refer to these painful ten years of existence in his cell. Yet from the very first letters, marking his imprisonment in 1926, until the last, written shortly before his death in 1937, Gramsci's condemnation to prison gave rise to his own capacity to resist, which was his sole means of living. The *Prison Notebooks* and *Letters* both are some of the most inspiring products of a human being's desire to achieve real usefulness. With the faith and steady growth of a great artist whose plans and endeavors were subsumed by prison, Gramsci found a way to penetrate to the heart of his own life, since he could no longer live *in* the world, without losing sight of the limits of that world, seen now in a radically different light. The world was "over" for him the instant something other, and painful, began.

---

1. Antonio Gramsci, *Letters from Prison* (New York: Harper and Row, 1973), 262. This quote appears in a letter dated January 25, 1936, and is addressed to Gramsci's wife. Like Keats, Gramsci was supremely conscious of circumstance or what he called "coercion." "Coercion in certain matters seems necessary, even a good thing," he writes to his wife in this same letter. "I have been in a similar situation for many years, from 1926 on, when I was arrested. Then, my own existence was brusquely channeled in one direction by external pressures; liberty grew possible only for the inner life, and my will became solely the will to resist."

Often an artist seems to approach possibility by contradictory means. But often he or she in fact is following the necessary if irrational steps that lead to some liberation of form and feeling that no other thing allows. For Keats, Negative Capability seemed to contain a kind of contradiction to the question of new life. How can something "negative" be capable, and of what? Yet its truth and usefulness exists in the redefinition and exactitude of perception which comes only from suspended certainty and dissolution of personality in favor of intense attention to objects presented to the mind. Keats chose particularly apt metaphors, often oxymorons, inspired by his intense study of Shakespeare, with which to speak of the world. As Harold Bloom has remarked, "The entry of the oxymoron...is the emblem of awakening into reality."[2] These lines from *Endymion* exemplify this fact:

> Happy gloom!
> Dark Paradise! where pale becomes the bloom
> Of health by due; where silence dreariest
> Is most articulate; where hopes infest;
> Where those eyes are the brightest far that keep
> Their lids shut longest in a dreamless sleep.[3]

These lines are from the Cave of Quietude passage, which became supremely important to the meaning of *Endymion* precisely because of the new term Keats discovered here. Paradox opened the way to a profound dimension of human existence.

Like his poems, Keats's letters also contain this powerful rhetoric of opposites by which his intention to explore and celebrate the world, as well as his sense of reality, is clearly expressed. The means of realizing the perfection of his *Way* came about quickly and early on, the result of such necessary elements as Negative Capability and Adam's Dream. In addition

---

2. Harold Bloom, *Visionary Company* (Garden City, N.Y.: Doubleday, 1961), 386. Hereafter cited as Bloom.

3. Stillinger, 208. From Book IV, 537-542.

to the overmuscled action of the human power he called the "egotistical sublime," Keats was somehow allowed to perceive the possibility of action as something lacking egotism, yet positive as a sign of the soul. And he was exhilarated by this bountiful contradiction or paradox. In fact he was so exhilarated that he seems to go to great lengths to dismiss other, imputedly truer, forms of knowledge, as when he exclaims, "Oh for a Life of Sensations rather than of Thoughts!" Poetry was no "irritable reaching after fact & reason." Nor was it dogma or analysis or philosophy ordinarily defined. Poetry in fact offered a perfect "negative" to the logical, rational model of knowing. Keats, however, had come to distrust the kind of poetry he had hitherto written, as evidenced by his comments on *Endymion* before and after the beginning of 1818.[4] If not distrust, then it is surely the sense that his poems up to then were preparatory to other efforts. Indeed, Keats wrote very little between finishing the first draft of *Endymion* on November 28, 1817 and beginning the corrections to it on January 6, 1818. With Negative Capability at the center of this period of time, there is a sense that Keats's patience would be its own reward, yielding a poetry to advance both his craft and vision.

With Tom and George in Teignmouth, Keats saw in the new year alone at Hampstead and continued to see much of his friends in town. At the same time, he was actively pursuing subscriptions from his friends for Charles Cripps, a young man whom he and Haydon had planned to apprentice to Haydon for training as an artist. While doing all this, Keats was hearing depressing news from all sides that winter. From Teignmouth he learned that the climate was almost as bad as that in London, and that Tom was spitting blood now. He was also getting miserable reports about the health of his good friend James Rice. And from a safe distance, he witnessed the

4. See, e.g., Keats's remarks to Haydon on September 28, 1817, to Hessey on October 8, 1818, to Taylor on February 27, 1818, and to his family in America on February 19, 1819.

quarrels between and among his other friends: Haydon and Reynolds were waging a war in letters over a slight in etiquette one had done to the other; Hunt and Haydon likewise fought over an "indelicacy" involving the return of borrowed silver; and Bailey and Haydon's falling out months before remained unchanged. The "World's Quarrels" went on, Keats wrote to his brothers, "Uproar's your only music" (January 13, 18, 1818). Yet through all this malady and opprobrium, he was undaunted in his mind. He was revising *Endymion* for publication and thinking of a new poem, of which "the march of passion and endeavor will be undeviating," as he tells Haydon in a letter of January 23, 1818.

Keats was referring to his proposed epic *Hyperion,* a totality of a work like that of *Paradise Lost,* the nature of which he wanted to treat "in a more naked and grecian Manner" than *Endymion*. When Keats wrote these words to Haydon, contrasting *Hyperion* to *Endymion,* he was anxious to put the latter poem aside, with its "deep sentimental cast," and to advance toward what would be a better poem. His pride is evident in the contrast. As for any actual writing, however, it was more a case of fits and starts than any passionate marching. *Hyperion,* in fact, was not to begin in earnest until the autumn of that year.

Just five days prior to his letter to Haydon, Keats wrote to his brothers that he could only write in "scraps & patches." Keats alludes to *Hamlet,* III.iv.103: "A king of shreds and patches," which may possibly have conjured up for him the mad king in the tempest scene from *Lear,* Keats's epitome of the intensity of art. His remark, coupled with the proposed poem on the Greek gods and titans, alludes to a preoccupation with a special sort of genius, one significantly seen through or existing in the rage of opprobrium and suffering. Indeed, Shakespeare's poems and plays, along with the discovery of Negative Capability, were to prove a "demand" answered in all of Keats's future work. Seen over the course of letters from January to May 1818, and in the development of poems over this same period of time, this demand involves a profound growth of heart and mind.

"Demand" is the word Keats himself uses in the letter to his brothers where he includes a sonnet he wrote as a preparatory to rereading *King Lear*: "I sat down yesterday to read King Lear once again the thing appeared to demand the prologue of a sonnet." This is the last of four letters Keats wrote on January 23 (the other three were to Haydon, to his publisher John Taylor, and to Bailey), and it was finished the next day late in the evening. Keats's letter to his brothers and that to Bailey testify to a growth or deepening of the heart and mind which was signaled by a new penetration into Shakespeare.[5] Both letters clearly show that what Keats is moving toward early in 1818 is a participation in evil and pain, an attitude that refuses to withdraw from life when life is most horrible and sorrowful. Sometimes this attitude seems to be a withdrawal from or renunciation of Keats's earlier cry, "O for a Life of Sensations rather than of Thoughts!" But then one is compelled to look at the remarkable wholeness of his life, whereby sympathy unites sensation and thought. In short, Keats's fall into Heart, barely a month before, becomes quite evident in these letters. For his feeling-thinking is of "Humanity alone," and it is humanity that comes from the heart alone.

Keats's letter to Bailey was in response to a letter Bailey had apparently written to him twelve days before on January 11 in which he communicated something about an "unfortunate Family." Keats asks Bailey how the family in question has lived through the twelve days since Bailey wrote. He ponders that "perhaps more goes through the human intelligence in 12 days than ever was written," and then goes on in a most fascinating vein of thought:

---

5. See Randall McLeod, "Editing Shakespeare," *Sub-Stance* 33/34 (1982), *passim*. McLeod examines intertextuality in some of Keats's letters, including that to his brothers where he inscribes the sonnet "On sitting down to King Lear once Again." Citing the problem involved in editing and transmitting Keats's poems and letters over time, McLeod argues for a critical restoration of the "exact physical situation" of texts and extends his argument to an approach concerning Shakespeare. Hereafter cited as McLeod.

> One saying of your's I shall never forget —you may not recollect it —it being perhaps said when you were looking on the surface and seeming of Humanity alone, without a thought of the past or the future—or the deeps of good and evil—you were at the moment estranged from speculation and I think you have arguments ready for the Man who would utter it to you—this is a formidable preface for a simple thing—merely you said; *"Why should Woman suffer?"* Aye. Why should she? 'By heavens I'd coin my very Soul and drop my Blood for Drachmas.!" These things are, and he who feels how incompetent the most skyey Knight errantry its to heal this bruised fairness is like a sensitive leaf on the hot hand of thought.

Keats uses the quotation from *Julius Caesar*, IV.iii.72-73, "By heavens, I had rather coin my heart / And drop my blood for drachmas," somewhat ostentatiously to demonstrate his sincerity in the matter at hand. But this ostentation is modulated by the sudden change of phrase and thought regarding the suffering of women. In answer to Bailey's question, Keats asserts with plain-faced certainty: "These things are." But immediately certainty becomes mysterious: "and he who feels how incompetent the most skyey knight errantry its [sic] to heal this bruised fairness is like a sensitive leaf on the hot hand of thought." This image—unchivalric, inward, almost secretive—is a "fine isolated verisimilitude" suggesting a state of heart and mind that is capable of a certain kind of action. Such action is a fearless availability to life. Though Keats seems to go waywardly through the rest of this part of his letter, the mention of his friends' quarrels leads him further into the "hot hand of thought," as the following sentences give witness to a definitive subject:

> Things have happen'd lately of great Perplexity—You must have heard of them—Reynolds and Haydon retorting and recriminating—and parting for ever—the same thing has happened between Haydon and Hunt—It is unfortunate—Men should bear with each other—there lives not the Man who may not be cut up, aye hashed to pieces on his weakest side. The

> best of Men have but a portion of good in them—a kind of spiritual yeast in their frames which creates the ferment of existence—by which a Man is propell'd to act and strive and buffet with Circumstance.

These words presage the central activity that was to claim Keats, and that he was to explore over the next several weeks. It's an activity, a process, in which the test of suffering would make possible the preparation of heart and mind to meet circumstance.

Like so many things about Keats, the troubles of the unfortunate family attracted him because it occasioned self-definition. Keats was feeling anything but Hazlitt's ideal of "disinterestedness." In fact Bailey's endorsement suggests Keats actually did something *for* the family in question.[6] Their misfortune or hardship helped Keats to define his own feelings on the nature of human life. It may likely have struck at the brooding hurt he felt over the violent dislocation of his own family: his father and mother both dead before Keats was fifteen; his sister Fanny forced to live with trustee and guardian Richard Abbey, who forbade her to see her brothers; Tom's lingering illness; and George's failure to find gainful work. Whatever the case, there was a growing recognition taking place in Keats's mind that life is fragile and, as the Gilgamesh poet wrote, that "the end of life is sorrow." But there was also a growing awareness that one must face all circumstance bravely, not with innocence but through judgment by selective inclusiveness. Keats finished his letter to Bailey and then turned to his brothers before ending his correspondence that day.

As he wrote to Tom and George, he sensed that "a little change has taken place lately in my intellect," and offered the sonnet he'd written the day before, while sitting down to read *King Lear*, as proof of his change. For Keats, possibility is identical to that spiritual yeast which creates the ferment of existence. It's as if possibility were witnessed in or through the

---

6. See Rollins, I, 209n.

dramatic structure of that possibility. Which is to say that writing a poem, such as the sonnet on rereading *Lear*, proves that writing a poem has considerable effect. "I wrote it," Keats says, "& began to read—(I know you would like to see it)." Here is "On sitting down to King Lear once again" as it appears in Keats's letter:

> O golden tongued Romance with serene Lute!
> Fair plumed syren! Queen! if far away!
> Leave melodizing on this wintry day,
> Shut up thine olden volume & be mute.
> Adieu! for once again the fierce dispute,
> Betwixt Hell torment & impassioned Clay
> Must I burn through; once more assay
> The bitter sweet of this Shakespeareian fruit
> Cheif Poet! & ye clouds of Albion.
> Begettors of our deep eternal theme,
> When I am through the old oak forest gone
> Let me not wander in a barren dream
> But when I am consumed with the Fire
> Give me new Pheonix-wings to fly at my desire

It isn't so much that Keats wanted to leave behind romance forever. The opening of his sonnet is explicitly romantic in subject and structure with its music, siren, and Petrarchan octave. What he most wanted and needed was to absorb into poetic speech both the sensuous music of romance and the insistent clarity or intensity of tragedy, as in the terms of Shakespeare's *King Lear*. It's no accident, then, that instead of the sestet we get the Shakespearean quatrain and couplet to close the poem.

Keats's injunction to Romance, "Leave melodizing" and "Adieu," must be read in the context of the "bitter sweet," a mode that is not at all unfamiliar to him ("once again…must I burn through; once more assay"). Indeed, the bittersweet is most powerfully argued in the final four lines where Keats, inspired by Shakespeare, the "Cheif Poet," formulates that intensity which vaporizes all but beauty and truth. It is an intensity of transformation or purification through the fire of poetry, and not just any poetry. Of all Shakespeare's work, *King Lear* showed Keats most vividly that paradoxical state known as the bittersweet, which led him to his own term of possibility, Negative Capability. That flight of desire after consuming fire is quintessential Shakespeare; it exists not unlike the way *The Tempest* (romance) issues from *King Lear* (tragedy), which Keats was supremely aware of. Romance, then, is not simply one form or procedure abandoned for another, as if it were a youthful thing Keats outpassed and felt a little ashamed of. It's a power he integrates in advancing toward a new horizon of conscious being.

What is important here is that which Keats himself is working toward or burning through to the end. As he tells Tom and George immediately after copying his sonnet: "So you see I am getting at it, with a sort of determination & strength." He is getting at nothing less than the application of all his speculations, the embodiment of both an imaginative space and activity therein. The fact that Keats's original draft of this sonnet was inscribed in the blank space between the end of *Hamlet* and the beginning of *Lear* in his folio volume of Shakespeare's plays does not necessarily mean that he was sitting down to "write" *King Lear*, as Randall McLeod argues.[7] Certainly Keats had a rude directness and ingeniousness as an artist, as well as a sense of the iconic that was singular and great. But I feel that the act of inscribing his sonnet in between *Hamlet* and *Lear* is the instinct for the greater truth of poetics reacting the moment he engaged the strange stirring inspiration of *Lear* once again. The "demand" of *Lear* was surely not to write another *Lear* nor to rewrite *Lear* to Keats's satisfaction. It was to advance toward his own system of feeling and thinking, his own poetics.

---

7. McLeod, 33. "By virtue of responding to its 'demand' and offering *Lear* the sonnet as 'prologue,' Keats had entered into collaboration with Shakespeare." This seems to attribute intellectual *vanitosa* to Keats which doesn't jibe with his reflectiveness and self-correctiveness, no matter how iconic he may have been.

For a discussion of the differences between the text of the sonnet in Keats's letter to his brothers and the text in the Shakespeare folio known as the Hampstead holograph, see Stillinger, 588-589.

It seems to me that whatever the physical circumstances, an internalization was taking place (the praxis of poetry), a schooling of the self that Keats was not afraid to conduct in public, especially in his letters. The sonnet on rereading *Lear* is proof of the inward turn Keats discovered earlier with Negative Capability. And what became crucial to this turn is the fact and consciousness of tragic mortality. Keats allows the world of circumstance to enter his own being and becoming, thus integrating it and making it his own. This event is the same as that of writing poems, which, always somehow coming from without, enter and exit the poet through "irrational doorways."[8] The truth of his sonnet is the truth of his soul: the soul cannot *make it through* "the old oak forest" (which is a symbol not a rational explanation of its goal) until it restores the text of *Lear* to its truth, which for Keats is a cosmic truth of transmutation.

On February 19, 1818, Keats enclosed the draft or copy of his sonnet "O thou whose face hath felt the winter's wind" in an extraordinarily beautiful letter to his friend John Reynolds, whom he had visited the day before. Reynolds had been ill with rheumatic fever for some time. He was "in the worst place in the world for amendment," Keats wrote to his brothers, "among the strife of women's tongues in a hot and parch'd room" (February 21, 1818). Keats was sensitive to all this when he wrote "to lift a little time from your Shoulders." His poem was composed that morning of February 19, evidently provoked on the spot by the beauty of the day and the song of a thrush while Keats mused in idleness. In his letter he says that the thrush had seemed to speak the words of the poem, words condoning his indolence and affirming the promise of some future harvest, some prospective light:

> 'O thou whose face hath felt the Winter's wind;
> Whose eye has seen the Snow clouds hung in Mist

---

8. The phrase is from William James, *The Varieties of Religious Experience* (New York: Modern Library, 1936), 374.

And the black-elm tops 'mong the freezing Stars
To thee the Spring will be a harvest-time—
O thou whose only book has been the light
Of supreme darkness which thou feddest on
Night after night, when Phœbus was away
To thee the Spring shall be a triple morn—
O fret not after knowledge—I have none
And yet my song comes native with the warmth
O fret not after knowledge—I have none
And yet the Evening listens—He who saddens
At thought of idleness cannot be idle,
And he's awake who thinks himself asleep.'

It's a soothing and firm piece of writing, and the only unrhymed sonnet among Keats's poems. In light of his letter, this sonnet answers the occasion of Keats's speculation about idleness which precedes it; it is grounded in and arises from the intense meditative preparedness which Negative Capability defined. Keats was entirely turned toward and attuned to the expression of thought in the form of poetry, whether it was in verse or prose. He sensed this poem and other efforts were self-impelling encounters between the inquiring spirit and its objects, leading him quickly into a formalization of artistic truth which he was not afraid to situate and correct in his letters. With typical self-effacing swagger, he closed off his sonnet by telling Reynolds, "all this is a mere sophistication."

Keats's letter to Reynolds can be seen on a plane equal to the poem it precedes and encompasses. It is poetry. And "since poetry is so much possibility and speculation in the making," Di Piero writes, "however self-contained or defined by the lineaments of occasion, the poetic form bears some exponential promise."[9] Like his poem, Keats's letter promises the development of a poetry one with the reality of beauty and the reality

9. Di Piero, 69.

of imagination, a poetry that accounts at once for what is really there and what the mind creates.[10] His letter begins:

> I have an Idea that a Man might pass a very pleasant life in this manner—let him on any certain day read a certain Page of full Poesy or distilled Prose and let him wander with it, and muse upon it, and reflect from it, and bring home to it, and prophesy upon it, and dream upon it—untill it becomes stale—but when will it do so? Never—When man has arrived at a certain ripeness in intellect any one grand and spiritual passage serves him as a starting post towards all "the two-and thirty Pallaces" How happy is such a "voyage of conception," what delicious diligent Indolence! A doze upon a Sofa does not hinder it, and a nap upon Clover engenders ethereal finger-pointings—the prattle of a child gives it wings, and the converse of middle age a strength to beat them—a strain of musick conducts to "an odd angle of the Isle" and when the leaves whisper it puts a "girdle round the earth. Nor will this sparing touch of noble Books be any irreverance to their Writers—for perhaps the honors paid by Man to Man are trifles in comparison to the Benefit done by great Works to the 'Spirit and pulse of good' by their mere passive existence. Memory should not be called knowledge—Many have original Minds who do not think it—they are led away by Custom—Now it appears to me that almost any Man may like the Spider spin from his own inwards his own airy Citadel—the points of leaves and twigs on which the Spider begins her work are few and she fills the Air with a beautiful circuiting: man should be content with as few points to tip with the fine Webb of his Soul and weave a tapestry empyrean—full of Symbols for his spiritual eye, of softness for his spiritual touch, of space for his wandering of distinctness for his Luxury—

10. Cf. Donald C. Goellnicht, "Keats on Reading: 'Delicious Diligent Indolence,'" *Journal of English and Germanic Philology* 88, 2 (1989), 190-210. Goellnicht addresses only Keats's "concept of reading" in this letter, a letter that as a whole involves far more than reading, i.e. "a sense of idleness" derived from not reading. For Keats, reading here becomes an imaginative/spiritual journey in search of meaning and wholeness of being. It is a "reading" in the largest possible sense, that of interpreting the whole cosmos.

One of the unique and striking phrases in this letter is that of "the two-and thirty Pallaces," whose origin Keats does not explain and which, for Northrop Frye, has an oriental ring to it.[11] Frye is looking for analogues, as indeed Keats himself is looking, that is, looking outside his own mind for metaphors to describe what a poet discovers in the writing of poetry or what one discovers in reading it. Shakespeare came most readily to his mind, as the quotations from *The Tempest* and *A Midsummer Night's Dream* here show. Poetry is a vast enchanted territory in which to wander like the characters in Shakespeare's magical plays. It is a spiritual treasure like the oriental opulence suggested by Keats's phrase. Art creates a world large enough to live in, which can be limited when the artist does not admit other things. But here Keats is talking about having "arrived at a certain ripeness in intellect" where "any one grand and spiritual passage serves [Man] as a starting post towards all 'the two-and thirty Pallaces.'" This "voyage of conception" is happy because luxurious, that is, its peregrine excess (Latin *luxus,* "excess" and *luxare,* "to dislocate") centers on a dislocation from the standard existence or method of life. Thoreau saw the very same luxury in his experience. His *"extra-vagance"*—an expression adequate to the truth of "whole new continents and worlds within"—expresses imagination as a purposeful wandering beyond the narrow limits of daily life.[12] The mind that makes this journey discovers—by traversing the landscape of its dreams or desires—the beneficence of its own operations.

---

11. Northrop Frye, *A Study of English Romanticism* (Chicago: University of Chicago Press, 1982), 157.

See Rollins, I, 231n. It does not seem either strange or impossible to me that Keats could have known anything about Eastern lore, whether Buddhism, Hinduism, or Confucianism. Various references in his *Letters* in fact testify to more than a passing knowledge of such lore. See, e.g., I, 349; II, 28; II, 103; II, 270.

12. Henry David Thoreau, *Walden* (New York: Norton, 1966), 214. In the "Conclusion" to his experiment in living, Thoreau speaks of journeying in the direction of dreams and wisdom in terms not unlike those of Keats. Of his *extravagance,* he writes: "I desire to speak somewhere *without* bounds; like a man in a waking moment, to men in their waking moments; for I am convinced that I cannot exaggerate enough even to lay the foundation of a true expression."

Keats's oxymoron "diligent Indolence" captures the heart of the meaning of poetic activity: the poet is most busy when he or she appears to be doing nothing. Concentration is work; it involves waiting, a disciplined expectancy. It's a form of attention (like memory which Keats dismisses as knowledge), an enthusiastic noticing of or alertness to the worlds within and without, at least for Keats, as he works over the possibilities of revelation here that yield such privileged moments as those which express the joy of voyaging toward new inner lands and which recommend "the Spirit and pulse of good."

What does Keats mean by "great Works"? He does not mean books, for the entire letter concerns "a sense of Idleness" derived from not having read any books. He means the works of nature, like the spider, flower, bee, and thrush. These, "by their mere passive existence," *benefit* "the Spirit and pulse of good." For the passivity of these things creates or performs an imaginative action in the human mind. Passivity demonstrates oneness and contentment. This is man's response to an example or experience which only nature can provide. First and foremost, such oneness and contentment can only result from encounter and association.[13] Keats had initially responded to nature's beneficence in his early poem "I Stood Tip-Toe Upon a Little Hill," written in 1816 and originally titled "Endymion." The happiness engendered by that response informed part of the need to write what became the "poetic romance" *Endymion* a year later. To find happiness, Keats learned that all things need to be explored inside and out:

---

13. See Martin Buber, *I and Thou* (New York: Charles Scribner's Sons, 1970), 109. Buber proposes the establishment of man's relation to God as an "I" and "You" relation, a relation which extends to man and nature. The relation of "I" and "it" results in the ignobility of "the capricious man [who] does not believe and encounter; he does not know association. He knows only the feverish world out there and his feverish desire to use it."

In connection with this destructiveness of being, see also Bloom, 362: "The man cut off from others and from his own true imagination is in hell, for the Romantic hell is neither other people nor oneself but the absence of relationship between the two."

> Wherein lies Happiness? In that which becks
> Our ready minds to fellowship divine,
> A fellowship with essence; till we shine,
> Full alchemiz'd, and free of space.[14]

The alchemy is one of relating, whether it be humanity and God, humanity and Nature, or the relationship among human beings. It's alchemy precisely because a new matter is created by the introduction of an entity or "essence" which prehends other objects. "Free of space" hints of a fundamental cosmic condition, a change returning one to origins. For what is at issue here is the work of reshaping the self.

The *essences* of these natural things in Keats's letter are *the* essences of transformation, of destiny, since they are to be found on the path toward "the two-and thirty Pallaces." What could be more suggestive than the motif of the spider that "spin[s] from his own inwards his own airy Citadel"? This kind of passivity is the action of the spirit, its *passion,* as it reshapes itself into its own true expressive form. Its weaving is both an activity and architecture, a self-portrait and dwelling. Such is the secret of happiness, of this kind of alchemy, that through its own creative agency the self achieves an image of sublime existence filled with symbols for instruction and inspiration.

However much it seems impossible for any commonality or mutuality to exist for human beings in relation to this condition, Keats does not resign himself to the narrowness of individual luxury. He believes in the larger, wider force of sympathy:

> The Minds of Mortals are so different and bent on such diverse Journeys that it may at first appear impossible for any common taste and fellowship to exist between two or three under these suppositions—It is however quite the contrary—Minds would leave each other in contrary directions, traverse each other in Numberless points, and all last greet each other at

---

14. Stillinger, 125. Book I, 777-780.

> the Journeys end—A old Man and a child would talk together and the old Man be led on his Path, and the child left thinking—Man should not dispute or assert but whisper results to his neighbour, and thus by every germ of Spirit sucking the Sap from mould ethereal every human might become great, and Humanity instead of being a wide heath of Furse and Briars with here and there a remote Oak or Pine, would become a grand democracy of Forest Trees.

By partaking of the selfsame benefit offered by the voyage—which is an odyssey in search of wholeness—all are capable of arriving at the same place. There is a sense here in Keats's figures of Old Man and Child of a circle that opens and closes in which a symbolic vision flowers.[15] It is a vision of association and intimacy: neighbors whispering "results" to each other. Such results may likely recount the stages of this journey to the Orient, a journey of *becoming* "a grand democracy of Forest Trees." All the metaphors in Keats's letter pass through this one idea. However, "become" is not a metaphor; it is a truth that is real, the most adequate statement for expressing the poet's sense of existence—and it is less a way of expressing than of illumining evidence of life other than our normalized state of being. To become is anything but a poeticism here. It is the capacity of life itself.

Keats's letter emerges not so much as a form of sensation versus knowledge, but as a testing of Negative Capability, especially in its aspect of passiveness and receptivity. That is, rather than reaching after fact and reason, Keats's capability here is that of feeding or being fed by what is not ordinarily perceived as knowledge:

> It has been an old Comparison for our urging on—the Bee hive—however it seems to me that we should rather be the flower than the Bee—for it is a false notion that more is gained by receiving than giving—no the receiver and the giver are equal in

---

15. See Corbin, *Avicenna and the Visionary Recital,* 29. This is what Corbin defines as the "hermeneutic circle."

> their benefits—The f[l]ower I doubt not receives a fair guerdon from the Bee—its leaves blush deeper in the next spring—and who shall say between Man and Woman which is the most delighted? Now it is more noble to sit like Jove that to fly like Mercury—let us not therefore go hurrying about and collecting honey-bee like, buzzing here and there impatiently from a knowledge of what is to be arrived at: but let us open our leaves like a flower and be passive and receptive—budding patiently under the eye of Apollo and taking hints from every noble insect that favors us with a visit—sap will be given us for Meat and dew for drink—

Hyder E. Rollins notes that Wordsworth's "wise passiveness" was in Keats's mind here.[16] The phrase appears in Wordsworth's poem "Expostulation and Reply" and stems from the poet's reply to a disquisition of sorts on idleness, whereby dreaming and not-dreaming are called into question. In the fifth and sixth stanzas Wordsworth answers his interlocutor with these words:

> "The eye—it cannot choose but see;
> We cannot bid the ear be still;
> Our bodies feel, where'er they be,
> Against, or with our will.
>
> "Nor less I deem that there are Powers,
> Which of themselves our minds impress;
> That we can feed this mind of ours,
> In a wise passiveness.[17]

In a letter of January 10, 1818, to Haydon, Keats had written: "I am convinced that there are three things to rejoice at in this Age—The Excursion Your Pictures, and Hazlitt's depth of Taste." *The Excursion* (IV, 687-765, 840-881) in particular has

---

16. See Rollins, I, 232n.
17. Ernest de Selincourt, ed., *The Poetical Works of William Wordsworth*, vol. 4 (Oxford: Clarendon, 1947), 56. Hereafter cited as de Selincourt.

been cited as the source of Keats's ideas about the function and nature of poetry, namely that it evokes the forceful imminence of the visible world.[18] Keats gleaned more than just this one idea from Wordsworth's work. The subject of his letter to Reynolds is truly a "wise passiveness," that is, a condition answering his experience of the world. All of Keats's borrowings throughout this period are indicative of his desire for the sustained simultaneous rush of intellection and sensation, for tragic knowledge and sensuous thrill. And as for "borrowing," Keats didn't borrow anything without making it his own, for a thing's only meaning or value to him was as *use*, a particular human use. If Keats was to do anything with what others had given him, it was to build on what was given and then go beyond or alongside the same. Keats plunged inside the borrowings from Wordsworth until they yielded his own propositional rhythm as expressed in his letter. Hence he symbolizes those Wordsworthian "powers," which impress themselves upon our minds, as forms of nature. We could even say Keats *mythologizes* those powers, since a good definition of myth involves the capacity to touch one's best consciousness and drench a fact with human truth.[19] This effort might seem at odds with indolence. However, indolence is actually *sympathesis*, the self in its experiencing of the world. Although

---

18. See John Barnard, ed. *John Keats: The Complete Poems* (New York: Penguin Books, 1973), 130.

Keats gave Wordsworth his "due," despite his admonition that we need not "be bullied into a certain Philosophy engendered in the whims of an Egotist," as Keats wrote to Reynolds in a letter of February 3, 1818. He also states to Reynolds his faith that "Poetry should be great & unobtrusive, a thing which enters into one's soul, and does not startle it or amaze it with itself but with its subject." This credo resonates with the passiveness and receptivity which distinguishes Keats's speculation on idleness, and which distinguishes him from his contemporaries, especially Wordsworth and Hunt, both of whom he criticized for what we can only call the sheer obtrusiveness of ideology. That is, the insistence that the reader should think the way they do. Keats balked at this "false coinage" and self-deception of supposing one's ideas are of overwhelming import. He did not gainsay Wordsworth and Hunt's value; he simply wanted something pure, the old poets' "grandeur & merit,...uncontaminated & unobtrusive."

19. See Sherman Paul, "Resolution at Walden," in *Walden*, 338. Professor Paul writes: "*Walden* was [Thoreau's] myth.... For him, only the fact stated without reference to convention or institution, with only reference to the self which has tasted the world and digested it, which has been 'drenched' and 'saturated' with truth, is properly humanized—is properly myth."

Keats can seemingly shift gears and speak of having "no enjoyment in the World but continual drinking of Knowledge" (April 24, 1818), isn't "drinking" a sensuous activity? "Such shifts of mood were to continue," Douglas Bush writes, "active assimilation of knowledge and ideas and passive receptivity to 'sensation' were both valuable and nourished each other."[20] By "knowledge" Keats often means "wisdom." That is, the soul's most intimate depths, experiences, and journeys. Over against the acquisitive reaching after knowledge as fact or reason, Keats pleads for contemplation, the nature of which for him is a living, exfoliating event, a conscious mature life that promises renewal, growth, and happiness.

One could argue that the song of the thrush, telling Keats he was "right" to be idle and speculative, sustains an anti-intellectual mood. But what it really says is the advocacy of something mysterious: "He who saddens / At thought of Idleness cannot be idle, / And he's awake who thinks himself asleep." These lines, in turning idleness and sleep into their contraries, reverse the assumptive wisdom about human efforts. "However it may neighbor to any truths," Keats says of his sonnet, it was written "to excuse my indolence." Yet how indolent is it to write a letter or poem of such extraordinary power of imaginative action? It's uncertain whether Keats was writing to Reynolds or himself, or both at once, in order to announce these "truths." In any case, one of these truths is that it was no false spring in the imagination which gave voice to Keats's thrush. He was moving closer every day to an equinox of sensation and thought in which he would encounter a nightingale whose voice would carry him to "embalmèd darkness." Another truth is that "the light of supreme darkness" was now revelatory of the human heart, wakeful and alert to the seemingly contradictory nature of existence, tense with its own desire to see into the heart of contradiction. "Humility like darkness reveals the heavenly lights," Thoreau quotes Confucius in his

20. Douglas Bush, *John Keats* (New York: Macmillan, 1966), 70. Hereafter cited as Bush.

plea for the greater truth of human life.[21] Perhaps this is the vista seen from the vantage point of "the two-and thirty Pallaces." Keats's dark light was the dawning of a great new life of happy struggle, one that brings the most difficult kind of purity or inner freedom there is.

21. *Walden*, 217.

From Feathers to Iron

Time, time for you to begin a new spiral

—H.D.
"The Walls Do Not Fall"

· IV ·

On March 13, 1818, Keats wrote to his friend Benjamin Bailey a letter headed only by the words "Teignmouth Friday." These two coordinates alone situate the immediacy of writing from Devonshire, a coastal town in the south of England where Keats had lately arrived from Hampstead to join his brothers. For the past three months, George and Tom had been residing in Devonshire, hoping the change of climate would improve Tom's health. Something happened there of enormous significance to Keats's poetry and poetics, something having to do with his growing awareness of tragedy, mortality, and the terms of a possibility of new life. At this stage in his life and career, the instructive discovery of Negative Capability, its testing as an intense meditative preparedness in both poems and letters, and the situation of Tom's slow descent to death from tuberculosis, all constitute the stuff of life which had entered Keats and which he transformed, through great pain and joy, into a vital and meaningful condition. This condition is contained or implied in a mysterious phrase appearing in his letter to Bailey: "We take but three steps from feathers to iron." It is a phrase proleptic of Keats's passage into the "Chamber of Maiden Thought," which is a room in life where we drink the light of differentiation as opposed to undifferentiated moods of sensation in the "infant chamber." More significantly, "from feathers to iron" involves a journey revelatory of humanity's relation to transcendence, a journey in fact that Keats had marvelously described earlier in a letter to Reynolds when he wrote of a spiritual passage towards "all the two-and thirty Pallaces" (February 19, 1818).

Now, barely a month later, he plunged into that journey to describe in detail what he was discovering along the way.

Writing from Teignmouth on Friday marks the vista or site of a vast mental depth which Keats bodies forth to his friend in Oxford. While we get plenty of information about Teignmouth, more importantly we get a demonstration of a world-making letter. Keats did not like to write short letters, as he told his brothers (February 21, 1818). He preferred a certain amount of space in which to compose the many diverse elements cramming his head, all of them having to do with poetry and poetics. As he wrote to Reynolds about his letters:

> If I scribble long letters I must play my vagaries. I must be too heavy, or too light, for whole pages—I must be quaint and free of Tropes and figures—I must play my draughts as I please, and for my advantage and your erudition, crown a white with a black, or a black with a white, and move into black or white, far and near as I please—I must go from Hazlitt to Patmore, and make Wordsworth and Coleridge play at leap-frog. (May 3, 1818)

With a blend of humor and seriousness, the composition of these kinds of things is what I take to be the creation of a world within the letter, the worldliness of which exists in the fact that it acknowledges both unity and disunity. So when Keats begins his letter to Bailey, his writing is not merely occasioned by the "abominable" Devonshire weather but by other weather *within*:

> When a poor devil is drowning, it is said he comes thrice to the surface, ere he makes his final sink if however, even at the third rise, he can manage to catch hold of a piece of weed or rock, he stands a fair chance,—as I hope I do now, of being saved. I have sunk twice in our Correspondence, have risen twice and been too idle, or something worse, to extricate myself—I have sunk the third time and just now risen again at this two of the Clock P.M. and saved myself from utter perdition—by beginning this, all drench'd as I am and fresh from the Water—and I would rather endure the present inconvenience of a Wet Jacket, than you should keep a laced one in store for me. Why did I not

> stop at Oxford in my Way?—How can you ask such a Question? Why did I not promise to do so? Did I not in a Letter to you make a promise to do so? Then how can you be so unreasonable as to ask me why I did not? This is the thing—(for I have been rubbing up my invention; trying several sleights—I first polish'd a cold, felt it in my fingers tried it on the table, but could not pocket it: I tried Chilblains, Rheumatism, Gout, tight Boots, nothing of that sort would do, so this is, as I was going to say, the thing.—I had a Letter from Tom saying how much better he had got, and thinking he had better stop—I went down to prevent his coming up—Will not this do? Turn it which way you like—it is selvaged all round—I have used it these three last days to keep out the abominable Devonshire weather—

Keats begins in a genial humor by way of explaining his silence to Bailey, to whom he had not written in nearly two months. The image of himself "all drench'd and fresh from the Water" is a self-exonerating one. It's also a hilarious mock baptism and an alternative to the image of being straitjacketed by the clerical Bailey who, it seems, was easily offended that Keats did not promise to visit him. Keats then commences to play one of his "vagaries" on Bailey, which turns out to serve quite a serious purpose: it comes to rest on his brother Tom's illness, and it doubles back as a kind of rhyme on the previous remark about saving himself. "Turn it which way you like," Keats says with a little vindication, "it is selvaged all round." "Selvage" is the edge of a piece of woven fabric finished so as to prevent unravelling. By sleight of word, in the very quick of the word, Keats has woven a fine piece of *coherence* or "holding together" that won't come unravelled in use. And he keeps the invention going as a safeguard against Devonshire as his letter now takes up describing the immediate scene:

> You may say what you will of devonshire: the thuth is, it is a splashy, rainy, misty snowy, foggy, haily floody, muddy, slipshod Country—the hills are very beautiful, when you get sight of 'em—the Primroses are out, but then you are in—the Cliffs are of a fine deep Colour, but then the Clouds are continually vieing

> with them—The Women like your London People in a sort of negative way—because the native men are the poorest creatures in England—because Government never have thought it worth while to send a recruiting party among them. When I think of Wordswo[r]th's Sonnet 'Vanguard of Liberty! ye Men of Kent!' the degenerated race about me are Pulvis Ipecac. Simplex a strong dose—Were I a Corsair I'd make a descent on the South Coast of Devon, if I did not run the chance of having Cowardice imputed to me: as for the Men they'd run away into the methodist meeting houses, and the Women would be glad of it—Had England been a large devonshire we should not have won the Battle of Waterloo—There are knotted oaks—there are lusty rivulets there are Meadows such as are not—there are vallies of femminine Climate—but there are no thews and Sinews—Moor's Almanack is here a curiosity—A[r]ms Neck and shoulders may at least be seen there, and The Ladies read it as some out of the way romance—Such a quelling Power have these thoughts over me, that I fancy the very Air of a deteriorating quality—I fancy the flowers, all precocious, have an Acrasian spell about them—I feel able to beat off the devonshire waves like soap froth—I think it well for the honor of Brittain that Julius Caesar did not first land in this Country—A Devonshirer standing on his native hills is not a distinct object—he does not show against the light—a wolf or two would dispossess him. I like, I love England, I like its strong Men—Give me a "long brown plain" for my Morning so I may meet with some of Edmond Iron side's descendants—Give me a barren mould so I may meet with some shadowing of Alfred in the shape of a Gipsey, a Huntsman or as Shepherd.

This passage is no mere demonstration of an invective sliding into a rhapsody on the fatherland. Nor is it simply an instance of what Keats termed "Fort-St-Hyphen de-Phrase" for these "troopings" of words reminiscent of Burton or Rabelais.[1] This

1. See his letter to George and Georgiana Keats, September 18, 1819: "I have been reading lately Burton's Anatomy of Melancholy; and I think you will be very much amused with a page I here coppy for you. I call it a Feu de joie round the batteries of Fort St Hyphen-de-Phrase on the birthday of the Digamma." Keats would have known of Rabelais from William Hazlitt's lectures if not from his own voracious reading in French literature.

long passage is consequential in terms of the "innumerable compositions and decompositions which take place between the intellect and its thousand materials before it arrives at that trembling delicate and snail-horn perception of Beauty" (April 8, 1818).

Once again in Keats's life and thought, a haven of beauty and truth is felt as something desired and necessary, and Keats sets about building this haven of intensity with language, aided as always by fancy or imagination. Imagination is the key to this construction which became a way to grapple effectively with the deterioration of humanity seen and felt at Devonshire. However one wishes to characterize the writing here, it is a tour de force of composition, weaving its diverse elements (literature, history, and nature) into a tapestry "selvaged" not by misanthropy but by the power of imagination. Keats is no misanthrope. "I admire Human Nature," he once wrote to Haydon, "but I do not like *Men*" (December 22, 1818). He is a lover of the noble spirit of humanity, of the ambitious pursuit of sublime discovery, such as that felt in his early sonnet "On First Looking into Chapman's Homer" (1816). Inspired by his own mention of Ironside and Alfred the Great, he goes on to say:

> Scenery is fine—but human nature is finer—The Sward is richer for the tread of a real, nervous english foot—the eagles nest is finer for the Mountaineer has look'd into it—Are these facts or prejudices? Whatever they are, for them I shall never be able to relish entirely any devonshire scenery—

What is suggested here is that identity or personality of life is what gives life meaning. Such meaning is hinted in Keats's repetition of "finer," echoing his "finer tone" of human life and its "spiritual repetition" (November 22, 1817). That Keats chose *walking* and *climbing* as images to express what is fine about human nature is no accident. These are central to the imaginative action in Keats's poetics; they represent the soul's journey and ascent toward sacralized existence. More than "prejudices" of intellectual being, they are "facts" of spiritual experience because they *renew* the practical religious imagination in art and poetry that reveals humanity's relation to transcendence. And renewal is crucial to Keats since human nature is susceptible to degeneration.

What began as "invention," the "selvage" of Keats's opening, has now disclosed something new that must be accounted for according to the needs of imagination:

> Homer is very fine, Achilles is fine, Diomed is fine, Shakspeare is fine, Hamlet is fine, Lear is fine, but dwindled englishmen are not fine—Where too the Women are so passable, and have such english names, such as Ophelia, Cordelia &—that they should have such Paramours or rather Imparamours—As for them I cannot, in thought help wishing as did the cruel Emperor, that they had but one head and I might cut it off to deliver them from any horrible Courtesy they may do their undeserving Countrymen—I wonder I meet with no born Monsters—O Devonshire, last night I thought the Moon had dwindled in heaven.

Keats may be echoing *Henry V*, II.ii.85: "These English monsters!" Or perhaps he is reminded of the "bruised fairness" of humanity he wrote about to Bailey in his last letter, in which he spoke of the test of suffering as a means of preparing the heart and mind to meet circumstance (January 23, 1818). In any event, Keats cannot help but see Devonshire as representative of what is insufferable about human life.

The more Keats writes of Devonshire, the more he is led into its opposite. In this oscillating or dialectical dynamic, Keats expresses a skepticism about poetry which apparently springs from the dissolution he feels all around him:

> I am sometimes so very sceptical as to think Poetry itself a mere Jack a lanthern to amuse whoever may chance to be struck with its brilliance.

In the context of his letter, the poetry Keats is sometimes so skeptical about might very well be his own or that of the immediate past and present. It's certainly not Shakespeare's poetry, for Keats will soon confer upon it the status of the "ethereal." This skepticism must be balanced by all that Keats thought and felt about poetry.[2] One cannot disregard, for example, what Keats had written to his publisher John Taylor while completing the final changes on *Endymion*:

> In Poetry I have a few Axioms, and you will see how far I am from their Centre. 1st I think Poetry should surprise by a fine excess and not by Singularity—it should strike the Reader as a wording of his own highest thoughts, and appear almost a Remembrance—2nd Its touches of Beauty should never be half way therby making the reader breathless instead of content: the rise, the progress, the setting of imagery should like the Sun come natural natural too him—shine over him and set soberly although in magnificence leaving him in the Luxury of twilight—but it is easier to think what Poetry should be than to write it—and this leads me on to another axiom. That if Poetry comes not as naturally as the Leaves to a tree it had better not come at all.
>
> (February 27, 1818)

The fact that he felt himself so far from the center of his ideal poetry may account in part for the skepticism he felt less than a month after writing to Taylor. More significantly perhaps, it is precisely his estrangement from poetry's sometimes blatantly garish colors ("a mere Jack a lanthern") that enables Keats to inquire further into the nature and use of poetry, to be more inclusive rather than exclusive.

The polarity in Keats's letter leads him now into a pursuit of "Ethereal thing[s]." "Ethereal" is a term found often in Keats's letters.[3] This is synonymous with or identical to the spiritual nature of humanity. It is both the "old Wine of Heaven," as he

---

2. For a refutation of Keats's so-called skepticism, see Ernest J. Lovell, "Keats the Humanist," *The Kentucky Review* 3, 2 (1982), 3-18. Hereafter cited as Lovell. This is a beautifully considered treatment of the *Letters* by the late Professor Lovell.

3. See, e.g., the following passages: May 11, 1817; November 22, 1817; and February 19, 1818.

referred to Bailey's orthodox religion, and the moment's possibility of sympathetic experience (November 22, 1817). The ethereal is broached here because Devonshire so vividly embodies the opposite: the failure of spiritual curiosity and the abnegating of consciousness itself. Keats tells Bailey:

> As Tradesmen say every thing is worth what it will fetch, so probably every mental pursuit takes its reality and worth from the ardour of the pursuer—being in itself a nothing—Ethereal thing may at least be thus real, divided under three heads—Things real—things semireal—and no things—Things real—such as existences of Sun Moon & Stars and passages of Shakspeare—Things semireal such as Love, the Clouds &c which require a greeting of the Spirit to make them wholly exist—and Nothings which are made Great and dignified by an ardent pursuit.

This is a very interesting set of ethereal things, revealing Keats's love of knowledge and sensation but above all that life of "allegory" he is beginning to understand more and more as he lives it. For as one reads these words slowly, one hears Keats aspiring to something quite different from the Cartesian thought tradition that posits Mind's independent existence even as thinking itself gives rise to consciousness of being. One hears, that is, a life flow that is its own creation and revelation apart from the order such ethereal things provide.

In a threefold order, Keats lays out things "real," "semireal," and "nothings." Viewed closely, these headings have too general a conception or structure to satisfy analysis. However, the peculiar relevance lies in the being, becoming, and contrivance each thing entails. Reality here is more a matter of "ardent pursuit" than intellectual thought or empirical consciousness alone.[4] For Keats, it is the pursuer's "ardour" (from Latin *ardere,* "to burn") which accounts for the degrees of realness and

4. See Berger, 100-101. Keats is a man of *eros* for whom reality is not necessarily either natural, human, or divine, but "what he decides it is after deliberation."

corresponds to "ethereal" (from Greek *aithos,* "fire"). All three ethereal things here absolutely depend upon passion which, together with imagination, gives rise to their reality and worth. Keats cares for passion, which the self-reflexive knot of Descartes does not include, because its intensity or fire is not such, as in the case of a jack-o'-lantern poetry, "to amuse whoever may chance to be struck with its brilliance." This ardent pursuit has little or nothing to do with *chance.* It is a form of spiritual work aroused by the *need* for a world more human than the given world, which Keats can imagine and construct. Such work of possibility corresponds to the life of poetry when poetry serves need.

This quest, Keats says, "by the by stamps the burgundy mark on the bottles of our Minds, insomuch as they are able to '*consec[r]ate whate'er they look upon*'." The "stamp" of these ethereal things upon our minds is the act of assigning them with the virtue of consecration (from Latin *consecrare,* "to make sacred together"), which caries an emphasis upon the endeavor of looking, of directing one's sight to a thing. Keats's figure of the mountaineer who has "look'd into" the eagle's nest, thereby making it "finer," recites this sense of reality and worth. This is what allegory requires: perceiving a truth under the image of a thing to return us to a most self-evident experience. Allegory is the basis of the "collateral nature" of the sonnet Keats now includes in his letter to Bailey:

Four Seasons fill the Measure of the year;
  Four Seasons are there in the mind of Man.
He hath his lusty spring when fancy clear
  Takes in all beauty with an easy span:
He hath his Summer, when luxuriously
  He chews the honied cud of fair spring thoughts,
Till, in his Soul dissolv'd they come to be
  Part of himself. He hath his Autumn ports
And Havens of repose, when his tired wings
  Are folded up, and he content to look

On Mists in idleness: to let fair things
Pass by unheeded as a threshhold brook.
He hath his Winter too of pale Misfeature,
Or else he would forget his mortal nature.

"Don't imagine it an a propos des bottes," Keats says. And indeed the sonnet is ancillary to his meditation on reality and desire, more of an accommodation than a form lived out by the poet. But the point is well taken: his sonnet is a "nothing" made "real" by the mind's consecration of the seasons in the life of man, a "nothing" made "Great and dignified" by the ability to see anew what is most familiar but abnegated by man's estrangement from himself.

The upshot is that the shift in emphasis from mental to emotional pursuit enables the making (poesis) of this reality of ethereal things. Without some suspicion of the ethereal, moreover, this shift in awareness cannot be pursued. In Devonshire's entirely desacralized reality, Keats immediately suspected the dwarfed human image to be a condition of soul, which unnerved him and provoked a formal interrogation that he had been practicing all along in his letters. The condition he aspires to here is a means or method of renewal in life rather than the old all-too-human belief in life after death. The means is difficult to grasp because it is the process of creativity itself. Although Keats had mocked his own "clerklike" manner of speculation in his letters, one feels that the adequacy of his language to express the reality he perceives is that of a religious scribe, someone who, like one of the tribe of Levi, possesses not a territorial but spiritual portion in life. He goes on to write:

> Aye this may be carried—but what am I talking of—it is an old maxim of mine and of course must be well known that evey point of thought is the centre of an intellectual world—the two uppermost thoughts in a Man's mind are the two poles of his World he revolves on them and every thing is southward or northward to him through their means—We take but three steps from feathers to iron.

Keats has gone through a whole universe of things connected by imagination and passion as he now hits this center of mystery. He has revolved on the two poles of his world-letter in an ever tightening circle until something new and mysterious results from his inwarding motion: "We take but three steps from feathers to iron."

W.J. Bate makes the interesting remark that these two uppermost thoughts are Milton and Wordsworth, polar opposites to be reconciled in order for Keats to find his way out of the "painful labyrinth" mentioned in his letter of May 3, 1818 to John Reynolds.[5] When he wrote the "Chamber of Maiden Thought" letter to Reynolds, Keats was still in Devonshire with Tom, and the misery he first experienced upon arriving there was still present but now transforming itself into a marvelous insight about the "Burden of the mystery," a phrase taken from Wordsworth's meditative poem "Tintern Abbey." Wordsworth and Milton for Keats both represented philosophy in the service of humanity's spiritual torment in this life. But whereas Milton had Religion in his mind, Wordsworth had Mystery. The latter for Keats was of utmost significance because of his romantic disbeliever's religion of transcendence. What Keats desired was to be in a condition whereby philosophy (human and divine) was not dogma, nor mystery anti-intellectualism or superstition (mystification). This desire must be seen in the light of Keats's life of allegory. For if we can but look with consecrating eyes at Keats's image—and a total faith in poetry demands belief in the *other* reality of being and feeling—we can see that "from feathers to iron" gestures toward that necessary change or differentiation in order to see into the heart and nature of humanity. To see, in other words, the allegory of a life of worth—"worth" here being a depth of heart and mind combined vis-à-vis the world of circumstance.

5. Bate, 329.

Keats's phrase "from feathers to iron" carries with it a sort of exasperating difficulty not unlike that associated with parable.[6] And yet it has the feel of a thing emerging whole and continuous like poetry. "From feathers to iron" is an image of crossing a boundary or limit—that limit, in fact, which is precisely the extent to which we ordinarily see, whether we call it the "chamber of infant thought," as Keats does, or something else. On the basis of the entire letter, this limit is reality or circumstance, which binds humanity or makes it over into a "degenerated race" aided by humanity's own self-alienating behaviors. Its opposite, then, is the reality of the spirit which, once seen, can possibly unbind humanity from circumstance. In other words, the boundary of understanding must first be drawn (as Keats does continually in the *Letters*) in order to surpass it.

How do we find our bearings here with Keats's remark? "We take but three steps from feathers to iron" sounds like a statement worthy of the oracle at Delphi—enigmatic, inescapable, divine. It's essentially both imagistic and oracular in that it presents and announces. But *what* exactly? Keats's letter contains or expresses the human condition as one of abuse by the world. Devonshire is the world, representative of harsh reality and of unmediated facts in the consciousness of humanity. Thus Keats pursues and strives for harmony, which makes him a successor in a long sapiential or wisdom tradition—such tradition, however, being more poetic than philosophic. The idea of limit, of measure, rests not on some notion of the Good but rather on Mystery.[7]

---

6. See John Dominic Crossan, *The Dark Interval* (Allen, Tex.: Argus Communications, 1975), 54-60, where he argues that parable is the opposite of myth, i.e. it is not meant to assure but rather to change us. It reminds us of limit in order to see that limit, to interpret or "read" it, and hence possibly to go beyond it. While Crossan doesn't discuss allegory at length, he does state that it is a change in the structure of parable, sometimes even "narrative overkill."

7. In Book III of the *Republic*, Plato's great triad (Music, Gymnastics, Number) is based on mathematical order or science, whereas what Keats contemplates and demonstrates is something far beyond the power of mathematics. He is (à la Simone Weil) a "geometer" with respect to the soul rather than to matter and energy alone. See B. Jowett, tr. *The Dialogues of Plato*, vol. 3 (London: Oxford University Press, 1931), 68-106. Hereafter cited as Jowett.

"Feathers to iron" is an image of transformation. Through its terms Keats suggests a capability of inward change. The shift from "feathers" to "iron" possibly corresponds to a change in spirit from lightness or frivolity of being to a strength or durability of character. It would be only slightly stretching the truth of Keats's words here to connect this image with the sought-after "new Phoenix wings" in the sonnet on *Lear*. [8] For it is only through the catharsis of tragedy that Keats could see himself arising or unfolding anew, consecrated by the event itself. "From feathers to iron" also suggests the two poles of any man's world, the binaries he either resolves or finds irreconcilable, thus reminding him of his limits.[9] Either way, Keats's statement does not yield its meaning through language analysis. And rather than teaching or illustrating, it demands faith for faith's sake. It demands that one clothe oneself in its mystery for the journey it leads one on—a journey through the immediacy and memory of the sacred.

Why does Keats say "three" steps? Does it recite his three ethereal things? Or does it mean a very quick transcendence as "forty" in the Bible represents a very long time, though no one knows exactly why "forty"? Number as the secret of things is central to and inseparable from the archaic past, whether it be part of Egyptian cosmology or Plato's Reason.[10] Is Keats swept into an immense field or heaven of significances here in

---

8. Recall Keats's sense of intensity with its aspect of evaporation, which is a transformation of reality.

9. The reconciliation or resolution of polar opposites for Keats will be a "differentiation" (see Chapter 5: The Chamber of Maiden Thought). This is the process of becoming different. The literal meaning of *differ* is "not to carry" or "to carry apart." Keats sticks to his terms of movement.

10. See Giorgio de Santillana and Hertha von Dechend, *Hamlet's Mill* (Boston: Gambit, 1969), *passim*.

Cf. John Clarke, *From Feathers To Iron: A Concourse of World Poetics* (San Francisco: Tombouctou/Convivio, 1987), 28, 31. Hereafter cited as Clarke. In the first part of a long and strikingly complex discourse on world poetics, Clarke makes the salient point that the special language of poetry or story in antiquity was once such that its images, objects, and symbols were more obvious before inscription. With specific reference to the Hebrew Bible, he states: "Narratively speaking, Noah sails for forty days and forty nights, *then* the three birds go out." And referring to the Gospels, he states: "Forty days and forty nights in the wilderness reduce, spatially, to three temptations."

his letter to Bailey? It would be easy to ignore this possibility because such a possibility may have little or nothing to do with our own world. But Keats's perspective involves "ethereal things," the allegory of "the Measure of the year," "the centre of an intellectual world," and "three steps from feathers to iron." He sets himself, and us, on a journey toward something which is not necessarily truth, yet at the same time is not falsehood or solipsism. And at the center of his mind is a single "point," a locus of power, though not as some abstract philosophical construct. It is a center of "ardour" or passion, where our minds are able to consecrate what they behold.

We stand before poetry when we stare at Keats's words here—poetry that offers us an image or metaphor of reality. Although we cannot initially know what the words precisely mean, we must take them seriously even if Keats ends his letter by stating: "I have not one Idea of the truth of any of my speculations—I shall never be a Reasoner because I care not to be in the right, when retired from bickering and in a proper philosophical temper." This remark is no proof of a lack of seriousness. On the contrary, Keats's seriousness is proven by the container his letter becomes, a container of thought and passion, a poem or *poesia seriosa*. Moreover, Keats is not unreasonable. He goes with reason as far as it can go, and then goes beyond reason toward mystery, not leaving it alone. His "proper philosophical temper" is a relaxation of mind, a spaciousness into which the real world flows and revolves by the power of imagination.[11]

With Keats the imagination is formally complex, not a whimsical or obsessive thing. It's certainly not naive or innocent. The language of imagination, above all, demands unending

11. Clarke, 25. Explaining his idea of "manifests of momentary incursion," Clarke states that it is the brief and irregular visitations of *negentropy*, the opposite of entropy. It's not epiphany per se but more like a penetration. In a world where the "ordering intervention" or totalizing system of a Homer or a Dante, for instance, has disappeared, it happens that individuals can become the recipients and beneficiaries of what has been lost but paradoxically isn't lost. As Blake said, "The Authors are in Eternity." One gathers knowledge, in other words, wherever one can find it. Keats's statement is more than a rubric for Clarke's "concourse on world poetics." It is the ground of his system-building project.

consideration. Indeed, it seems to be a hieroglyphic language, which is both a true report and transfiguration of the real. For as Keats said of poetry in a review of Edmund Kean's return to the stage:

> A melodious passage in poetry is full of pleasures both sensual and spiritual. The spiritual is felt when the very letters and prints of charactered language show like the hieroglyphics of beauty;—the mysterious signs of an immortal freemasonry! 'A thing to dream of, not to tell!'[12]

This passage speaks eloquently of Keats's perception of the reality of poetry. As he had written to Reynolds just a few weeks prior to this time, "Poetry [is a] great & unobtrusive...thing which enters into one's soul" (February 3, 1818). The entrance of poetry is always in its literal shape as a sign or an inscription.[13] Furthermore, poetry as an "hieroglyphics of beauty" exists not simply in picturelike terms but in the mysterious way "the very letters and prints of charactered language" produce an effect in or leave a trace upon the soul. It is a lure as suggested by Keats's choice of "pleasure." What poetry lures us to is thought in search of belief. In the high business of the poet, the exegesis of a dimly perceived thing, especially "a thing of beauty," is always attempted because of the exaltation of existence it brings. Such is the action of Keats's words that appear in his letter.

When Keats concludes by stating, "you must not stare if in any future letter I endeavor to prove that Apollo as he had a cat gut string to his Lyre used a cats' paw as a Pecten," he is humorously expressing the serious knowledge that imagination proves the truth of anything felt to be real. For in art the more

---

12. Reprinted in H.B. Forman, ed. *The Poetical Works and Other Writings of John Keats,* vol. 5 (New York: Scribner, 1938-9), 229. Hereafter cited as Forman.

13. The very inscribing is at once a violent act, that is, a scratching or carving that cuts or wounds its material, and a marvelous new creation of sacred dimensions that heals the soul.

Cf. Edmond Jabès' "blessure" ("wound") in *The Book of Questions,* 2 vols. (Middletown: Wesleyan University Press, 1990); also Lorca's "borde" ("rim") in "Play and Theory of the Duende," 50.

one imagines the more one paradoxically approaches truth, that is, the imagination's truth of beauty. An immortal freemasonry is indeed the quest of art. Yet the imagination, as Keats knew, "lives in the world of what's possible with the constant persuasion of impossibility."[14] And as he would discover only two months from now, impossibility itself could stir the imagination to create an everlasting good for the soul.

14. W.S. Di Piero, *Out of Eden* (Berkeley: University of California Press, 1991), 237.

The Chamber of Maiden Thought

Dear Reynolds, I have a mysterious tale
And cannot speak it. The first page I read
Upon a lampit rock of green sea weed
Among the breakers.—'Twas a quiet eve;
The rocks were silent—the wide sea did weave
An untumultuous fringe of silver foam
Along the flat brown sand. I was at home,
And should have been most happy—but I saw
Too far into the sea; where every maw
The greater on the less feeds evermore:—
But I saw too distinct into the core
Of an eternal fierce destruction,
And so from happiness I far was gone.
Still am I sick of it: and though to-day
I've gathered young spring-leaves, and flowers gay
Of periwinkle and wild strawberry,
Still do I that most fierce destruction see,
The shark at savage prey—the hawk at pounce,
The gentle robin, like a pard or ounce,
Ravening a worm.—Away ye horrid moods,
Moods of one's mind! You know I hate them well,
You know I'd sooner be a clapping bell
To some Kamschatkan missionary church,
Than with these horrid moods be left in lurch.
Do you get health—and Tom the same—I'll dance,
And from detested moods in new romance
Take refuge.

—John Keats
"Dear Reynolds, as last night I lay in bed"

In my Father's house are many mansions:
if it were not so, I would have told you.
I go to prepare a place for you.

—The Gospel According to John, 14:2

·V·

LITERARY HISTORY records that when Keats first met William Wordsworth, who was visiting London during the winter of 1817-1818, Keats recited his "Hymn to Pan" from *Endymion* at the entreaty of his friend the artist Robert Benjamin Haydon, a reading which drew the chilly response from the elder poet, "a very pretty piece of paganism."[1] Keats had other meetings with Wordsworth that winter, even a chance meeting while walking over Hampstead Heath one day, all of which left a bad aftertaste. In a letter to his brothers, Keats wrote: "I am sorry that Wordsworth has left a bad impression wherever he visited in Town—by his egotism, Vanity, and bigotry—yet he is a great poet if not a Philosopher" (February 21, 1818). Though Keats criticized Wordsworth as severely as he did Leigh Hunt, one of his early mentors, and came in time to distinguish Wordsworthian poetical character as the "egotistical sublime," there remained a positive side to the effect Wordsworth had on Keats. For Wordsworth, the compassionate poet of the human heart, had explored the deep and darkened side of the modern world as no one had done before. And through his phrase "the burthen of the mystery" from "Tintern Abbey," he had shown something to Keats that furthered his poetics and illumined his encounter with the inner and outer worlds.[2]

Keats first used Wordsworth's phrase in speaking of the need for knowledge in a world of sorrow. He was writing to his

---

1. Bate, 179, 265; Ward, 157; Bush, 65.

2. Benjamin Bailey reports Keats's notice of this phrase; see Rollins, *The Keats Circle*, II, 275.

friend John Reynolds, whom Keats had met through Leigh Hunt in 1816. Reynolds was a fellow poet, one with whom Keats talked about poetry. Even after taking up law in 1817, Reynolds remained one of Keats's steadfast correspondents. His tombstone proclaims him "The friend of Keats." Reynolds suffered prolonged bouts of illness and had written to Keats in the spring of 1818 while under the gloomy spell of rheumatic fever. This fact was utmost in Keats's mind as he replied to Reynolds. His letter, addressed to Christ's Hospital in London, begins thus:

> What I complain of is that I have been in so an uneasy a state of Mind as not to be fit to write to an invalid. I cannot write to any length under a dis-guised feeling. I should have loaded you with an addition of gloom, which I am sure you do not want. I am now thank God in a humour to give you a good groats worth—for Tom, after a Night without a Wink of sleep, and overburdened with fever, has got up after a refreshing day sleep and is better than he has been for a long time; and you I trust have been again round the Common without any effect but refreshment.
>
> (May 3, 1818)

Although Keats did not speak a great deal about his past in his letters, he brings up his medical training in his letter to Reynolds to shed light upon the state of mind engendered by painful reality and occasioned by Wordsworth's phrase. Medicine, as part of "an extensive knowledge," can possibly aid the human condition in a time of great misery, physical illness.[3] Thus Keats writes:

> Were I to study physic or rather Medicine again,—I feel it would not make the least difference in my Poetry; when the Mind is in its infancy a Bias is in reality a Bias, but when we have acquired more strength, A Bias becomes no Bias. Every

3. For an account of Keats's healing mission and its significance to his poetry, with a focus upon the shamanistic tradition, see Michael E. Holstein, "Keats: The Poet-Healer and the Problem of Pain," *The Keats-Shelley Journal* 36 (1987), 32-49.

> department of knowledge we see excellent and calculated towards a great whole. I am so convinced of this, that I am glad at not having given away my medical Books, which I shall again look over to keep alive the little I know thitherwards; and moreover intend through you and Rice to become a sort of Pip-civilian. An extensive knowledge is needful to thinking people—it takes away the heat and fever; and helps, by widening speculation, to ease the Burden of the Mystery: a thing I begin to understand a little, and which weighed upon you in the most gloomy and true sentence in your Letter. The difference of high Sensations with and without knowledge appears to me this—in the latter case we are falling continually ten thousand fathoms deep and being blown up again without wings and with all [the] horror of a bare shoulderd Creature—in the former case, our shoulders are fledged, and we go thro' the same air and space without fear. This is running one's rigs on the score of abstracted benefit—when we come to human Life and the affections it is impossible [to know] how a parallel of breast and head can be drawn—(you will forgive me for thus privately treading out my depth and take it for treading as schoolboys tread the water—it is impossible to know how far knowledge will console us for the death of a friend and the ill "that flesh is heir to"—

Keats wants to believe that knowledge wedded to sensation will help take away "the heat and fever" of life. But he knows he is merely projecting a wish, that is, a wish rigged out and ready for action on a plane of abstraction. It's important to recall that Keats was caring for his brother in Teignmouth. Tom, "overburdened with fever," was helplessly sick with consumption. Keats was all too familiar with this predicament. He had nursed and watched his mother die of consumption eight years earlier. Keats feels the impossibility of the consolation of knowledge in a world of suffering and death, "where but to think is to be full of sorrow," as he will write in the "Ode to a Nightingale" a year from now. The fact of death, and the consciousness of suffering (as Keats's quote from *Hamlet*, III.i.63 attests) overburden the sense of human life and its affections which Keats considers in this passage of his letter.

At this point Keats includes his fragment "Ode to May" as a "ratification" of his sympathy for Reynolds and of his thoughts about "the affections and Poetry." This gesture of tenderness comes perhaps in a desire to exchange poems: earlier in his letter Keats asks Reynolds for "a peep at your Spencerian," that is, Reynolds's "The Romance of Youth," later published in *Gardens of Florence* (1821). The "Ode" also draws one's attention to the verse epistle Keats had written to his friend only six weeks earlier. In that poem he describes himself there at Teignmouth picking flowers in early spring, unable to shake the terrifying vision of seeing "too far into the sea." The vision follows on the heels of a reluctance "to philosophize / I dare not yet!" and of a belief that "Things cannot to the will / Be settled, but they tease us out of thought." All these things somehow dovetailed in his mind, resulting in the present letter to Reynolds which gave Keats not so much a "refuge" as a new "mystery" to ponder. He continues thus:

> You may be anxious to know for fact to what sentence in your Letter I allude. You say "I fear there is little chance of any thing else in this life." You seem by that to have been going through with a more painful and acute zest the same labyrinth that I have—I have come to the same conclusion thus far. My Branchings out therefrom have been numerous: one of them is the consideration of Wordsworth's genius and as a help, in the manner of gold being the meridian Line of worldly wealth,—how he differs from Milton.—And here I have nothing but surmises, from an uncertainty whether Miltons apparently less anxiety for Humanity proceeds from his seeing further or no than Wordsworth: And whether Wordsworth has in truth epic passion, and martyrs himself to the human heart, the main region of his song—

Keats has concluded, along with Reynolds, that there is little else in this life but the "burden" of human life—one that is labyrinthine in its structure and meaning. The maze as a figure for life has endless suggestions. Whether Keats is thinking of Greek mythology or some other lore, the labyrinth itself is a thing that implies a technique for getting out of it.[4] And here I see Keats's earlier remark about the mind in its "infancy" and subsequent strength as proof of his technique for escape: the numerous "Branchings out" from his lugubrious conclusion. And with Wordsworth's genius "as a help," he places the burden of the mystery within a meaning that enlarges the world of sorrow and knowledge, with the human heart at the center of this region of darkness.

Why Keats should pair Milton and Wordsworth in thinking about the fact and nature of human suffering bears some scrutiny.[5] Certainly he thought of both men as great poets.[6] But it was precisely because their greatness lay in a depth of intelligence and compassion. As he would write to Sarah Jeffrey over a year later: "One of the great reasons that the english have produced the finest writers in the world; is, that the English world has ill-treated them during their lives and foster'd them after their deaths. They have in general been trampled aside into the bye paths of life and seen the festerings of Society" (June 9, 1819). What is at issue here between Wordsworth and Milton are the two poles of Keats's mind as these are consonant with knowledge and sorrow. What Keats seeks is to see into the mystery of the human heart as best as he possibly can. For this he needed Wordsworth's martyrdom, his anxiety and elegiac tenor:

> In regard to his genius alone—we find what he says true as far as we have experienced and we can judge no further but by larger experience—for axioms in philosophy are not axioms

4. Labyrinth comes from the Greek root *labrys*, the double-axe found in ancient Crete. Among the many suggestions are those of return to a beginning, of circuits or paths (as in a text), of hardship, and of initiation and process, i.e., the transformation of death. See Kerényi, 90-118.

5. See Susan J. Wolfson, *The Questioning Presence* (Ithaca: Cornell University Press, 1986), 191-198. In a subsection of Chapter 8 titled "Philosopher vs. Poet: Milton and Wordsworth," Wolfson provides an excellent treatment of the relation between Wordsworth and Milton in Keats's mind. She does not specifically discuss the Chamber of Maiden Thought.

6. See, e.g., Keats's remarks about Milton in the following letters: January 23, 1818 (I, 211); March 24, 1818 (I, 255); April 27, 1818 (I, 274). See also his marginalia on *Paradise Lost* in Forman, V, 292-305.

> until they are proved upon our pulses: We read fine— things but never feel them to thee full until we have gone the same steps as the Author.—I know this is not plain; you will know exactly my meaning when I say, that now I shall relish Hamlet more than I ever have done—Or, better—You are sensible no man can set down Venery as a bestial or joyless thing until he is sick of it and therefore all philosophizing on it would be mere wording. Until we are sick, we understand not;—in fine, as Byron says, "Knowledge is Sorrow"; and I go on to say that "Sorrow is Wisdom"—and further for aught we can know for certainty! "Wisdom is folly"—So you see how I have run away from Wordsworth, and Milton; and shall still run away from what was in my head, to observe, that some kind of letters are good squares others handsome ovals, and others some orbicular, others spheroid—and why should there not be another species with two rough edges like a Rat-trap? I hope you will find all my long letters of that species, and all will be well; for by merely touching the spring delicately and etherially, the rough edged will fly immediately into a proper compactness, and thus you may make a good wholesome loaf, with your own leven in it, of my fragments—

Why does Keats "relish" *Hamlet* more than he has done so before? I think it's for the reason that now, in the spring of 1818, after stretching his poetic powers beyond the limits of his first published work (*Poems,* 1817) and then *Endymion,* Keats had gone "the same steps" as Shakespeare (or Milton or Wordsworth for that matter). He had begun with lyric poetry and was moving toward epic and dramatic poetry. And in doing so, he had been coming to terms with "the heartache, and the thousand natural shocks that flesh is heir to." This poetic passage—from lyric to epic, or romance to tragedy—is not simply a matter of exchanging genres or conventions. It is a matter of content, of understanding both the "conscience," as Hamlet says, which "does make cowards of us all," and "the native hue of resolution," toward which Keats's affections were tending.

Did Reynolds know exactly Keats's meaning with respect to *Hamlet*? To make himself clearer ("Or, better") he provides another example of extensive knowledge: "no man can set down Venery as a bestial or joyless thing until he is sick of it." Keats wants and needs to judge by "larger experience," whether it be poetry or venery, in order to arrive at a "full" understanding that is both axiomatic and proven. Thus Keats takes Byron's "Knowledge is Sorrow" (from *Manfred,* I.i.10) a step further. Indeed, he steps from one pole of thought to the other in saying that "Sorrow is Knowledge." But Keats goes further still to say that "for aught we can know for certainty! 'Wisdom is folly.'" Now it seems that Keats, like Hamlet in his "madness," has gone too far. But the point of it all is to give his mind free rein with these ideas, not to draw in the reins on his mind. For freedom means creativity and inventiveness which, in relation to Wordsworth and Milton, is something as different from their sonorous philosophies as a rattrap is different from ovals and spheroids. Keats says, "If I scribble long letters I must play my vagaries." All this play or rhetoric engages the formalizing power of imagination in the humorous but serious moment of catching his own mind suffused with imaginative possibility. In the process, he is enacting what he has run to in running away from Wordsworth and Milton: Shakespeare, the supreme creator and master of playing vagaries.

Keats breaks off at this point in his letter; when he resumes he commences with a bit of virtuosity, employing the simile "like the Gull I may *dip*" to dip from one page of his letter to another. "This crossing a letter is not without its association," Keats writes. And indeed, as kinetic energy it joins or forms a union with the human crossing that lies just ahead in Keats's letter. For now he returns to Wordsworth and the burden of the mystery in order to see whether or not

> he has an extended vision or a circumscribed grandeur—whether he is an eagle in his nest, or on the wing—And to be more explicit and to show you how tall I stand by the giant, I will put down a simile of human life as far as I now perceive it; that is, to the point to which I say we both have arrived at 'Well—I compare human life to a large Mansion of Many

> Apartments, two of which I can only describe, the doors of the rest being as yet shut upon me—The first we step into we call the infant or thoughtless Chamber, in which we remain as long as we do not think—We remain there a long while, and notwithstanding the doors of the second Chamber remain wide open, showing a bright appearance, we care not to hasten to it; but are at length imperceptibly impelled by the awakening of the thinking principle—within us—we no sooner get into the second Chamber, which I shall call the Chamber of Maiden-Thought, than we become intoxicated with the light and the atmosphere, we see nothing but pleasant wonders, and think of delaying there for ever in delight: However among the effects this breathing is father of is that tremendous one of sharpening one's vision into the heart and nature of Man—of convincing ones nerves that the World is full of Misery and Heartbreak, Pain, Sickness and oppression—whereby This Chamber of Maiden Thought becomes gradually darken'd and at the same time on all sides of it many doors are set open—but all dark—all leading to dark passages—We see not the ballance of good and evil. We are in a Mist—*We* are now in that state—We feel the "burden of the Mystery."

Keats's words here are poetic and mysterious, no less than Jesus's words on the eve of his death: "In my Father's house are many mansions: if it were not so, I would have told you. I go to prepare a place for you" (John 14:2). Rollins makes this comparison, and it is an apt one.[7] For the life of the soul is at issue here; and the fact of Christ's passion and death only deepens the relevance. But in Keats's simile of human life, a new understanding rather than dispensation, and a passing to mystery rather than religious certainty, are of utmost importance.[8]

---

7. Keats was very knowledgeable not only of the Bible but of Anglican doctrine as well. See, e.g., his letter to his sister on the eve of her confirmation, March 31, 1819, II, 49-51.

8. See Robert Pack, "Keats's Letters: Laughter as Autobiography," *New England Review and Bread Loaf Quarterly* 7, 2 (1984), 182, where Pack draws the connection between the Chamber of Maiden Thought letter, that is, its darkness and mystery, and the "Ode to a Nightingale" in which "Keats envisions in language of felt uncertainty what he literally cannot see."

The Chamber of Maiden Thought is a room in life where we drink the light of differentiation as opposed to the "infant and thoughtless Chamber" where all concerns the undifferentiated, wayward moods of erotic sensation. This thoughtless stage translates, Clarence Thorpe claims, to Keats's "feeling for poetic experience [in *Endymion*] as one of detachment in an ideal dreamworld existence, abstracted and separated from the visible and real."[9] Once we pass into the Chamber of Maiden Thought, however, what was delightful becomes transformed; our vision sharpens to perceive that "the World is full of Misery and Heartbreak, Pain, Sickness and oppression." Differentiation is this sharpening or penetration (recalling the Penetralium of Mystery) into the burden of the mystery, which is the necessary precondition for an understanding of or "vision into the heart and nature of Man." This vision or understanding is resonant with Keats's earlier remark that "Man is propell'd to act and strive and buffet with Circumstance" (January 23, 1818). Moreover, the change from sensation into knowledge of the world's unyielding force exemplifies Keats's ambition to actively assimilate both into a model that would allow man to equal the violent force of the world with a strength all his own of heart and mind combined. But this is no easy change.

Keats perceives "mystery" as simultaneously darkness and the openness of movement within such darkness. He tells Reynolds: "this Chamber of Maiden Thought becomes gradually darken'd and at the same time on all sides of it many doors are set open—but all dark—all leading to dark passages." Darkness is the burden of mystery, that is, of not knowing with certainty or "consequitive reasoning." Here as elsewhere, one thinks of Keats's distrust of dogmatic and self-assertive methods of grasping reality. As Ernest J. Lovell reminds us, men like William Godwin were "the enemy," not only of Negative Capability but of the whole concept of humanity.[10] "They

9. Clarence Thorpe, *The Mind of John Keats* (New York: Russell and Russell, 1964), 47. Hereafter cited as Thorpe.

10. Lovell, 5.

want to hammer their nail into you," Keats will write to his family in America a little over a year from now, "and if you turn the point, still they think you wrong. Dilke will never come at a truth so long as he lives; because he is always trying at it. He is a Godwin-methodist" (September 24, 1819). In opposition to "trying at it," Keats proposes mystery as a means of arriving at truth, well aware that it means or contains more than just mistiness. Mystery in its Greek origin is *mystos,* "keeping silence," from *myeín,* "to be closed (as of the eyes or lips)." It is the myth or story of the Ineffable Presence in everyday life. As long as we remain thoughtless in our infancy (an altogether different kind of silence that comes from Latin, *infans,* "incapable of speech"), this visionary feeling is in exile. Mystery is the province of knowledge and wisdom, the "gradual evolutionary, educative process, in which the intellect expands from a thoughtless stage" and achieves insight and understanding.[11]

"To this point was Wordsworth come," Keats says, "when he wrote 'Tintern Abbey'." In that poem (composed on July 13, 1798) Wordsworth recaptured an original visit to the Wye valley and ruins of Tintern Abbey in Monmouthshire. The poem as meditation seems to have impressed itself on Keats's mind for several reasons, among which is the knowledge of human suffering that purifies in the presence of nature. To the forms of nature's beauty Wordsworth attributes a certain "gift":

> To them I may have owed another gift,
> Of aspect more sublime; that blessed mood,
> In which the burthen of the mystery,
> In which the heavy and the weary weight
> Of all this unintelligible world
> Is lightened:—that serene and blessed mood,
> In which the affections gently lead us on,

11. Thorpe, 46.

Until, the breath of this corporeal frame,
And even the motion of our human blood
Almost suspended, we are laid asleep
In body, and become a living soul:
While with an eye made quiet by the power
Of harmony, and the deep power of joy,
We see into the life of things.[12]

In "Tintern Abbey" an integration occurs, not of any sure points of reason but from "all objects of all thoughts" (line 101) which nature provides to one long absent from her beauties, as if they were forms "to a blind man's eye." This nature is a "thou," and her gift is that which engenders the central Romantic motif of blessing, the restoration of the Self-Other relation.[13]

Such restoration or "harmony" for Wordsworth is the power that "quiets" the mind's eye and "leads" humanity toward vision. It's a vision for Keats not in spite of but because of darkness. The forms seen in blindness (the words that came to Wordsworth upon recollecting the past) become for Keats the inspiration for the Chamber of Maiden Thought. Perhaps more directly, Wordsworth's lines, "When thy mind / Shall be a mansion for all lovely forms" (139-140) became for Keats the authentic expression of reality. It seems to me that the difference between the two poets' thinking is one of emphasis: Wordsworth stresses the leading on from the mind's mansion; Keats reveals that mansion as a space in which the mind is changed, a place he comes to in order that he may know and understand. Keats's thinking *into* the human heart ends with those dark passages that are set open all around the Chamber of Maiden Thought, whereas Wordsworth's "genius

---

12. De Selincourt, II, 260.

13. See "The Rime of the Ancient Mariner," *The Collected Works of Samuel Taylor Coleridge*, vol. 16 (Princeton: Princeton University Press, 1983). In Part 4, the Mariner blesses the water-snakes—a pivotal moment that changes the entire direction of his voyage and narration.

Cf. Lewis Hyde, *The Gift: Imagination and the Erotic Life of Property* (New York: Vintage Books, 1979).

is explorative of those dark passages." But Keats anticipates an *exodus* from such passages:

> Now if we live, and go on thinking, we too shall explore them. he is a Genius and superior [to] us, in so far as he can, more than we, make discoveries, and shed a light in them—Here I must think Wordsworth is deeper than Milton—though I think it has depended more upon the general and gregarious advance of intellect, than individual greatness of Mind—From the Paradise Lost and the other Works of Milton, I hope it is not too presuming, even between ourselves to say, his Philosophy, human and divine, may be tolerably understood by one not much advanced in years, In his time englishmen were just emancipated from a great superstition—and Men had got hold of certain points and resting places in reasoning which were too newly born to be doubted, and too much opposed by the Mass of Europe not to be thought etherial and authentically divine—who could gainsay his ideas on virtue, vice, and Chastity in Comus, just at the time of the dismissal of Cod-pieces and a hundred other disgraces? who would not rest satisfied with his hintings at good and evil in the Paradise Lost, when just free from the inquisition and burning in Smithfield? The Reformation produced such immediate and great benefits, that Protestantism was considered under the immediate eye of heaven, and its own remaining Dogmas and superstitions, then, as it were, regenerated, constituted those resting places and seeming sure points of Reasoning—from that I have mentioned, Milton, whatever he may have thought in the sequel, appears to have been content with these by his writings—He did not think into the human heart, as Wordsworth has done—Yet Milton as a Philosopher, had sure as great powers as Wordsworth—What is then to be inferr'd? O many things—It proves there is really a grand march of intellect—, It proves that a mighty providence subdues the mightiest Minds to the service of the time being, whether it be in human Knowledge or Religion—

This passage is directly concerned with comparing the virtues of Milton and Wordsworth on the grounds of their humanitarian or humanistic natures and from the perspective of the long view.[14] Wordsworth is "deeper" or more profound than Milton because he has been able to stand upon the greatness of the past—a greatness that is Christian in nature, Lovell stresses. From this Keats concluded that the "grand march of intellect" was the doing of "a mighty providence that subdues the mightiest Minds [like Wordsworth's] to the service of the time being, whether it be in human Knowledge or Religion." Man is essentially Adamic for Keats, though not necessarily a fallen creature in need of theology exclusively. Adam is the Soul or Imagination, and therefore in need of both God and poetry, of a balance of spirit and body.

For the truth of "the time being" demanded such a unity of god and poetry, one that can be overwhelming in its intensity.[15] Yet such intensity for Keats was exactly what he was alternately struggling with and against. It was both the pain of suffering and the joy of life. The allegory of his life was a hunger for discovery of the unknown, an eagerness to explore the world's dark passages, precisely for a vision of "the ballance of good and evil." He did not have long for this exploration. He would be dead in less than three years from this time. Perhaps that is what accounts for the "march" already present in Keats's life early in 1818. The present and future work is what he elected to advance toward with the few remaining years he possessed. And we feel that choice in Keats's art with all the drivenness of destiny.

At this time, Keats was in fact writing "Isabella," which achieved an initial difficult task of creating precision, economy, beauty, and terror, all at once. "Isabella" is the story of two star-crossed lovers, taken from Boccaccio's *The Decameron* and rendered in *ottava rima.* Keats altered, while remaining faithful to, Boccaccio's narrative, developing it into a "new" Poetic Romance that succeeds in fulfilling his artistic requirement of

---

14. Lovell, 7. Cf. Laurence S. Lockridge, "Keats: The Ethics of Imagination," in *Coleridge, Keats, and the Imagination,* eds. J. Robert Barth and John L. Mahoney (Columbia: University of Missouri Press, 1989), 143-173.

15. Recall Plato's *Ion,* where he describes the "divine madness" of the poet. See Jowett, I, 491-511.

"intensity": to bury or obliterate all repulsiveness called forth by the story of murder, while exciting beauty and a marvelous depth of speculation. The spiritual in "Isabella" triumphs in one line alone, according to Ridley, a line "which for richness of content and beauty of music is surpassed by few others that Keats ever wrote."[16]

And thou art distant in Humanity.

That is the ghost of Lorenzo addressing his forlorn Isabella in the dull gloom of midnight. It's a painfully realized speech, and the poem overall indeed contains, as Keats wrote to Woodhouse, a "sober-sadness about it." Though Keats worried "Isabella" was "too smokeable" and "a weak-sided poem," he qualified his opinion by stating, "I enter fully into the feeling" (September 22, 1819). Looking at the range of possibilities between his letters and his poems, one wonders if Lorenzo is a premonition of that "Vision in the form of Youth, a Shadow of reality to come," of which he had written to Bailey six months before. One wonders if Isabella is the embodiment of Keats's reply to Bailey's question, "Why should Woman suffer?" Though one cannot say for certain, the possibility is intensified by the triumph Ridley discusses—Humanity alone, which Keats certainly worked on in all his writings.

"By widening speculation," in both letters and poems, Keats made his way through the "labyrinth" of life, and in this way discovered a method that is in fact what he was always seeking.[17] The *Letters* in particular are "an act of poetic trust" in thinking of information (or truth) as connected to where one gets it.[18] Proceeding by analogy (human life compared to a mansion of many rooms), Keats moved toward a content that

---

16. Ridley, 42.

17. Or as Novalis writes, "That which is sought after—is the method whereby it is found." That is, one acts within one's belief, and what one wants to do finally happens unquestionably. This is a "strengthening method" for the exhausted imagination. Quoted in Clarke, 31. See Friedrich Phillip von Hardenberg, *Allgemeine Brouillon,* Book IX.1720.

18. Clarke, 26.

helped him move on in ever more meditative twisting paths. Almost exactly a year from this time, he would begin a long and complex letter to his brother and sister-in-law in America, a letter written over three months in which the "Ode to Psyche" first appeared. It was in this same letter that Keats's "system of salvation" first came into existence as a "prooving" of the human heart in a world of "Circumstance," a world, that is, in which Keats found himself "straining at particles of light in the midst of a great darkness—without knowing the bearing of any one assertion of any one opinion" (March 19, 1819). From the "Chamber of Maiden Thought" to the "vale of soul-making," Keats's artistic and ethical passage is a poetics best illumined in his letters where the uncertainties, instabilities, and solitude of life are spread out like vast zones.

Letter writing was but one, if the more advanced, of two ways of getting to and through the labyrinth. Equally, it seems, Keats often wrote letters to remedy unhappy situations. Keats's letter to Reynolds was meant to help ease his friend's long hours of illness. As Keats knew from Tom, Reynolds, and *Hamlet,* illness (and well-being) was a cosmological proposition to be answered by a creative process regardless of the mediations of medicine. Amid the world's misery, heartbreak, pain, sickness, oppression, and death, there is a place and role for a beauty that restores the soul, a beauty impossible to think of without images discovered in this life. One such image is the "Mansion of Many Apartments" as opposed to the "endless labyrinth of woe" that Blake envisioned.[19]

"After all there is certainly something real in the World," Keats says to Reynolds in the manner he had proposed to him earlier: "Man should not dispute or assert but whisper results to his neighbour" (February 19, 1818). "The truth is there is something real in the World Your Third Chamber of Life shall be a lucky and a gentle one—stored with the wine of love—and the Bread of Friendship." As Lovell asserts, this third and last chamber of life is as significant as the other two. "Although he

19. Erdman, 174. *Jerusalem,* Chapter 2, line 19.

gave it but one isolated sentence [since Keats at this time could only describe two], it is obviously a chamber of redemption or salvation."[20] A salvation, but without a saviour, I would add. This third chamber is "real," and the emphatic sense of "real" here is not only prospective but actual: it is the friendship between Keats and Reynolds. And the "luck" he refers to, I think, does not qualify the realness of this chamber. For the sense is directly tied to the physical and metaphysical health of Keats's friend, whose gloom, I dare say, would have lifted upon receiving this extraordinary letter.

20. Lovell, 7.

The World Out There

I was never afraid of failure.

—John Keats to J.A. Hessey
October 8, 1818

• VI •

ON THE DAY Keats arrived at Teignmouth to be with Tom, George left for London, eager to set out on his own after having nursed Tom for so long, thus allowing his older brother time to write poetry. The day after Keats wrote to Reynolds on the Chamber of Maiden Thought (May 3, 1818), word came from London that George had decided to marry and leave England for America. After trying to decide what to do for many months, the climax had now come about for Keats's brother, who had been "more than a brother to me, he has been my greatest friend" (August 6, 1818). John and Tom started off quickly for London, a journey of a hundred and fifty miles, normally a twenty-seven hour trip by coach in those days. But because of Tom's poor health, the two brothers did not arrive home for a week; they had to travel in stages, spending nights at various hamlets and towns between Teignmouth and London. At Bridport in Dorset, Tom had a severe hemorrhage, an episode which must have caused extreme fear and tension in both brothers. They reached Hampstead by May 11, and shortly thereafter, probably on May 28, George and his fiancée, Georgiana Wylie, were married.

While Keats rejoiced in his brother's marriage, he was vexed by strange and not easily quieted moods. In a letter to Bailey around this time, he writes: "I am never alone without rejoicing that there is such a thing as death" (June 10, 1818). This note of bitterness was occasioned by Bailey's two articles on *Endymion*, preemptive attempts to defend against the attacks Bailey and Keats both knew were mounting by the press. Or rather, the reason Keats spoke so sharply to Bailey was "because the world is malignant enough to chuckle at the most honorable Simplicity. Yes on my Soul my dear Bailey you are too simple for the World—and that Idea makes me sick of it." Keats's "morbid" nature alone is not the cause of such bitterness. There were also "a thousand Circumstances" which contributed to his "incendiary spirit": "I have two Brothers one is driven by the 'burden of Society' to America the other, with an exquisite love of Life, is in a lingering state."

All three brothers had originally planned to embark on separate journeys that summer: George of course to America with his new wife; John to northern England and Scotland with Charles Brown; and Tom had developed a plan to visit Italy, "there to remain until I have acquired a stock of knowledge and strength which will better enable me to bustle through the world."[1] But by the time Keats wrote to Bailey, Tom was worse. "[He] is taken for a Madman," Keats writes to the Jeffrey sisters, which madness could have been any one of a number of complications of tuberculosis.[2] Nevertheless, twelve days after Keats's letter to Bailey, he and Brown went ahead with plans to tour northern England and Scotland together after Tom gave his brother brave assurances that he would be all right alone. So with Brown, Keats accompanied George and Georgiana by coach to Liverpool where they arrived on June 23 late in the afternoon. He said his last goodbyes that night. Early the next morning, while George and Georgiana slept, Keats and Brown took a coach for Lancaster, the starting point of their Scottish tour and, for Keats, the first step toward a unifying experience.

Throughout the walking tour of Scotland, the experience that emerges in Keats's letters constitutes not only a further development of his poetics but also a further envisioning of his

1. See Rollins, I, 350. Letter to Mariane Jeffrey, May 17-18, 1818.

2. I'm told by those in the medical profession that tumors of all kinds, including those in the brain, are still a common development in cases of tuberculosis.

For an account of the pathology of the Keats family, see William Hale-White, *Keats As Doctor and Patient* (London: Oxford University Press, 1938).

spiritual journey in the bittersweet world of human existence. Put another way, the poetics Keats was making during the Scottish tour received a major contribution from the experience he gained and recorded during this time, which tutored his life as nothing else before. Keats had now at his disposal an experience involving the themes and witness of the moral lesions and spiritual turbulence of dislocation, dispossession, displacement. These letters speak especially to those of us who are near descendents of displaced populations and cultural estrangements. But more important to all readers of Keats, the letters of June to August 1818 reveal the poet of Negative Capability furthering his consciousness (the central fact of Keats's work, early or late) with yet another journey of his adventurous, moving spirit. The journey now was neither the dizzying chariot ride of "Sleep and Poetry" nor the "slow journeying with head on pillow" of *Endymion*. It was the movement through the heavy and tragic tonings of sheer waking life, the troubles of mortality. In these letters, Keats's acute perception of natural and human detail becomes, one might say, modernized, for though Keats never rejects a general synthesis of the human and the elemental universe, he now sees a bitter enough alienation of life in the lowlands and highlands of Scotland. Bitter though it is, the experience evokes some of the warmest and wisest remarks Keats has yet written in his letters. And since these are mostly addressed to his brother Tom, one feels that, consciously or not, he was blending his impressions of misery and heartbreak, pain, sickness, and oppression with an exquisite love for his family.

Keats and Brown spent a total of six weeks together touring what, as Aileen Ward says, was "still a foreign country to the Englishmen of that time."[3] The letters Keats wrote during his walking tour register not only the "foreignness" of Scotland and part of Ireland but more importantly the desire to gain more experience. Keats defined his purpose to Bailey in a letter

---

3. Aileen Ward's chapter, "Mist and Crag," 182-209, from which I draw heavily, gives an excellent account of Keats and Brown's walking tour of Scotland.

written toward the end of the tour: "I should not have consented to myself these four Months tramping in the highlands but that I thought it would give me more experience, rub off more Prejudice, use [me] to more hardship, identify finer scenes load me with grander Mountains, and strengthen more my reach in Poetry, than would stopping at home among Books even though I should reach Homer" (July 22, 1818). Experience, prejudice, and hardship, especially, would materialize in startling forms, despite the fact that Keats and Brown would not spend the total four months together in Scotland. They cut short their tour by two and a half months: foul weather and a persistent sore throat took their toll on Keats. Nevertheless, the experience gained from the trek among the "mist and crag" of Scotland was crucial. It would prove to be the staging for *Hyperion* and the later great poems, and it would initiate Keats to the life he would share with his dying brother upon his return.

In these letters from Scotland, Keats was writing enrichments both for his ailing brother and for his own poetic health. These letters are, to be sure, no different from his previous letters; they contain both imagination and speculation. But in writing these, I think he wanted to work out rough formulations of what he should do as an English poet living at that point in time. He wanted experience, something all young poets crave, though they may not be totally prepared for it. The experience Keats says he hoped to gain was meant to form a conversation with the rest of his life, especially needful in the pause following George's departure and the recognition of Tom's impending death. Keats, for all his identification with Hamlet, was never indecisive. He continually threw himself into action, whether direct, swift action, such as that of going to Scotland, or the ardor of mental pursuit. All his letters indeed converse with themselves and with the poems that issue from or constellate around them. It's interesting to note that Keats wrote a relatively greater number of poems for inclusion in his letters during the walking tour than at any other period in his letter-writing days. And although the poems bear the pinchmarks of this occasion, many individual lines from these poems and many words from these letters constitute the greater clutter of things Keats was to select from and articulate almost immediately upon returning to Hampstead. These find their way directly and indirectly into both *Hyperion* poems, into the "Ode to a Nightingale," and later into the "Bright Star" sonnet.[4] They are the gems of the experience in Scotland which studded Keats's sympathies and grasp of truth.

Keats was astonished by all he saw in Scotland and Ireland, by "the intellect, the countenance of such places," as he tells Tom during the first three days of the walking tour. The scenes he saw were forms of realism and living, charged presences. "I live in the eye; and my imagination, surpassed, is at rest" (June 27, 1818). This does not mean, one should not assume it means, that Keats does not care about what he sees. He knew from the start that there could be no imagined obliging transcendent Other here to offer promise of new life. His condition in the here-and-now is that of living completely in the webwork of earthly existence, without any struggle to imagine the divine. So his astonishment was actual, passionate, frontal. He looked into life, into other lives, to see not so much singularly but comprehensively through the embodiment of single, weighty life.

Keats tells Tom: "Let any of my friends see my letters—they may not be interested in descriptions—descriptions are bad at all times—I did not intend to give you any; but how can I help it?" (June 27, 1818). Indeed, he could not help it. He therefore conveys immediacy and spontaneity, an on-the-spot transcription of color, motion, solidity. He describes, for example, the waterfall at Ambleside with such fine details that his description is a responsive instrument:

> First we stood a little below the head about half way down the first fall, buried deep in trees, and saw it streaming down two more descents to the depth of near fifty feet—then we went on a jut of rock nearly level with the second fall-head, where the first

4. See discussion of other images and phrases that echo in both *Hyperion* poems, the odes, and other works, in Bate, 358-360. His chapter on the Scottish tour has filled in many gaps in my reading of the letters.

> fall was above us, and the third below our feet still—at the same time we saw that the water was divided by a sort of cataract island on whose other side burst out a glorious stream—then the thunder and the freshness. At the same time the different falls have as different characters; the first darting down the slate-rock like an arrow; the second spreading out like a fan—the third dashed into a mist—and the one on the other side of the rock a sort of mixture of all these. (June 27, 1818)

For the most part Keats writes not so much description as "a fine isolated verisimilitude," caught from the *countenance* or *intellect* of the place, which rattled him with its concentrated feeling. With Keats, one always feels that, no matter how self-conscious he is, his activity in these letters is not limited to analysis or speculation but includes dramatization or actualization of every jot of poetry unfolding before his eyes. Looking upon the face of Scotland, what he sees is beautiful, unspoilt nature: forests, valleys, streams, lakes, cataracts, islands, mist, mountains, clouds, crags, and chasms. As he tells Tom, these sights, surpassing imagination and defying memory, are vital to poetry. They are the stuff of it. "I shall learn poetry here," he continues in this same letter, "and shall henceforth write more than ever, for the abstract endeavor of being able to add a mite to that mass of beauty which is harvested from these grand materials, by the finest spirits, and put into etherial existence for the relish of one's fellows." Poetry is a creation and a contribution to the lore of Beauty, and its existence is ethereal in the sense Keats had proposed earlier, that is, as the first of the three "real" things that enrich human life.

But the other face Keats beholds is arrestingly human—that of the Scottish and Irish people of the villages and towns along the walking tour. As for his relation to this human element, the eye alone would reveal the tone, color, and weight of earthly existence, and nearly all in as calm a way as that of nature's scenes. Which is to say that Keats brought a clarity to his descriptions. Yet Keats did not make that "most devastating and impious assumption" of certain poets, that "the world in all its hard bright particulars exists so that we can write poems about it. (Or that it exists by virtue of language's capacity to make statements about it.)"[5] On the contrary, it seems to me that he managed to give the things he saw a dignity in words they were so lacking in life, an emotional veracity that was hitherto unknown and undiscovered.

I'm thinking of his letter to Tom on July 9, 1818, which tells of one particular "isolated verisimilitude" that tested Keats's desire for experience. Indeed, this letter singles out a dramatic moment in the experience of the tour, a moment that entails the precise relation between art and life, between possibility and impossibility. Keats and Brown had entered the English town of Carlisle on July 1, thence crossing over into Scotland via coach to Dumfries. By July 6 they had walked a total of sixty miles from Carlisle to Portpatrick, and the next day they crossed the North Channel in a passage boat to Belfast, Ireland. While there, Keats wrote of the disfigurement of poverty, comparing and contrasting the Scots and the Irish he had seen:

> I can perceive a great difference in the nations from the Chambermaid at this nate Inn kept by Mr Kelly—She is fair, kind and ready to laugh, because she is out of the horrible dominion of the Scotch kirk—A Scotch Girl stands in terrible awe of the Elders—poor little Susannas—They will scarcely laugh—they are greatly to be pitied and the kirk are greatly to be damn'd. These kirkmen have done scotland good (Query?) they have made Men, Women, Old Men Young Men old Women, young women boys, girls and infants all careful—so that they are formed into regular Phalanges of savers and gainers—such a thrifty army cannot fail to enrich their Country and give it a greater appearance of comfort than that of their poor irish neighbours—These kirkmen have done Scotland harm—they have banished puns and laughing and kissing (except in cases where the very danger and crime must make it very fine and gustful). I shall make a full stop at kissing for after that there should be a better parent-thesis: and go on to remind you of the

5. Di Piero, 75.

> fate of Burns. Poor unfortunate fellow—his disposition was southern—how sad it is when a luxurious imagination is obliged in self defence to deaden its delicacy in vulgarity, and riot in thing[s] which are not. No Man in such matters will be content with the experience of others—It is true that out of suffrance there is no greatness, no dignity; that in the most abstracted Pleasure there is no lasting happiness: yet who would not like to discover over again that Cleopatra was a Gipsey, Helen a Rogue and Ruth a deep one? I have not sufficient reasoning faculty to settle the doctrine of thrift—as it is consistent with the dignity of human Society—with the happiness of Cottagers—All I can do is by plump contrasts—Were the fingers made to squeeze a guinea or a white hand? Were the Lips made to hold a pen or a kiss? And yet in Cities Man is shut out from his fellows if he is poor, the Cottager must be dirty and very wretched if she be not thrifty—The present state of society demands this and this convinces me that the world is very young and in a very ignorant state—We live in a barbarous age. I would sooner be a wild deer than a Girl under the dominion of the kirk, and I would sooner be a wild hog than be the occasion of a Poor Creatures pennance before these execrable elders.

It's a perceptive rendering of the facts stated in a decisive mood. What Keats perceived was twofold. First, he became aware of the severe effects of the Kirk or presbytery, which ruled over almost all the Scottish people by the middle of the eighteenth century. These were the Calvinists whom Robert Burns (one of Keats's heroes of the heart as we shall see) had satirized in a number of poems for the ironic contrasts and sore inadequacy of a full and warm humanity their orthodoxy created. Second, Scotland presented the historical situation of the displacement of populations from common lands caused by enclosure laws. These facts dominated the condition of wretchedness that Keats was witness to in 1818 in both Scotland and Ireland.[6]

---

6. See the essay "Enclosure Movement," *Encyclopedia Americana*, vol. 10 (Danbury, Conn.: Grolier, 1989), 329; and the *Cambridge History of the British Empire*, vol. 2 (Cambridge: Cambridge University Press, 1940), 438, 440.

The whole state of affairs was so organized that for Keats being an animal was preferable to being one of these people who were destroyed by a heartless, civilized insanity. One cannot underestimate this sentiment that is at the heart of Keats's life and work, that is, a sense of justice lacking in the social order. His words here show that he knew himself to live in a society of such absolute denial of the commonest human forms of feeling and consociation, a society of such vicious alienations and errors, that one of its most exacting punishments for nonconformity (like the "crime" of love in Keats's letter) is to isolate by a thousandfold the individual or group in poverty and ignorance; this is a kind of torture that breaks the spirit, and, as Keats seems to have recognized, is a torture in which any one of us are equal participants by virtue of the terrible silence or laughter that denies rather than defends against that torture.

Keats and Brown found the cost of living in Ireland to be "thrice the expense of Scotland," another manifestation of conditions beyond parallel at that time.[7] So they returned quickly to Portpatrick where Keats found a welcome letter from Tom. From Portpatrick they walked to Ballantrae where Keats then wrote the following to Tom on July 9 about the visit to Ireland:

> On our walk in Ireland we had too much opportunity to see the worse than nakedness, the rags, the dirt and misery of the poor common Irish—A Scotch cottage, though in that some times the Smoke has no exit but at the door, is a pallace to an irish one—We could observe that impetiosity in Man and boy and Woman—We had the pleasure of finding our way through a Peat bog—three miles long at least—dreary, black, dank, flat and spongy: here and there were poor dirty creatures and a few strong men cutting or carting peat. We heard on pasing into Belfast through a most wretched suburb that most disgusting of all noises worse than the Bag pipe, the laugh of a Monkey, the chatter of women *solus* the scream of [a] Macaw—I mean the

7. This is a phenomenon in our own time brilliantly elucidated by Michael Harrington, *The Other America* (New York: Macmillan, 1963).

> sound of the Shuttle—What a tremendous difficulty is the improvement of the condition of such people—I cannot conceive how a mind 'with child' of Philantropy could gra[s]p at possibility—with me it is absolute despair.

It may be that Keats's own sense of isolation is as much a part of this "despair" as the witnessing of these conditions. Yet conditions were almost beyond despair; there was so much fear and distrust prevalent that Keats and Brown were mistaken for jewellers, razor sellers, spectacle vendors, and excisemen. Keats was even taken for a man with a price on his head by two men at a roadside tavern between Donaghadee and Belfast, one of whom had apparently said "he was ready to take it," that is, to sell out his fellow man to raise himself even one jot. But perhaps the essential key to all this description is forthcoming in Keats's letter as he now tells Tom of a most staggering incident:

> On our return from Bellfast we met a Sadan—the Duchess of Dunghill—It is no laughing matter tho—Imagine the worst dog kennel you ever saw placed upon two poles from a mouldy fencing—In such a wretched thing sat a squalid old Woman squat like an ape half starved from a scarcity of Buiscuit in its passage from Madagascar to the cape,—with a pipe in her mouth and looking out with a round-eyed skinny lidded, inanity—with a sort of horizontal idiotic movement of her head—squab and lean she sat and puff'd out the smoke while two ragged tattered Girls carried her along—What a thing would be a history of her Life and sensations.

What a history indeed! Another writer might have written a poem on this lamentable condition of human life. But Keats was too decent-minded to write a poem out of this dispossession. He "kept his vision clear of speck," as a line of his own verse has it, kept "his inward sight unblind."[8] Certainly this is

8. This is from the final line of a poem Keats included in a letter to Bailey on July 2, 1818; see Rollins, I, 345. It can also be found in Stillinger, 275-276, under the title "There is a joy in footing slow across a silent plain."

a sober and sombre moment of the tour, yet it is neither "marvelous" nor "picturesque."[9] It is a moment greater than we are, which makes a poet's words unimportant in that they do not, or cannot, willfully alter or arrange the figuration and pattern that is woefully *there.* It is a moment, above all, whose urgency of language makes it a completed image of the experience of memory, pain, and desire.

Without knowing or admitting it, Keats is employing memory—memory which, as he told Tom, was defied by the flux of images, and which, as he had argued to Reynolds five months before, was not knowledge.[10] Yet memory is part of all the history-bound matter of intellection and sensation that was stirring in the imperious present for Keats. The old woman is a figure of memory within the margins of time that nevertheless seems to burst out of efforts to contain it. Keats writes to Reynolds a few days after this incident: "The short stay we made in Ireland has left few remembrances—but an old woman in a dog-kennel Sedan with a pipe in her Mouth, is what I can never forget" (July 13). As part of the structure of Keats's journey, it bestowed an instance of "surface drama" commensurate with the interior complex of relations that concerns the world out there.

Keats was reading the Henry Cary translation of Dante's *Divine Comedy*, which is "a remembered journey," whose subject is "the acquisition of knowledge."[11] This three-volume miniature set was the only book Keats took with him on the walking tour. As he told Bailey before leaving England, "those minute volumes of cary...will go into the aptest corner" (June 10, 1818). In Keats's description/narration of the Duchess of Dunghill, Dante occupies a very apt corner indeed. Dante's telling is felt in the way that Keats's letter gives evidence of an unveiling and recovery reminiscent of the *Comedy*.

---

9. Bate, 355.

10. In his letter to Reynolds, February 19, 1818, he states that "memory should not be called knowledge."

11. Di Piero, 121.

As in Dante's poem, where even the most incidental detail implies the grand pattern of all three canticles, Keats's letter focuses upon an incident that patterns the entire journey. The gazing or staring at the old woman is just that, a staring. But it's also the medium for unveiling the import of what was seen and recollected. Keats unveils what happened, and in doing so presents in miniature the law of matter and motion—the squalor, inanity, imprisonment, and dispersion, all results of poverty and oppression—which governs the experience in Ireland. This unveiling is a prefiguration of the moment, in both *Hyperion* poems, of gazing upon the countenance (albeit divine) of sickness and doom. No special pleading is needed to see likeness here. The difference of course is that the deep and pained sympathy for the fallen titans in the first *Hyperion* is to be transcended by the "more excellent, more true and beautiful" nature transfigured by their fall.[12] But in Ireland, Keats's concentration on the face of dispossession remains a negative presentation of untransfigured human nature stuck in the "mud of history."[13]

For the first time in his life, Keats finds here that possibility is impossible, that is, his original expectation or desire to "learn poetry here" was brought up against the relentless ways of life. Or rather, the poetry that did come to mind and the poetry that he wished for but could not realize were hopelessly separated by a chasm of ignorance or misunderstanding. Keats was not repulsed by this gulf in his makeup. Or if repulsed, he was not afraid to confront it and struggle with it. Indeed, the letters of the Scottish tour show that Keats walked bravely into this *selva oscura*, with no guide but his own heart, to set straight his path toward a poetry all his own. And as happens to every sensitive traveler in a strange land, Keats found himself in this journeying, and in the process he would begin to understand far more than he had ever before.

---

12. Bloom, 385.
13. The phrase is from the Nicaraguan poet Pablo Antonio Cuadra.

On July 10, Keats and Brown walked from Ballantrae to Girvan, passing the mountains of Arran, one of the Hebrides, and Ailsa Rock on the way. On July 11, they visited the cottage birthplace of Robert Burns in Alloway, a few miles south of Ayr. Before reaching Ayr, Keats began a letter to Reynolds in the town of Maybole and, two days later, resumed writing after having taken in the full effect of the visit to "the Bardies Country." This is an extraordinary letter on several levels, first because it contains reflections on Scotland's greatest bard, whose tomb Keats and Brown had visited earlier on July 1. At that time, Keats had enclosed in a letter to Tom a sonnet written ostensibly to pay homage to one of Keats's beloved poetic predecessors:

> —On visiting the Tomb of Burns—
> The Town, the churchyard, & the setting sun,
> The Clouds, the trees, the rounded hills all seem
> Though beautiful, Cold—strange—as in a dream,
> I dreamed long ago, now new begun
> The shortlived, paly summer is but won
> From winters ague, for one hours gleam;
> Through saphire warm, their stars do never beam,
> All is cold Beauty; pain is never done.
> For who has mind to relish Minos-wise,
> The real of Beauty, free from that dead hue
> Fickly imagination & sick pride
> [?*Cast*] wan upon it! with honor due
> I have oft honoured thee. Great shadow; hide
> Thy face, I sin against thy native skies.

Though certainly not one of his best poems, "On Visiting the Tomb of Burns" reflects a most complicated recognition by Keats about the Scottish tour as a whole. He explains its origin in his July 1 letter to Tom:

> You will see by this sonnet that I am at Dumfries, we have dined in Scotland. Burns' tomb is in the Churchyard corner, not

> very much to my taste, though on a scale, large enough to show they wanted to honour him—Mrs Burns lives in this place, most likely we shall see her tomorrow—This Sonnet I have written in a strange mood, half asleep. I know not how it is, the Clouds, the sky, the Houses, all seem anti Grecian & anti Charlemagnish—I will endeavour to get rid of my prejudices, & tell you fairly about the Scotch.

The somewhat dismissive remark about his "prejudices" suggests quite strongly that something profound had happened before the tomb of Burns that he did not expect to happen. In his sonnet, the question between an old dreaming "new begun" and the power of the eye sans fancy is a real conflict. That the entire experience in Scotland and Ireland embodied this conflict over the reality Keats saw (and his desire to use it) is evidenced in this sonnet to Burns.

From the very beginning, Keats is more concerned with the "cold Beauty" his mind perceives than with the object of his poem, the tomb of Burns. And yet the two are of a piece, because the process of perceiving all that enclosed the grave reestablishes or recapitulates the dreaming which is precisely of the reality perceived. Keats realizes he is seeing another graveyard on top of the one he is presently visiting. The paradox continues with the "cold" and "paly" attributes of winter relayed to summer. Summer here has a wintry "gleam," while winter has fever, "ague." Things are out of joint. Ward argues that both this visit and Keats's response to it in verse signal the shock of recognition of St. Stephen's Cemetery in London where Keats's parents lay buried. That certainly explains the almost somnambular mood in which the poem was written. So too does Ward's insight that, already laden with a presentiment of his own death, the self-reproach at the close of the poem concerns Keats's "sin" of pride, fancying that he "stood not by Burns' grave but his own."[14] Thus Keats ends the octave

---

14. Ward, 197-198.

with the realization, "All is cold Beauty, pain is never done," a line that resonates both backward (to his parents' tomb) and forward (to the denatured portrait of the "Cold Pastoral" that lay ahead in "Ode on a Grecian Urn").

With the third quatrain, Keats begins to argue the revelation of cold beauty and does so in a way that again reveals the underpinnings of the experience in Scotland. His mention of Minos obliges the myth of the great and just king who, after his death, became judge of the dead in Hades. It justifiably occasions the question of "that dead hue" which imagination and pride cast upon beauty. Quite apart from Boccaccio's moralization of Minos in *The Genealogy of the Gods,* wherein Boccaccio shows the great lessons of Christian morals beneath the pagan fables, the figure of Minos here is Dantesque in its effect.[15]

In the fifth canto of the *Inferno,* Minos is an image of remorse and of the most severe judgment as it appears to impenitence and despair. Minos is a judge in the Tartarus of Vergil's *Aeneid* (VI.582ff.), but there is no other likeness to that image in Dante's poem. Dante's encounter with the awful judge begins:

> Thus I descended from the first circle down into the second, which bounds a smaller space and so much more of pain that goads to wailing. There stands Minos, horrible, snarling, examines their offences at the entrance, judges and despatches them according as he girds himself; I mean that when the ill-born soul comes before him it confesses all, and that discerner of sins sees what is the place for it in Hell and encircles himself with his tail as many times as the grades he will have it sent down. Always before him is a crowd of them; they go each in turn to the judgment; they speak and hear and then are hurled down.[16]

---

15. See Jean Seznac, *The Survival of the Pagan Gods* (Princeton: Princeton University Press, 1953), 224. Boccaccio's allegorization, Seznac argues, was in line with the thought of the Middle Ages insofar as its general conception, sources, and methods go. "Yet here and there symptoms of new time may be found." The *Genealogy* "is essentially a work of transition."

16. See John D. Sinclair, tr., *The Divine Comedy* (New York: Oxford University Press, 1939), 73. From Canto V.

In Keats's poem, the Minos-like mind is the ultimate moral impossibility, given that beauty for humanity is "shortlived" and "won" from death only "for one hour[']s gleam." We are subject, in other words, to an order of life on earth such that our sense of beauty (or intensity) is burdened with the knowledge that time causes the decay of all beauty. As Bate precisely puts it: "What human mind is able, as though it were a judging Minos, to separate beauty objectively from the knowledge of brevity and death that suffuses our experience of beauty?"[17] Into this drama "fickly imagination & sick pride" cast a "dead hue" upon beauty. Why "fickly" and "sick"? As the entire journey makes evident, imagination must not be false or deceiving if it is ultimately to confront the reality of death. If imagination seeks only to obtain fame and glory, then indeed what is dreamt will become "cold" and "dead." This is like the justice of *contrapasso* meted out to the sinners in Dante's inferno. It is like the irony that made Hamlet, recalling the dead Yorick whose skull he clutches in V.i.175, cry out, "And now how abhorred in my imagination it is!" So too Keats condemns his motives of memory and poetry before Burns's grave.

While Keats claimed it to be surpassed and at rest, imagination was so strong in him that, when it arose as here before Burns's tomb, he was in great conflict. His greeting of the dead poet is telling: "Great shadow, hide / Thy face, I sin against thy native skies." It is despairing and repentant. Yet this is a pathos that shows the good of the intellect, which is the knowledge or truth that while life *is* always lyric or poetic, poetry can never enforce a deliberate momentariness without assuming the burden of corrupt moral motives. Give up the fiction of continuity and the freshness of possibility, and you will feel yourself in a wilderness or in a grave as Keats did. What Keats called "prejudice" before the tomb of Burns is really more like horror or repugnance at his poetic imagination, which brought forth "Grecian" and "Charlemagnish" qualities impossible here at the grave of his poet-hero. This prejudice, as well as that misery

17. Bate, 352.

and death which had insinuated themselves in his mind since the journey began, would not "rub off," even before the birthplace of Burns. It was triggered by the arrival there.

Why was Keats so compelled by the life and death of Robert Burns? And what has this to do with his poetry or poetics? First, I think his knowledge of and love for Burns's poetry underwent a severe trial with the experience in Scotland. His love and enthusiasm are seen untroubled at the start of the journey. On July 1, when he had visited a country dance in Ireby, remarking that this brisk, twirling affair was "no new cotillion fresh from France," he was quoting Burns's "Tam o' Shanter" which was running through his head. And on July 11, when he stood upon the bridge across the river Doon in Ayrshire, facing the entire breathtaking entrance to Burns's native land, he was filled with Burns's "The Banks o' Doon" and "It Was Upon a Lammas Night."[18] As Harold Bloom has remarked, the ideal for Keats is to be poised before experience.[19] Here he is seen literally poised on the bridge between his past and future life.

But Keats was too honest to hold strictly to enthusiasm or any one thing. He did not think singularity in poetry or art a desirable thing. The farther he had come here in Scotland, the more intense became the Minos quality that in Dante concerns the dispatch of all the modes of suffering. The visit to Burns's cottage indeed marks a turning point in Keats's journey, as Ward asserts. The experience of visiting both the grave and birthplace seems to have disclosed self-recognition, which is precisely what Keats had wanted to get away from when he wrote to Reynolds on July 11 from the town of Maybole: "One of the pleasantest means of annulling self is approaching such a shrine as the Cottage of Burns." Yet he could not annul his own feelings, though he tried as he approached Burns's cottage: "We need not think of his misery—that is all gone—bad luck to it—I shall look upon it hereafter with unmixed pleasure as I do upon my Stratford on Avon day with Bailey." His letter

18. Rollins, I, 323.
19. Bloom, 407.

to Reynolds continues on July 13 from Kingswells with a description of what transpired there at Burns's cottage:

> We went to the Cottage and took some Whiskey—I wrote a sonnet for the mere sake of writing some lines under the roof—they are so bad I cannot transcribe them—The man at the Cottage was a great Bore with his Anecdotes—I hate the rascal—his Life consists in fuz, fuzzy, fuzziest—He drinks glasses five for the Quarter and twelve for the hour,—he is a mahogany faced old Jackass who knew Burns—He ought to be kicked for having spoken to him. He calls himself "a curious old Bitch"—but he is a flat old Dog—I shod like to employ Caliph Vatheck to kick him—O the flummery of a birth place! Cant! Cant! Cant! It is enough to give a spirit the guts-ache—Many a true word they say is spoken in jest—this may be because his gab hindered my sublimity—The flat dog made me write a flat sonnet.

The sonnet Keats wrote beneath the roof of Burns's cottage is filled with irony, which is a disguise and a disclosure of the feelings he had been harboring since embarking for Scotland. He did not include this sonnet in his letter to Reynolds, claiming that it was so bad he could not copy it. Instead, he later burned it (the fate suffered only by some of Keats's earliest verse), though fortunately not before Brown had copied it in his note-crammed journal where it bears the title, "Written in the Cottage where Burns was Born":

This mortal body of a thousand days
  Now fills, O Burns, a space in thine own room,
Where thou didst dream alone on budded bays,
  Happy and thoughtless of thy day of doom!
My pulse is warm with thine old barley-bree,
  My head is light with pledging a great soul,
My eyes are wandering, and I cannot see,
  Fancy is dead and drunken at its goal;
Yet can I stamp my foot upon thy floor,
  Yet can I ope thy window-sash to find
The meadow thou hast tramped o'er and o'er,—

Yet can I think of thee till thought is blind,—
Yet can I drink a bumper to thy name,—
O smile among the shades, for this is fame![20]

Keats's poem answers several questions, such as why he was angered at the old man who had known Burns. Certainly part of the reason is that "the flat dog made me write a flat sonnet." But Keats's poem is not as bad as that; it breeds its own adversity and seems to ask what it needs. No, Keats was overcome by something more covert.

Keats was so much alive in Burns's cottage—drinking the whiskey Burns had loved, looking out over his beloved hills of Ayrshire—while that absence in the cottage was itself so present and yet now made over into a terrible irony, namely the old man with his anecdotes and whiskey. I think he felt caught between the two, while simultaneously feeling a presentiment of his own death figured in the first line of his sonnet. The feeling this time, however, was not derived from fancy, if we take Keats's word for it. Keats tells Reynolds: "Fancy is indeed less than a present palpable reality, but it is greater than remembrance." And in his poem "Fancy is dead and drunken at its goal," that is, at the cottage shrine of Burns's birth. Perhaps death here is a true disclosure, initially or wholly at the primary ground of Keats's relation to Burns, a relation itself whose immediacy as love, work, and act may have informed him, as he wrote, in a manner and context impossible until now.

Like Burns, Keats was terribly hurt by the circumstances in which he lived and wrote his most memorable poetry. Unlike Burns, Keats was not an immediate literary success. Even before the reviews of *Endymion* appeared, which was after his return to England, he knew he had been marked out for attack, as evidenced by the series of articles "On the Cockney School of Poetry" published in *Blackwood's Edinburgh Magazine* in 1817.[21] The savage attacks and vicious abuse directed at Keats

20. Stillinger, 272.

21. See *The Romantics Reviewed*, vol. 1 (New York: Garland, 1972), 90-95. See also Ward, 184; Bate, 224-226.

over time have been largely due to his "youthfulness" and "tenderness," as if these were qualities somehow ludicrous in a poet or in poetry. It is this quality that Keats shares with Burns, a very sweet and loving man by all accounts who, like Keats, was made to feel the burden of his vocation.

There is a story that Burns was once asked the perennial imbecilic question, "How about a poem?" To which he responded by writing on the smudged windowpane of a tavern. Whether or not true, the story calls attention to itself because a master was asked to render that which he strives to realize completely but in a far more transitory and impermanent mode than pen on paper. Imagine the barmaid wiping the pane clean after hours. The irony of throwing away a poem—not merely on a napkin or tablecloth but on a smudged windowpane—is what is terrible. Keats's poem is no less terribly ironic, having been occasioned by yet another idiot barking for a poem. Indeed, it is more ironic for the fact that "This mortal body of a thousand days" would survive less than a thousand days from this time. And of course that last line of the poem is horribly ironic ("O smile among the shades, for this is fame"), revealing how great Keats's misery was for it to intrude here at Burns's cottage. But precisely here, I think, for the reason that it was Burns's birthplace, a "shrine" as Keats called it, which suggests that his deeper misery lay in being caught or feeling caught (indistinguishable in the experience) in steel nets at this sacrificial altar of love. As he says in his letter, "O the flummery of a birth place!" And it *is* flummery or nonsense. But it is also true that the spirit was in turmoil there. Feeling caught in a net or swirl within which no rational or previous structure can provide aid or power to understand what is happening is truly relevant to Burns. Keats continues his letter to Reynolds:

> One song of Burns's is of more worth to you than all I could think for a whole year in his native country—His Misery is dead weight upon the nimbleness of one's quill—I tried to forget it—to drink Toddy without any Care—to write a merry Sonnet—it wont do—he talked with Bitches—he drank with Blackguards,

> he was miserable—We can see horribly clear in the works of such a man his whole life, as if we were God's spies.

The echo of *King Lear*, V.iii.17 ("And we'll take upon 's the mystery of things / As if we were God's spies") reflects the eternal nature of witnessing temporal truths that, for Keats, concern the "works" of such a man as Burns—not only his poems but all his words, acts, loves. I believe that's why he asks, referring to Burns's wife Jean Armstrong, "What were his addresses to Jean in the latter part of his life," which in turn sparks thoughts about marriage:

> I should not speak so to you—yet why not—you are not in the same case—you are in the right path, and you shall not be deceived—I have spoken to you against Marriage, but it was general—the Prospect in those matters has been to me so blank, that I have not been unwilling to die—I would not now, for I have inducements to Life—I must see my little Nephews in America, and I must see you marry your lovely Wife—My sensations are sometimes deadened for weeks together—but believe me I have more than once yearne'd for the time of your happiness to come, as much as I could for myself after the lips of Juliet.—From the tenor of my occasional rhodomontade in chitchat, you might have been deceived concerning me in these points—upon my soul, I have been getting more and more close to you every day, ever since I knew you, and now one of the first pleasures I look to is your happy Marriage—the more, since I have felt the pleasure of loving a sister in Law. I did not think it possible to become so much attached in so short a time—Things like these, and they are real, have made me resolve to have a care of my health—you must be as careful—

What does he mean, "I should not speak so to you"? Does he mean not speak of Burns's misery, or the whole substance of his letter? It's not clear, though surely Reynolds's was not "the same case" as Burns, that is, economic hardship, poor health, and loneliness. "You are in the right," Keats says, "and you shall not be deceived." Deceived by what or whom? As Ward suggests, "probably far below the level of his awareness, was the fear that to love a woman wholeheartedly meant only to risk betrayal and loss—the legacy of his attachment to his mother."[22] I'm not qualified to judge the truth of that assertion, but it's quite possible that such fear existed in Keats.

Howsoever he believed marriage to be a loss of freedom and solitude, Keats was also cognizant that the problem was not with women—theirs was another story—but with men themselves. "I am certain I have not a right feeling towards Women," he writes to Bailey from Inverary on July 18. "Is it because they fall so far beneath my Boyish imagination?" He was aware, for example, that his brother's wife was more than just an exception to the "generallity of women" who are made over or buy into the image men have created of them. Georgiana's "disinterestedness," by which Keats meant a freshness of mind and spirit, and a lack of meretriciousness, was attractive to him and served to disassemble his obstinate prejudice toward women. As he says to Reynolds: "I have felt the pleasure of loving a sister in law." That love, apparently, was real.

So when Keats says he has not been unwilling to die, the reason is his own prospects for marriage have been so "blank." Indeed, they were so blank that on July 10, just the day before his letter to Reynolds, tears had sprung to his eyes when a wedding party passed him by in Ballantrae. He wrote to Tom about it in verse that reminds one of Burns:

> An every heart is full on flame
> An light as feather
> Ah! Marie they are all gone hame
> Fra happy wedding
> Whilst I—Ah is it not a shame?
> Sad tears am shedding—

This admission of the blankness of his life was undoubtedly difficult to make; it could be taken as self-pity or as soliciting pity from Reynolds. Nevertheless, Keats did make such admissions

22. Ward, 201.

in order to school himself and adjust or temper his thinking by his more loving attitude toward Georgiana, whose loyalty to and faith in George must have offered him a new and worthy model for the power of his love.

There is sadness in his words here that we need not ennoble or overlook. To understand his misery we should simply remember that his family was breaking up with George's departure and Tom's impending death; that his warm circle of friends who shared his interests and ambitions was also dissolving with the onset of quarrels but also with marriage; and, deeper still, that his desire to write great poetry, epic poetry, of which the march of passion and endeavor would be undeviating, was threatened now by a foreboding of his own death. All this bore down on him as he wrote to Reynolds, prompting the longed-for happiness of marriage and the resolve "to have a care for my health."

After visiting a number of sights, Keats and Brown came by ferry to Staffa, an isle of the Inner Hebrides. Keats writes to Tom of the difficulty of the trip, but he never once mentions that he has caught a cold and sore throat from all the exertion and exposure. On July 26 he writes:

> Well—we had a most wretched walk of 37 Miles across the Island of Mull and then we crossed to Iona or Icolmkill from Icolmkill we took a boat at a bargain to take us to Staffa and land us at the head of Loch Nakgal whence we should only have to walk half the distance to Oban again and on a better road—All this is well pass'd and done with this singular piece of Luck that there was an intermission in the bad Weather just as we saw Staffa at which it is impossible to land but in a tolerable Calm Sea—But I will first mention Icolmkill—I know not whether you have heard much about this Island, I never did before I came nigh it. It is rich in the most interesting Antiqu[i]ties. Who would expect to find the ruins of a fine Cathedral Church, of Cloisters, Colleges, Mona[s]taries and Nunneries in so remote an Island? Columba in the Gaelic is Colm signifying Dove—Kill signifies church and I is as good as Island—so I-colm-kill means the Island of Saint Columba's Church.

The beauty of the place was exceeded only by its antiquity. Keats's knowledge of Scottish history, whether coming from the guide, one of the locals, or his own voracious reading, was good. He knew he was standing on ground that had been inhabited and fought over for centuries by a host of peoples and tribes—from the complex Druids, to the simple Picts, to the warring Norse and later Romans. He seems to have been impressed with all of them, as when he tells Tom about the burial grounds of the old kings at Icolmkill, including the "many tombs of Highland Chieftains—their effigies in complete armour face upwards—black and moss covered."

Keats now describes Staffa at this point in his letter. Again, he cannot help but describe to Tom, though surely he had little else to offer his sick brother:

> I am puzzled how to give you an Idea of Staffa. It can only be represented by a first rate drawing—One may compare the surface of the Island to a roof—this roof is supported by grand pillars of basalt standing together as thick as honey combs The finest thing is Fingal's Cave—it is entirely a hollowing out of Basalt Pillars. Suppose now the Giants who rebelled against Jove had taken a whole Mass of black Columns and bound them together like bunches of matches—and then with immense Axes had made a cavern in the body of these columns—of course the roof and floor must be composed of the broken ends of the Columns—such is fingal's Cave except that the Sea has done the work of excavations and is continually dashing there—so that we walk along the sides of the cave on the pillars which are left as if for convenient Stairs—the roof is arched somewhat gothic wise and the length of some of the entire side pillars is 50 feet—About the island you might seat an army of Men each on a pillar—The length of the Cave is 120 feet and from its extremity the view into the sea through the large Arch at the entrance—the colour of the columns is a sort of black with a lurking gloom of purple therein—For solemnity and grandeur it far surpasses the finest Cathedrall—

Here at Fingal's Cave, the walking tour began to draw to a rapid close. With his sore throat, which would plague him until the first sign of tuberculosis sealed his fate, Keats approached in a rented boat this vast, titanic sanctuary that appears a year later in *The Fall of Hyperion.*[23] It's as if Keats were meant to arrive at this bourne of physical and spiritual realms; as if the experience in Scotland were waiting for him to be in it, so that it could be the thing it really was, a test of greater understanding; so that he could traverse through it and, in turn, meet the next thing his life proposed. And what that next thing was is already intimated here at Staffa, and then, a week later, at Ben Nevis, the highest point in Great Britain, on August 2.

Ben Nevis was the last and culminating vista of which Keats wrote to Tom on August 3. After describing the ascent to the summit in wonderfully dynamic ways, he writes: "There is not a more fickle thing than the top of a Mountain," and suddenly begins a most unusual tale:

> There was one Mrs Cameron of 50 years of age and the fattest woman in all inverness shire who got up this Mountain some few years ago—true she had her servants but then she had her self—She ought to have hired Sysiphus—

It's not certain if Keats made up this story on the spot. He goes on to say that Mrs. Cameron had a conversation with the old bespectacled mountain who wants to make love with the mountain of a fat lady, and proceeds to render this comic situation in heroic couplets, picturing the waking of a god and, at the close of these lines, invoking the muses:

> O Muses weep the rest—
> The Lady fainted and he thought her dead
> So pulled the clouds again about his head
> And went to sleep again—soon she was rous'd
> By her affrigh[t]ed Servants—next day hous'd
> Safe on the lowly ground she bless'd her fate
> That fainting fit was not delayed too late

---

23. See Stillinger, 363. Canto I, 61-71.

It seems a rehearsal for the titanic scenes and the great speeches of Keats's dramatic poem *Hyperion,* which he will begin writing in November 1818, three months from now.

Perhaps this seems an odd moment to be writing at all. However, it also seems that another kind of conversation took place atop Ben Nevis. For Keats wrote another poem there (and no one knows which came first), a sonnet that, placed beside the verse narrative of Mrs. Cameron, seems to challenge the other's anthropomorphic comedy with its mysterious impulses. Keats closed his letter to Tom with this originally untitled sonnet and mailed it on August 6 from Inverness, two days before he sailed from the nearby port of Cromarty for home. It reached London only six days before Keats. Here is the text of the poem from Keats's letter:

> Read me a Lesson muse, and speak it loud
> Upon the top of Nevis blind in Mist!
> I look into the Chasms and a Shroud
> Vaprous doth hide them; just so much I wist
> Mankind do know of Hell: I look o'erhead
> And there is sullen Mist; even so much
> Mankind can tell of Heaven: Mist is spread
> Before the Earth beneath me—even such
> Even so vague is Man's sight of himself.
> Here are the craggy Stones beneath my feet;
> Thus much I know, that a poor witless elf
> I tread on them; that all my eye doth meet
> Is mist and Crag—not only on this height
> But in the World of thought and mental might—

This is the only other Shakespearean sonnet Keats wrote during the Scottish tour ("This mortal body" being the first). It may have been an impromptu piece of versifying, as were the other efforts amid the walking tour. But like the sonnets to Burns, "Read me a Lesson muse" offers difficulties of interpretation, not the least of which is its relation to the experience in

Scotland as a whole. Keats says nothing about it in his letter to Tom. We have only Brown's testimony from his *Life of John Keats*: "He sat on the stones, a few feet from the edge of that fearfull precipice, fifteen hundred feet perpendicular from the valley below, and wrote this sonnet."[24]

Blindness or ignorance is the heart of this "soberly reflective" poem, as horror is the core of that "teasing problem of the imagination and actuality" in the sonnets to Burns.[25] After all the experience in Scotland and Ireland, Keats says here, at the terminal point of his journey, that he knows so little of man, heaven, earth, and hell. Had he come all this way to look into nothingness, as Ward asserts, to see with his own eyes the meaninglessness of existence and experience? Was this moment a reprise of that moment back in March at Teignmouth, of seeing "too far...too distinct into the core" of things, of being "lost in a sort of Purgatory blind" where he could not "refer to any standard law of either earth or heaven" (March 25, 1818)? The very question presupposes that he had. Yet this "lamest of the five lame sonnets he wrote on the trip," as Ward claims, is neither unsuccessful nor "significant as summing up the summer's meaning."[26] Keats's sonnet deserves and demands a fuller treatment.

The very first line reveals exactness of balance on a level of alliteration, assonance, and sense: "Read me a Lesson muse, and speak it loud." The lesson Keats wants uttered to him would supposedly clear the "shroud vaprous" from his blind vision and give him sight to a truth about the world. Herein lies the problem: is it literal seeing he wants or spiritual vision? When he says "just so much I wist," he uses the past tense of the archaic *wit*, "to know," not only making a rhyme with "Mist" in line two, but more importantly changing the drama of the

24. Charles Brown, "The Life of John Keats," in *The Keats Circle*, ed. Hyder E. Rollins, vol. 2 (Cambridge: Harvard University Press, 1948), 63. Hereafter cited as Brown.

25. Bush, 85.

26. Ward, 208.

poem. Climbing Ben Nevis and peering down into the chasms only confirms visually what he has already known or come to know, that man's knowledge of hell is essentially nothing:

> just so much I wist
> Mankind do know of Hell: I look o'erhead
> And there is sullen Mist; even so much
> Mankind can tell of Heaven: Mist is spread
> Before the Earth beneath me—

Keats now completes a looking in three cosmological directions (Hell, Heaven, and Earth) which instructs us to consider the poem not as a strictly personal order but as something more. He begins the third quatrain (interlocked like the second by enjambment) which includes man himself in this cloud of unknowing:

> Even so vague is Man's sight of himself.
> Here are the craggy Stones beneath my feet;
> Thus much I know, that a poor witless elf
> I tread on them...

"A poor witless elf," Keats writes. That "elf" came to him from *Endymion* (II.277, 464) and from "Isabella" (LVII.453). It is a favorite word of Keats that appears in other poems with varying senses.[27] Here "elf" reminds us of Spenser's use to refer to his knights in their "faerie" land. Keats, to some degree, had consciously imagined his journey through Scotland in heroic or mock heroic terms, as when he referred to Brown as "the Red Cross Knight."[28] He was on an adventure in Scotland as any knight would be in a foreign land. Indeed, the character of the

---

27. In *Endymion* "fog-born elf" means a dwarfish malignant spirit, and "curious elf" in "Isabella" has a similar meaning. But in "The Eve of St. Agnes," "La belle dame sans merci," "Lamia," and "Ode to a Nightingale," the sense is different. It is connected with not only the faery lands of the past but the ambiguously attractive and frightening.

28. See Rollins, I, 361-363. Letter from Charles Brown to C.W. Dilke, August 7, 1818.

lyric poet is expressed in the knight's quest for adventure.[29] According to James in *Varieties of Religious Experience,* the poet "owns nothing but his lyre," and his essence is "to dip into another kingdom, to feel an invisible order."[30]

But it seems that in his quest for poetry itself Keats discovered the limit of poetry in the Highlands of Scotland. Or rather, he discovered that adventure alone does not make for either poetry or life, and that poetry's false claims must be rejected. That is the "lesson" he was seeking since he first announced his desire to "learn" poetry here. Keats's sonnet *is* the lesson. For the prospect on Ben Nevis is one of his own elfin smallness or insignificance against a world that refuses to be easily swayed by poetic desire. Against the huge blankness of countenance or intellect which the world often shows us, poetry *alone* seems an improper ambition for any man or woman. It's no wonder then that Keats says

> all my eye doth meet
> Is mist and Crag—not only on this height
> But in the World of thought and mental might—

Descending Ben Nevis, Keats writes to Tom, "shook me all to pieces" because now the way—downward and backward, a terrible direction—led toward his brother's suffering and death, and his own struggle to salvage some deeper understanding out of all his difficult experience.

Keats and Brown reached Inverness on August 6, whereupon Brown called a doctor for Keats. He was fevered, his throat ulcerated, his body thin and worn out. The next day they took a coach to Beauly and then to Cromarty. On August 8, Keats boarded a smack at Cromarty alone, leaving Brown on shore to

---

29. Di Piero, 66, writes: "The character of the lyric poet is expressed in Lancelot's first question to the unknown damsel he meets in the forest after a long journey: 'Fayre damsel, know ye in this countrey ony adventures nere hande?'"

30. Quoted by Di Piero, 83. The full quote comes from a manuscript page of *The Varieties of Religious Experience* and reads: "It comes home to one only at particular times.... The more original religious life is always lyric—'the monk owns nothing but his lyre'—and its essence is to dip into another kingdom, to feel an invisible order."

complete the tour, and sailed nine days to London. It was a devastating conclusion to the journey. His first sea voyage was marked by high waves, bad food, and a toothache, as if fate had conspired to make every iota of circumstance miserable for him. But more devastating was the news, awaiting Keats at Wentworth Place when he arrived in London on August 18, that Tom was much worse than when he left almost two months and a world ago. It must have seemed a world ago in the face of his brother's life, now a suffering thing which looked to him as its only comfort and which he could not refuse. The following day he wrote, though without many details, to his fifteen-year old sister, telling her of Tom's condition and that he would ask her guardian, Richard Abbey, for permission to bring her to Hampstead.

In all its emanations, the subject of the letters from Scotland is experience—experience that led nowhere, to a blind mist on a mountain top. There is no reason to doubt what Keats says. But one must look at all that he says, from beginning to end, and not simply judge by the end. The experience he gained coexists with or subsumes the ending of looking into nothingness. In toto, he took an important step toward greater understanding, toward fusing his creative and corrective powers into one ambition. For by stating at the outset that he would live in the eye, how could he not reproach himself when his imagination would not be still? No "muse" read him a lesson. But that is not a know-nothingness. Or if Keats did recognize that there may be no purpose whatsoever to life, it was not necessarily a bleak recognition. On the contrary, it can be the most refreshing news of all whereby man is free of any outlook which excludes any aspect of a personality of life—personality, that is, which quite transcends one's ordinary circumstances. Such a recognition, initially, can shake one all to pieces. But Keats earned his own lesson by undergoing a cunningly unifying experience amid the astonishing scenes in Scotland and Ireland. The power of literal seeing is not enough. It must live with the power of inner vision which, as Wordsworth knew, "sees into the life of things."

The Vale of Soul-Making

·VII·

WHEN KEATS'S younger brother Tom died of tuberculosis in 1818, months of terrible suffering had at last come to an end. From August to December, Keats had nursed Tom day and night, giving him what little comfort and solace he could. During this time Keats was writing *Hyperion*, his epic poem about divine suffering. He called this concentration on his work a "plunge into abstract images to ease myself of [Tom's] countenance his voice and feebleness" (September 21, 1818). And yet it is probably Tom's face that is seen in *Hyperion* where Saturn shouts to Thea: "I see thy face; / Look up, and let me see our doom in it."[1] Poetry became the seeming "crime" of these days, as Keats referred to his poem. He would sit beside his bedridden brother while he wrote, never leaving him for more than a short time, so that by the end of November he had composed the greater part of *Hyperion*. On the morning of November 30, Tom fell "in a very dangerous state," as Keats wrote to their sister Fanny. Thereafter he worked very little on the poem, giving it up completely in April of the following year. By then Keats had experienced a great change in his heart and mind that had everything to do with Tom's suffering and death, and with a new urge to write.

Tom went easily, at eight o'clock in the morning, December 1, 1818, perhaps in his brother's arms. He had just turned nineteen. Six days later on December 7, Tom was buried in St. Stephen's Cemetery in London, where Keats's parents and

1. Stillinger, 332. From Book I, 97.

grandparents lay at rest. There is no information that Keats engaged a minister for the burial, but perhaps he or someone near him insisted in the moment. All that is certain is that between December 16, 1818 and January 4, 1819, Keats wrote a long letter to his brother and sister-in-law in America that mercifully says nothing of Tom's wasting away or anything of the daily sorrow and ache that weighed on Keats while nursing him. It begins with these words:

> You will have been prepared, before this reaches you for the worst news you could have, nay if Haslam's letter arrives in proper time, I have a consolation in thinking the first shock will be past before you receive this. The last days of poor Tom were of the most distressing nature; but his last moments were not so painful, and his very last was without a pang—I will not enter into any parsonic comments on death—yet the common observations of the commonest people on death are as true as their proverbs. I have scarce a doubt of immortality of some nature of other—neither had Tom.

Whatever happened during this time, he saw it through and tried anything to dispel the morbid longface gloom over the death of his brother Tom who, George remarked, understood Keats better than any other human being.[2]

When Tom died, it seems there was nothing left but the nothing, so that Keats's words to his family in America, however merciful, are also nagged by or impatient with grief and the shroud of death. His statement on immortality has been seen as "a hope as wan as the English sun in December," and as a "declaration. . .the result of grief rather than a steady conviction."[3] However one looks upon Keats's words here, there is no question that four months later he was to take immortality for granted in his account of "Soul-making" on April 21,

---

2. *The Keats Circle,* I, 285. Letter from George Keats to C.W. Dilke dated April 20, 1825.

3. Ward, 230; Bush, 93-94.

1819. This taking of immortality for granted, however, was "for the purpose of showing a thought which has struck me concerning it." The "thought" Keats was struck by is contained in the phrase "the vale of Soul-making" which appears in an entry of a journal-letter written to George and Georgiana between February 14 and May 3, 1819:

> Call the world if you Please "'The vale of Soul-making" Then you will find out the use of the world (I am speaking now in the highest terms for human nature admitting it to be immortal which I will here take for granted for the purpose of showing a thought which has struck me concerning it) I say *'Soul making'* Soul as distinguished from an Intelligence—There may be intelligences or sparks of the divinity in millions—but they are not Souls till they acquire identities, till each one is personally itself. I[n]telligences are atoms of perception—they know and they see and they are pure, in short they are God—how then are Souls to be made? How then are these sparks which are God to have identity given them—so as ever to possess a bliss peculiar to each ones individual existence? How, but by the medium of a world like this? This point I sincerely wish to consider because I think it a grander system of salvation than the chryst[e]ain religion—or rather it is a system of Spirit-creation—
>
> (April 21, 1819)

"The vale of Soul-making" is a proposition to countervail what Keats believes to be the world's "misguided and superstitious...'vale of tears' from which we are to be redeemed by a certain arbitrary interposition of God and taken to Heaven." Unlike other propositions in his letters, Christian doctrine is the occasion of his speculation here, in particular the doctrine of salvation which he calls "a little circumscribe[d] straightend notion!" Why does he dissent from or take exception to the Christian concept of immortality? For Keats, it is a question of what the soul actually desires. In both December 1818 and April 1819, the soul's grief needed expression and transformation within the "vale of tears," which he considered deeply, I think, after the death of his brother.[4] As Keats rightly understood, the vale of tears is not life's final qualification. For death (and the grief it brings) is the soul's initial recognition of awakening to the complete absence of something other than grief or loss, namely "salvation."

Keats had spoken of "salvation" the year before in a letter to his publisher John Hessey: "The Genius of Poetry must work out its own salvation in a man" (October 8, 1818). Keats meant that poetry must save one from failure, which was all around in various cunning forms, as the recent trip to Scotland had made clear to him. He felt that poetry must keep one safe from the praise or blame that others, indeed the poet himself, invariably impose upon it. Praise and blame are essential features of lyric, as W.R. Johnson explains, they give it scope.[5] But they are not the poet's redemption from the world of circumstance. Into the precarious drama of living with and singing of some understanding and sympathy, there must enter more than inspiration or the Muse, who can easily take her leave, leaving the poet without her forms, exhausted.[6] There must also enter the possibility of religious expression, "man's best anger, bile, and weeping," as García Lorca called it.[7]

---

4. The vale of tears expression possibly derives from Psalm 23:4, where King David says: "Yea, though I walk through the valley of the shadow of death. . . ." Or even earlier, from the Genesis story. In the popular devotion of the Rosary, there is a prayer to the mother of Christ known as "Hail, Holy Queen," which makes reference to the Fall: "To you [Blessed Virgin Mary] we do cry, poor banished children of Eve: to you we send up our sighs, mourning and weeping in this vale of tears." The Hebrew name for Eve (*hawwa*) is related to the word for "living" (*hay*). Thus the first mother of life is invoked in a prayer to the mother of the redeemer of life; the two are linked by the fallen state of humanity that proceeds from the first Eve and is changed forever by the second Eve. As we shall see, the pains and sorrows associated with Eve (Life) are of utmost importance to Keats's letter.

5. W.R. Johnson, *The Idea of Lyric* (Berkeley: University of California Press, 1982), 24-75. Praise and blame are essential features of all Greek poetry, not just the lyric.

6. Shakespeare knew this fact vividly. In his *Sonnets,* especially 100, 101, and 103, the Muse's abandonment and the poet's trial with a new mode of poetic and spiritual triumph over death is explicitly described.

See Duncan McNaughton, "Love Triumphant: Meditations on Shakespeare's *Sonnets,*" dissertation, SUNY Buffalo, 1973. Hereafter cited as McNaughton. McNaughton's reading of Shakespeare's *Sonnets* is a most needed and beautifully composed exegesis of a poetics centered on love.

Cf. Lorca, "Play and Theory of the Duende," 42-53.

7. Lorca, 50.

Having been present to the instant of death with Tom, Keats began to see through it to a place where his total faith in the authenticity of poetry could find deeper, more ardent expression in the service of life. Salvation was a symbolic yet practical ground of the poet's existence. In Elaine Pagels's words, "religious insights and moral choices, in actual experience, coincide with practical ones."[8] When Keats had written to George and Georgiana in December 1818—"I must again begin with my poetry for if I am not in action mind and body I am in pain"—salvation was a practical act with profound consequences. Now in April 1819, Keats was speaking of a "system" of salvation, which was not limited to poetry but included the whole life of humanity. Or rather, poetry and life for Keats were not only equal but identical. In our inheritance, poetry (though not all poetry by any means) is no more than an expression of the need to be in particular instances or constellations of being. What is at issue here in Keats's letters and poetics is a justice of life: all of human life becomes the terrain of the heart's habitation. Keats is *working* that terrain in his letters—and more so than in the poems, I feel—searching for anything that makes the objective reality of the soul concrete.

Keats's "system" (Greek *sustema,* "to stand together") is best understood as an organized whole for saving the soul of humanity from what would exhaust or destroy it, namely the mortal pain all humans are prey to. As Keats had written in the Chamber of Maiden Thought letter, we all live in a world "full of Misery and Heartbreak, Pain, Sickness and oppression" (May 3, 1818). Keats's "simile of human life," the Mansion of Many Apartments, is an apprehension of the justice which addresses life in its deepest, most concrete dimensions of the soul. The Vale of Soul-making letter, then, with its system of salvation, refuses what is sterile or degrading in the world, such as conventional religion, morality, and so on, those cruel perversions that seemed to Keats only by-products of conventional

---

8. Elaine Pagels, *Adam, Eve, and the Serpent* (New York: Vintage Books, 1988), xxvii. Hereafter cited as Pagels.

hypocrisies. Christian claptrap, as in the doctrine of salvation, is precisely what Keats is trying to shake out of, or expel from, a tradition that has kept alive a flicker of the justice of life in a world that too often discredits the soul's desire.

Keats was not alone in perceiving a certain quality of modern life in response to which he conceived his system of salvation. His contemporary, the great Italian poet Giacomo Leopardi (1798-1837), had seen the nature of the world as that of illusion and evil. In the *Pensieri,* a book of reflections and aphorisms based on his personal experience, Leopardi identified *noia* or *ennui* as one of the most compelling subjects (and problems) of Western culture throughout the nineteenth century. *Noia* is not idleness or boredom but spiritual pain resulting from a world that, as Leopardi says, "is satisfied by appearances. . .never satisfied by *substance*: it does not care about substance and often absolutely refuses to tolerate it."[9] More and more what Leopardi saw in life was a grim kind of "struggle—where it's one against all and all against one."[10] Like Keats, he recognized or realized that heroism had become a capacity of human feeling to possess meaningful spirit not in spite of but because of the world. Keats may have been less absolute about the evil nature of the universe than Leopardi. But his will to speculate about possibility, to transform into poetry the painful nature of life and consciousness, is no less staggering than Leopardi's great courage of mind and heart to explore human illusions. And while Keats admitted he was "morbid," that morbidity, it must be remembered, was something he always contested and hoped to defeat. This is shown in his effort alone to find a system not of "perfectibility" but possibility—a system that refused outright the consolations of Christian belief, as well as his earlier unqualified allegiance to classical norms, in an attempt to explore what truth might be hidden in either or both.

---

9. Giacomo Leopardi, *Pensieri* (New York: Oxford University Press, 1984), 105. Hereafter cited as Leopardi.
10. Leopardi, 151.

What had helped to crystallize Keats's thinking into a system of salvation were two books he was reading: William Robertson's *The History of America* (1777) and Voltaire's *Le Siècle de Louis XIV* (1751). The first is a history of man in simple existence; the second of man in a highly civilized state. In both cases, Keats found overwhelming the "mortal pains" with which humanity had to bear. As he writes to his family before expounding his system of salvation:

> The whole appears to resolve into this—that Man is originally 'a poor forked creature' subject to the same mischances as the beasts of the forest, destined to hardships and disquietude of some kind or other. If he improves by degrees his bodily accomodations and comforts—at each stage, at each ascent there are waiting for him a fresh set of annoyances—he is mortal and there is still a heaven with its Stars abov[e] his head. The most interesting question that can come before us is, How far by the persevering endeavours of a seldom appearing Socrates Mankind may be made happy—

Keats ponders, in effect, the same age-old question of the consolation of philosophy that he had pondered in the Chamber of Maiden Thought letter over a year before. But now the question has behind it all the force of his brother's suffering and death, and all the experience gained over a year's time. He continues:

> I can imagine such happiness carried to an extreme—but what must it end in?—Death—and who could in such a case bear with death—the whole troubles of life which are now frittered away in a series of years, would the[n] be accumulated for the last days of a being who instead of hailing its approach, would leave this world as Eve left Paradise—

Eve left Paradise in pain, punished for her disobedience with the pangs and sorrows of childbearing. This reference is quite apt; the expulsion from Paradise in disgrace and pain, indeed the whole story of "original sin," addresses the question of humanity's suffering and death that Keats's letter raises and attempts to answer through a kind of gnostic inversion of salvation—that is, a mental process that runs counter to the orthodox teachings enjoining repentance and obedience to a Law.[11]

When Keats exclaims, "I do not at all believe in this sort of perfectibility—the nature of the world will not admit of it—the inhabitants of the world will correspond to itself," he is denying the blissful promises of an afterlife offered by either philosophy or religion, and intimating an idea of moral responsibility that is the true birthright of humanity:

> Let the fish philosophise the ice away from the Rivers in winter time and they shall be at continual play in tepid delight of summer. Look at the Poles and at the sands of Africa, Whirlpools and volcanoes—Let men exterminate them and I will say that they may arrive at earthly Happiness—The point at which Man may arrive is as far as the paralel state in inanimate nature and no further—For instance suppose a rose to have sensation, it blooms on a beautiful morning it enjoys itself—but there comes a cold wind, a hot sun—it can not escape it, it cannot destroy its annoyances—they are as native to the world as itself: no more can man be happy in spite, the world[l]y elements will prey upon his nature—The common cognomen of this world among the misguided and superstitious is 'a vale of tears'.

Without bitterness or meanness, Keats had a tough mind that permitted no falsifications. He saw the world for what it truly is, a vale of tears, harsh and tragic and sometimes bitterly ironic. But above all it is a mystery that he unfailingly attempted to

---

11. Pagels, 127, shows that there has been widespread belief that "pain, oppression, labor and death are punishments that we (or our ultimate ancestors) *brought upon ourselves.* 'In the beginning' the willful choice of the first man and woman changed the nature of nature itself, and all mankind thereafter suffered and died."

But in contrast to the orthodox belief that Eve is to blame for the Fall, gnostic interpretation posits Eve as revelatory of spiritual awakening. It seems to me that Keats's identity, salvation, and humanity did not awaken until the period of beginning with Tom's death, leading up to the Vale of Soul-making letter—a change that gave way to the composition of the odes and all the other great poetry thereafter.

know or be reconciled with rather than live ignorant of its power and beauty. He knew that real happiness and any specific belief in life (whether as a vale of tears or as soul-making) are two different things fused only by desire and will.

In an earlier entry, two months prior to his sketch of salvation, Keats had written that famous passage, perhaps the most famous passage in his letters, about a life of "allegory." He tells George and Georgiana:

> A Man's life of any worth is a continual allegory—and very few eyes can see the Mystery of his life—a life like the scriptures, figurative—which such people can no more make out than they can the hebrew Bible. Lord Byron cuts a figure—but he is not figurative—Shakspeare led a life of Allegory; his works are the comments on it—
>
> (February 19, 1819)

Life is not simply interestingly occasioned, as Keats bears witness to Byron. It is as mysterious as that great code of art known as the Bible. But what "mystery," what "allegory" is possible in a world where man and inanimate nature both, in terms of "earthly Happiness," arrive at a "paralel state," that is, prey to nature, "and no further"?

To perceive the deepest implications of Keats's "allegory" and their relation to his "system of salvation," I draw heavily upon C. Kerényi's study of ancient Crete, *Dionysos: Archetypal Image of Indestructible Life.* In this discussion of human experience reflected in a totality of religion and art, Kerényi speaks of language enabling a prephilosophical wisdom common to all humans who use language. Of the ancient Greeks, his subject, he writes:

> In their everyday language the Greeks possessed two different words that have the same root as *vita* but present very different phonetic forms: *bios* and *zoë*. . . . The word *biologos* meant to the Greeks a mime who imitated the characteristic life of an individual and by his imitation made it appear still more characteristic. . . . A Greek definition of *zoë* is *chronos tou einai,* but

> not in the sense of an empty time into which the living creature enters and in which it remains until it dies. No, this "time of being" is to be taken as a continous being which is framed in a *bios* as long as this *bios* endures—then it is termed "*zoë* of *bios*"—or from which *bios* is removed like a part and assigned to one being or another. The part may be called "*bios* of *zoë*."... Plotinus called *zoë* the "time of the soul," during which the soul in the course of its rebirths, moves on from one *bios* to another.... If I may employ an image for the relationship between them, which was formulated by language and not by philosophy, *zoë* is the thread upon which every individual *bios* is strung like a bead.... This experience differs from the sum of experiences that constitute the *bios,* the content of each individual man's written or unwritten biography.... Actually we experience *zoë,* life without attributes, whether we conduct such an exercise or not. It is our simplest, most intimate and self-evident experience.[12]

This *zoë* is the "Penetralium of mystery" Keats had divined in his famous Negative Capability letter of 1817. That is, *zoë* is identical with the Penetralium because the latter contains the distinguishing thing about *zoë*-life: the time and being of the soul. Recall that the Penetralium embodies the condition that revealed to Keats the shift from a self-centered "irritable reaching after fact & reason" to an absolute surrender to uncertainty. This shift is like that of which Kerényi speaks—from *zoë* of *bios* to *bios* of *zoë* —for it disclosed the most intimately familiar thing of one's own being: life that exceeds all the assumptions erected by fact and reason.

Keats sees the connection between his own *zoë* -life and *bios* -life, which is what he needed to see in order to negate and transform the emptiness of "time." Allegory (Greek *allegoría*, "speaking otherwise," and *allegoros,* "the other speaking") stands in place of the nothingness of a life "time." It is the thread or string through those beads of experience that constitute an individual human story. Keats's "life of worth" is a *zoë* -life allegory whose nature or scope is "figurative," that is, narrative, and therefore

---

12. Kerényi, xxi-xxvi.

in need of interpretation. As he said of Shakespeare's life of allegory, "his works are the comments on it." That is, comments as interpretation or exegesis of a life "time" encompassing the whole human world, from comedy and history to tragedy and romance.

Now the system of salvation in Keats's Vale of Soul-Making letter is a deepening of that life of allegory. Salvation here is not unlike the immortality Blake spoke of in his last letter to George Cumberland, written shortly before his death in 1827:

> I have been very near the Gates of Death & have returned very weak & an Old Man feeble & tottering, but not in Spirit & Life not in The Real Man The Imagination which Liveth for Ever. In that I am stronger & stronger as this Foolish Body decays.[13]

Blake's "Real Man" translates to Keats's salvation, and it is given in all his "works," both poems and letters. Salvation, or more specifically, the "system of Spirit-creation," is part of the "Mystery" of life that very few eyes can see unless they are trained upon both the *zoë* and *bios* sides of life.

Keats takes for granted—and *takes* in the sense of bringing into relation—the Christian belief of salvation for the purpose of articulating his own idea of spiritual possibility, an idea or method that seems contradictory in that the spiritual is formed and practiced through the nonspiritual. Jeffrey Baker asserts that this is a "spontaneous theology."[14] If spontaneous, then it is in the primary sense of formal engagement, and that engagement is not so much with theology (*theós,* "god") as with thought (*théa,* "sight, contemplation"). For though it includes the divine, Keats's system of salvation really is, as Baker claims, "non-Messianic." It is an order of existential purpose, the outgrowth of all his earlier speculations on the self and world, from Negative Capability to the Chamber of Maiden

13. Erdman, 783. Letter to George Cumberland, April 12, 1827.

14. Jeffrey Baker, *John Keats and Symbolism* (Sussex: Harvester Press; New York: St. Martin's Press, 1986), 23. Hereafter cited as Baker.

Thought, down to the Vale of Soul-Making. Keats begins his description of the process of soul-making thus:

> This is effected by three grand materials acting the one upon the other for a series of years—These three Materials are the *Intelligence* —the *human heart* (as distinguished from intelligence or Mind) and the *World* or *Elemental Space* suited for the proper action of *Mind and Heart* on each other for the purpose of forming the *Soul* or *Intelligence destined to possess the sense of Identity*. I can scarcely express what I but dimly perceive—and yet I think I perceive it—that you may judge the more clearly I will put it in the most homely form possible—I will call the *world* a School instituted for the purpose of teaching little children to read—I will call the *human heart* the *horn Book* used in that School—and I will call the *Child able to read, the Soul* made from that *school* and its *hornbook*. Do you not see how necessary a World of Pains and troubles is to school an Intelligence and make it a soul? A Place where the heart must feel and suffer in a thousand diverse ways! Not merely is the Heart a Hornbook, It is the Minds Bible, it is the Minds experience, it is the teat from which the Mind or intelligence sucks its identity—As various as the Lives of Men are—so various become their souls, and thus does God make individual beings, Souls, Identical Souls of the sparks of his own essence—This appears to me a faint sketch of a system of Salvation which does not affront our reason and humanity—I am convinced that many difficulties which christians labour under would vanish before it—There is one wh[i]ch even now Strikes me—the Salvation of Children—In them the Spark or intelligence returns to God without any identity—it having had no time to learn of, and be altered by, the heart—or seat of the human Passions—

This passage is very rich with evidence that has often been overlooked or ignored. While Keats's system of salvation is certainly *religious*, there is also a pedagogical level whereby orthodox Christian terms are brought into a new set of metaphors or images. Out of this pedagogy (and pedagogy here simply means how to live a lifetime under any circumstance), Keats leads humanity forth from the heart rather than into any machinelike system.

"Soul-making" is, first of all, a "making," namely poesis (Greek *poiesis*, "creation, poetry, poem"). Keats is doing more here than simply giving "assent" to some religious principle.[15] He is bringing forward poetic action for meeting the problem of death head-on. Death denies life. But the making of a soul involves the acquisition of "identity" (something Keats does not take for granted), an identity "so as ever to possess a bliss peculiar to each ones individual existence." There would be no "bliss" possible if there were no world "like this," that is, full of misery, heartbreak, pain, sickness, oppression, and death. It is a paradox that some find impossible to accept or even see.[16] One must start from Keats's own premises if one is to see, with the eyes of inner vision, the allegory of life Keats spoke of. Always with Keats's words, one must take them at face value, asking what they can possibly mean and excluding nothing.

What does it mean to "school" an intelligence in order to make it a soul? Who or what schools the mind to give it confidence for its descent into the heart, where a door or gate then opens onto all of what else exists, namely the soul, identity, destiny? Keats writes that it is "the *World* or *Elemental Space*" which constitutes our school, the same world of "Circumstance" he had been speculating on for over a year now. This world is that same world of *King Lear*, especially in its central

---

15. Baker, 23. Although Baker argues that Keats's salvation is non-messianic, he gives a peculiarly Calvinist interpretation of that salvation, asserting that in Keats's system "salvation has thus been preordained by God." Keats, however, is not talking about a chosen few or preexisting set of conditions that allow soul-making to take place.

16. See John Jones, *John Keats' Dream of Truth* (London: Chatto and Windus, 1969), 88. Jones argues that "the automatic nature of the process [Keats's system of salvation] is what strikes an observer first. . . . Provided one stays alive one cannot help growing into a soul, and a saved soul. The scene therefore appears theologically as well as morally empty." Indeed it would strike an "observer," who did no more than observe, as "automatic." Keats, however, was providing for entrance to a deeper level of participatory life, which is anything but automatic, because submitting oneself to the trials of the world is an act of the greatest heroism.

Cf. Katherine M. Wilson, *The Nightingale and the Hawk* (New York: Barnes and Noble, 1964), 112. Hereafter cited as Wilson. Discussing the vale of soul-making letter, Wilson claims that "the pains of life gradually prepare us for death. We experience its deprivations piece-meal and so by easier stages than if death came suddenly to end a life of bliss. . .So [Keats] suggests it is better to look at life as a vale of Soul-making, this being its purpose. He says we are all intelligences, but we have to make ourselves souls."

tragic symbol of the tempest. *Lear* shows a world where man, as Keats quotes, is originally "a poor, bare, forked animal." It's fascinating that Keats quotes from the storm scene when Kent, the Fool, and Lear take shelter in Edgar's hovel, which is symbolically, as Martin Lings points out, "a palace of wisdom."[17] For as Tom o' Bedlam, Edgar holds out a mirror for Lear to look into with these words that reply to Lear's question, "What hast thou been?":

> A servingman, proud in heart and mind; that curled my hair, wore gloves in my cap; served the lust of my mistress' heart, and did the act of darkness with her; swore as many oaths as I spake words, and broke them in the sweet face of heaven. One that slept in the contriving of lust, and waked to do it. Wine loved I deeply, dice dearly; and in woman out-paramoured the Turk. False of heart, light of ear, bloody of hand; hog in sloth, fox in stealth, wolf in greediness, dog in madness, lion in prey.... (III.iv.81-89)

To which the king replies, as the storm continues to rage:

> Thou wert better in a grave than to answer with thy uncovered body this extremity of the skies.... Unaccomodated man is no more than a poor, bare, forked animal as thou art. (III.iv.96-102)

The world in *Lear* is no longer Britain; it is not even man's home but his exile, as the tempest vividly exemplifies. Lings sees an "inextricable interpenetration of Hell and Purgatory" reflected in the storm, "which both voices the anger of Heaven and purifies by the elements."[18] But the tempest is also reflected in Lear himself: "The tempest in my mind / Doth from my senses take all feeling / Save what beats there." It humbles and universalizes him into a representation of Everyman or the human soul.

---

17. Martin Lings, *The Secret of Shakespeare* (New York: Inner Traditions, 1984), 77. Hereafter cited as Lings.
18. Lings, 76.

Shakespeare's tragic salvation—the soul accepting the fate that defines it—is translated into Keats's system of salvation as a drama of choice and decision. Man does not choose to suffer and die, but his heart does learn from the world, and it teaches his mind to become a soul if man so chooses. Though the tempest of this world may strip away man's hubris and blindness, as it does in *King Lear*, it is man's acceptance of this tempest-change that matters most to his identity and spiritual life. Shakespeare dramatizes soul-making; Keats articulates it. And his terms for articulating the kind of heroism that acceptance involves are uniquely his own.

Heroism, at least in modern times, implies a capacity of the heart or a vision of the world's evil. Yet even so long ago as the eighth century B.C.E., one sees in the Homeric poems a depth of heart that has never failed to hold our attention through the ages since. According to Seth Schein, Homer has a "double view." That is, he sees the frivolous existence of the gods in contrast to the tragic reality of human strivings for heroism and meaning in life—a truly critical, human vision.[19] By Keats's time, however, great deeds are wholly locked in the distant past, or worse, are synonymous with contemporary, evil events such as the Napoleonic wars. Heroism becomes that interiorized condition which Leopardi understood better than most men, then or now. Leopardi and Keats both were living at a time when, as Lionel Trilling says, "the sickness of Europe began to be apparent." Trilling defines an adverse sense of relation between the self and culture, a sense that has extended to our own time. This sickness, together with historical events, "have destroyed [the Romantic] commitment" to the self, he argues. Thus we "find it all too easy to explain why Keats's heroic vision of the tragic life and the tragic salvation will not serve us now."[20]

---

19. Seth Schein, *The Mortal Hero* (Berkeley: University of California Press, 1984), passim. According to Professor Schein, the Greek sense of hero is someone who flourishes in his prime and then dies—life's brevity in other words.

20. Lionel Trilling, "The Poet as Hero: Keats in His Letters," *The Opposing Self* (New York: Harcourt Brace Jovanovich, 1979), 43. Hereafter cited as Trilling.

Keats's heroism is unmistakably a matter of the heart. The heart is central in Keats's life and thought; he felt it to be truly real. Just a month prior to his speculations on the vale of soul-making, he had said, quoting Wordsworth's poem "The Old Cumberland Beggar": "'we have all one human heart'—there is an ellectric fire in human nature tending to purify—so that among these human creature[s] there is continually some birth of new heroism—The pity is that we must wonder at it: as we should at finding a pearl in rubbish" (March 19, 1819). In this Biblical image of "the pearl of great price," we see the great tragedy of values in Western culture, that the purifying quality of the heart is dismally lacking or lost in the world of circumstance and human limitations. So the heart becomes even more central and dominant in the Vale of Soul-making. It stands precisely between the world and the soul, worked upon by the first and, along with the action of mind or intelligence, giving rise to the second.

In Keats's "homely" terms, the heart is the "Hornbook" used in the school of the world to help make a soul. A hornbook is a primer, specifically a single page of paper or sheet of parchment mounted on a panel of wood and protected with a covering of a transparent sheet of horn. It was commonly used in English schools from the fifteenth to the eighteenth century. Shakespeare and other English writers mention the hornbook.[21] Keats aptly chose this object to stand for the heart because it is the heart which schools the mind in order to make a soul. As the mind's "Bible," the heart contains the script of all human "experience" which the world writes or dictates. The heart is a text—a text to be written in or on by the world as well as read and interpreted by the mind. In the Book of Jeremiah, this im-

---

21. "Horn" in its Latin form *cornu* is related to the Greek word *keras* or "hart" in English which means "horned beast," as in a male deer or stag. As for "heart," the Indo-European base *kerd* or *krd* is represented also by the Greek *kêr* as in *kardía, kradía,* and the Latin *cord, cor.*

Cf. *Love's Labour Lost,* V.i.44: "Yes, yes! He teaches boys the hornbook."

The New Standard Encyclopedia states that the hornbook traditionally contained "as a safeguard against evil, an invocation to the Holy Trinity." So some religious significance was attached to the hornbook as well.

age of the heart as text appears when the prophet receives the word from God of a new covenant with Israel: "I will put my law in their inward parts, and write it in their hearts" (Jer. 31:33). This is a radical new image of the law as intimate, unmediated scripture to be read and interpreted solely by each person; no scribe or priestly tribe is needed for this new relation.[22] So too Keats, who is often spoken of as bookish, as having lived the major part of his life in books, possesses but one text now, the human heart, written upon by the hand of the world. He too needs no scribe or author save that of the world's experience.

The mind's action upon the heart is not an intellectual endeavor because one's feelings are an adequate articulation of being. For in Keats's terms, it's not the heart that is put to school but the intelligence, which must learn from what the heart has felt and suffered, must take its lessons of identity from the pain and death that the world has in store for each human being. Keats says that the heart "is the teat from which the mind or intelligence sucks its identity." Ward points out that this image of suckling "is supremely characteristic of Keats in implying that the assimilation of experience beyond all conscious endeavour is what makes wisdom in the end."[23] And yet what is absolutely conscious is the endeavor to achieve identity and thus salvation. For it does occur to one that identity is what can possibly unbind one from some afterlife existence or principle. The mind in Keats had been informed and urged by the heart to orient himself away from the mistaken despair that religious orthodoxy argues, because any one fixed outlook does exclude the aspect of a personality of life.

It could be argued that Keats's Vale of Soul-making, with its focus on the acquisition of identity, contradicts or cancels out his earlier statement on Negative Capability, with its corollary view of poetical character as having "no self," "no character," "no

---

22. Of all the prophets in the Hebrew Bible, Jeremiah is the most humanely radical, angered by hypocrisy and forgiving of repentant sinners. He, like Keats, was a letter writer, teaching the Hebrews "thoughts of peace, and not of affliction." He put his prophecy from God in a book.

23. Ward, 277.

identity" (October 27, 1818). But such an argument would be untenable because Negative Capability truly means an inwarding, an intense concentration on objects presented to the mind, without the obtrusiveness of the ego. In the context of soul-making, identity is not the same thing Keats rejected in speculating on the "gusto" that "delights the camelion Poet" (October 27, 1818). Whereas before Keats was speaking of identity as "an unchangeable attribute" (whether in "the Sun, the Moon, the Sea [or] Men and Women"), now he is speaking of a dynamic process leading not to simple happiness on earth or in heaven, but to a new sense of human vitality. When Keats says, "Call the world if you Please 'The vale of Soul-making' Then you will find out the use of the world," he is speaking of "use" in the sense of desiring to make known what is a hidden treasure, like the "pearl in rubbish," namely the soul destined to possess its own identity, its bliss. This is far removed from the ordinary identity that most persons observe in themselves and others. It is certainly not "the wordsworthian or egotistical sublime" that Keats opposed in his view of the poetical character. Identity, or the character of life, is what any man or woman of achievement struggles for, even to the end. Indeed, only a month before, Keats had written a sonnet, the conclusion of which contained a most striking realization:

> Why did I laugh tonight? No voice will tell:
> No god, no Deamon of severe response,
> Deigns to reply from heaven or from Hell—
> Then to my human heart I turn at once—
> Heart! thou and I are here sad and alone;
> Say, wherefore did I laugh? O mortal pain!
> O Darkness! Darkness! ever must I moan
> To question Heaven and Hell and Heart in vain!
> Why did I laugh? I know this being's lease
> My fancy to its utmost blisses spreads:
> Yet could I on this very midnight cease,
> And the world's gaudy ensigns see in shreds.
> Verse, fame, and Beauty are intense indeed
> But Death intenser—Deaths is Life's high meed.

There is a clash felt by Keats between pain and heroism in both halves of the sonnet (octave and sestet). But the beauty and truth of the last line destroys or obliterates any suggestion of irony. Moreover, it points to the order of Keats's system of salvation when you think of death as that toward which all our earthly existence is leading and which any man or woman must meet with all resource and identity. Intensity indeed reaches its final degree in death; thus death is "Life's high meed," for intensity gives purpose to our mortality, and that is the whole import of the Vale of Soul-Making.

Keats had prefaced the inclusion of this sonnet to George and Georgiana on March 19, 1819 thus:

> I am ever affraid that your anxiety for me will lead you to fear for the violence of my temperament continually smothered down: for that reason I did not intend to have sent you the following sonnet—but look over the last two pages and ask yourselves whether I have not that in me which will well bear the buffets of the world. It will be the best comment on my sonnet; it will show you that it was written with no Agony but that of ignorance; with no thirst of any thing but knowledge when pushed to the point though the first steps to it were throug[h] my human passions—they went away, and I wrote with my Mind—and perhaps I must confess a little bit of my heart—

These words are a good comment on this entire period in Keats's life, when he questioned his own "love of gloom" and alienation, seeking a greater sense of relatedness by freeing the self. His "first steps" to knowledge must be seen to be through the chambers of the "human passions," where Keats's heroism was fully defined.

In the Vale of Soul-Making letter, then, that "little bit of my heart" became more pronounced. Keats visualized the heart as the hornbook, Bible, and teat of identity for the mind. "Faint" though it may be, his entire sketch of a system of salvation provides an exact apprehension of the heart through metaphors that are not in the least gratuitous. "For a genuine poet," Nietzsche wrote, "metaphor is not a rhetorical figure but a vicarious image that he actually beholds in place of a concept."[24] Keats conceives of the heart as the seat of everything: Negative Capability, mystery, myth, and, most important of all, love. The *amor perfectissimus* of the heart is very much like what Hyemeyohsts Storm calls "the Give-Away," which is not the Christian sacrificial love but real sympathesis.[25] That is, true sympathy belongs to or originates in the heart, which is the place of all life.

One begins to understand the role of sympathesis in Keats's work only by realizing that heart is neither some kind of compensatory psychological consolation in a world of pains and troubles, nor simple wish-fulfillment. It is a force that gets through to the mind, pointing to some dimension of life other than empirical assumption. Imagination is not lacking in all this. It is part of intelligence, and its power is consolidated when heart teaches mind to become soul. Born at a time when the ethos of the two centuries since Shakespeare had been that of satire and science, Keats with his sensuous nature invoked the heart as the core of his life and art. This invocation became a virtuality of spirit-creation by means of his whole life's efforts, as though experience were a rehearsal or necessary thing to undergo in advance of something else, though not that supposition of heavenly joy. He envisaged the heart's empowerment and did so through the very thing it enabled, namely a reorientation away from both religious certainty and philosophical empiricism.

Here it may seem that Keats revised his earlier statement on that happiness "repeated in a finer tone here after." But then as now, he was not referring to an afterlife wonderland. The "spiritual repetition" of life was to be experienced in the "here" after "here"—in other words, again and again while we live. It

---

24. Friedrich Nietzsche, *The Birth of Tragedy* (New York: Vintage Books, 1967), 63.

25. Hyemeyohsts Storm, *Seven Arrows* (New York: Harper and Row, 1972), 5. Storm defines the Medicine Wheel as an image of the Total Universe. He writes: "Our teachers tell us that all things within this Universe Wheel know of this Harmony with every other thing, and know how to *Give-Away* one to the other, except man. Of all the Universe creatures, it is we alone who do not begin our lives with knowledge of this great Harmony."

is the activity of reclaiming the sacred from what is present in human toil. As for the real promoter of an afterlife, Christianity, Keats's letter continues:

> It is pretty generally suspected that the chr[i]stian scheme has been coppied from the ancient persian and greek Philosophers. Why may they not have made this simple thing even more simple for common apprehension by introducing Mediators and Personages in the same manner as in the hethen mythology abstractions are personified—Seriously I think it probable that this System of Soul-making—may have been the Parent of all the more palpable and personal Schemes of Redemption, among the Zoroastrians the Christians and the Hindoos. For as one part of the human species must have their carved Jupiter; so another part must have the palpable and named Mediator and saviour, their Christ their Oromanes and their Vishnu—If what I have said should not be plain enough, as I fear it may not be, I will but you in the place where I began in this series of thoughts—I mean, I began by seeing how man was formed by circumstances—and what are circumstances?—but touchstones of his heart—? and what are touch stones?—but proovings of his hearrt?—and what are proovings of his heart but fortifiers or alterers of his nature? and what is his altered nature but his soul?—and what was his soul before it came into the world and had These provings and alterations and perfectionings?—An Intelligence—without Identity—and how is this Identity to be made? Through the medium of the Heart? And how is the heart to become this Medium but in a world of Circumstances?—There now I think what with Poetry and Theology you may thank your Stars that my pen is not very long winded.

This whole passage reminds one of a kind of catechism. But it is not a parody of religious dogma uttered by rote.[26] It is a creed whose lessons lead from circumstance and touchstones

---

26. He may have had a sort of parody in mind for his lesson here, namely Shakespeare's *1 Henry IV*, V.i.130-141, where Falstaff recites his "catechism." Falstaff's speech, however, concerns a very serious element of the *Henriad*, namely the *ars moriendi* tradition in which death is seen not as a means of obtaining *kléos* or glory, but as a symptom of a moribund nation-soul.

to provings and alterations, back to the world of circumstance. These words come from the Book of the Heart, as though it were a mouth catechizing (teaching by word of mouth) on life's most important lesson, identity.

I do not think that souls in this scheme are formed unless the intelligence awakens or is alive to the "fortifiers or alterers" of one's nature. More is involved here than simply *knowing* that one has pains and troubles in life. Such "knowledge" can disappear as suddenly as one's troubles. Keats's "perfectionings" are the completion or achievement of the heart's ordeal; they confirm the heart's role as life's most vital organ and its place as the center of life itself. To perfect the soul through the medium of the heart means that the soul's life gets made and cannot be unmade. Where before it possessed only intelligence, now the soul has identity. Its perfection is not an "unchangeable attribute" but a purpose, a goal that one struggles for all one's life, even unto death. As Keats said in the Chamber of Maiden Thought letter, it is up to us "to live and go on thinking," exploring our way into life's dark passages through the vale of tears and joys.

Nine days after Keats wrote of the Vale of Soul-Making, he tells his family that "[Charles] Brown has been rummaging up some of my old sins—that is to say my sonnets." He then includes the three "lately written sonnets" ("On Fame," "Another on Fame," and "To Sleep"), followed by a line drawn across the page, below which appears the "Ode to Psyche." As Stillinger notes, the chronological order of these poems is far from certain.[27] It seems likely, however, that the "ode" belongs to a later date, though not just because of that separating line. For the subject of Psyche's suffering and transformation into the goddess of the soul, rendered as a poem by Keats, follows what appears to be a necessary clarification of his new approach to and understanding of life. Or rather, the "ode" comes into existence only after Keats's somewhat backward glance at the

27. Stillinger, 648-650.

subject of fame. Fame had been his love, fame of poetry. Yet he had already begun to see it as a "crime." This glance back at fame is a gesture which places it squarely in the present and, in light of what all three poems say, constitutes a vital link between the Vale of Soul-Making and the first of the great odes of that spring of 1819.

All three poems stand in intimate relation to the great odes which they precede by only a few days or weeks. The first of these, "On Fame," is headed by a proverb: "You cannot eat your cake and have it too." It has a remarkable calm and poignancy in contrast to the tormented mood of "Why did I laugh?" There is a connection to the earlier sonnet, not in terms of a dramatic situation but as consequence of meditating on man's "lease" in this life. Although the poem doesn't "surprise by a fine excess," it has a meaning which anticipates the later investigative work in the odes:

> How fever'd is that Man who cannot look
> Upon his mortal days with temperate blood
> Who vexes all the leaves of his Life's book
> And robs his fair name of its maidenhood
> It is as if the rose should pluck herself
> Or the ripe plum finger its misty bloom
> As if a clear Lake meddling with itself
> Should cloud its pureness with a muddy gloon
> But the rose leaves herself upon the Briar
> For winds to kiss and grateful Bees to feed
> And the ripe plumb still wears its dim attire
> The undisturbed Lake has crystal space—
> Why then should Man leasing the world for grace
> Spoil his salvation by a fierce miscreed

This poem has all the graceful, naturalistic details of a proverb. And yet its overall import clearly is that man's "lease" on this earth really concerns "salvation"—a salvation from the overmuscled action of ego which vexes the book of life and art. One is reminded here of Keats's balk at Wordsworth, of his objection to the "egotistical sublime" in the elder poet's character. In this first trial run as it were, Keats is approaching the form and content of the great odes by clearing the ground of being of that which "spoils" its "grace," namely an austere exclusiveness.

Wordsworth provided several exemplary lessons for Keats, both positive and negative. In Keats's next sonnet, "Another on Fame," he ingeniously borrows Wordsworth's "gipsey," and in borrowing from him Keats comes to his own thought, as he had done so often before. He makes it his and gives it a use of his own to show the wayward nature of ambition:

> Fame like a wayward girl will still be coy
> To those who woo her with too slavish knees
> But makes surrender to some thoughtless boy
> And dotes the more upon a heart at ease—
> She is a Gipsey will not speak to those
> Who have not learnt to be content without her
> A Jilt whose ear was never whisper'd close
> Who think they scandal her who talk about her—
> A very Gipsey is she Nilus born,
> Sister in law to jealous Potiphar.—
> Ye lovesick Bards, repay her scorn for scorn.
> Ye lovelorn Artists madmen that ye are,
> Make your best bow to her and bid adieu
> Then if she likes it she will follow you—

With gentle humor, Keats names the bards and artists as unrequited lovers in this comedy of fame. But he does not reject the fact of fame; he chooses not to pursue it. Let it come to him who does not seek it, he decides. Free of the idea of fame or success, Keats became more aware than ever of the formal problems confronting a superior artist and of his or her response to those pressures.

The third sonnet he composed, "To Sleep," is the best of the three. In it there is no explicit reference to the subject of fame. The liberation from fame has allowed the poet to search for a subject that lies elsewhere than in the "leased" world. Keats's "salvation" now begins to gather both the consciousness of the Vale of Soul-making and the need for the greater reality of a poet's working moments. Keats goes directly to the heart of this "crystal space" which becomes night's mausoleum or crypt:

> O soft embalmer of the still midnight
> Shutting with careful fingers and benign
> Our gloom-pleas'd eyes embowered from the light,
> Enshaded in forgetfulness divine—
> O soothest sleep, if so it please the close
> In midst of this thine hymn my willing eyes,
> Or wait the amen, ere thy poppy throws
> Around my bed it[s] dewy Charities—
> Then save me or the passed day will shine
> Upon my pillow breeding many woes.
> Save me from curious conscience that still lords
> Its strength for darkness, borrowing like a Mole—
> Turn the key deftly in the oiled wards
> And seal the hushed Casket of my Soul.

This "hymn" bears some resemblance to the "Ode to May."[28] But it is less an act of worship than a place longed-for, prospecting the "midnight hours" of the "Ode to Psyche" as well as the "embalmed darkness" of the later "Ode to a Nightingale." Here Keats has finally shuffled off fame's encumbrances and found pause to dream of life and poetry in far deeper terms. "To Sleep" reveals how the form-making impulse—seeking to fuse with the absolute, loving surrender to the world which Keats exemplified in his system of salvation—led directly to his experimentation with what had for almost a century been called "the greater ode."[29]

---

28. Ian Jack, *Keats and the Mirror of Art* (Oxford: Clarendon, 1967), 203. According to Jack, other antecedents include the early "Ode to Apollo," and the hymns to Pan, Neptune, and Diana in *Endymion*.

29. Bate, 496; see also Lawrence John Zillman, *John Keats and the Sonnet Tradition* (New York: Octagon Books, 1970).

Fame indeed is a "fierce miscreed" of human existence in these sonnets. As Katherine Wilson writes in *The Nightingale and the Hawk,* it is "a mistaken madness driving the poet, when he ought to live like a rose without letting ambition drive him, finding his salvation or soul through alterations in his attitudes induced by circumstances."[30] Wilson believes that Keats's was "a desire [for fame] so exorbitant that it asked for perpetuation of his works long after death."[31] This is certainly true of many artists. Rare is the writer, since Spenser fashioned our idea of a poetic vocation, who does not write in any sense for the future. Whether the impulse be memory or enthusiasm, writing is a medium of plenitude even if its content involve the opposite of plenitude. Most writers think of their efforts as that which matters and can be contained. Keats aspired to be "among the English poets" after his death, and his desire for fame was matched by his industry and commitment to truth. As time went on, however, present circumstance and eternal glory began to seem hopelessly unrelated; in fact, circumstance worked against fame. But as Keats discovered, it's not the cursedness of circumstance that determines how we live, but the imagination, which wants to save itself from withering by responding to the world as fully as it can. Desire was not abandoned or taken away from him; it was transmuted to a new urge to write. For if one believes that Keats truly discovered a sense of wholeness out of all the mortal struggles and divine intimations of the past two years of his life, then it is wholly logical, indeed necessary, that his creativeness, far from being lost, took hold of his own newly fashioned identity. We have, as testament to this development, all the great poems, especially the odes, which balance perfectly Keats's new-found identity with the procedure of intense attention to the objects presented to his mind. And the first of these, the "Ode to Psyche," is very much relevant to all that Keats had hitherto written about the world, heart, and soul. Keats inserted it now after the three sonnets on fame at the end of his letter.

---

30. Wilson, 112.
31. Wilson, 113.

Keats explains to George and Georgiana that unlike his previous poems, which had been written quickly and hurriedly, the "Ode" has been composed with greater patience and deliberation: "I think it reads the more richly for it and will I hope encourage me to write other thing[s] in even a more peacable and healthy spirit." It was truly a major development for Keats at the age of twenty-four. He was becoming more respectful not only of inspiration and motif, but also of the sustaining power of words, of the life of words in poetry. Though not as profound an investigation as the other odes, "Ode to Psyche" constitutes a making and initiation for Keats of the human soul, which is what he needed to advance both life and art.

Keats explains to his family: "You must recollect that Psyche was not embodied as a goddess before the time of Apuleius the Platonist who lived afteir the Agustan age, and consequently the Goddess was never worshipped or sacrificed to with any of the ancient fervour—and perhaps never thought of in the old religion—I am more orthodox than to let a hethen Goddess be so neglected." In his discussion of the "Ode to Psyche," Di Piero says that Keats was both *taking on* a subject, as attested by his amused remark about "orthodoxy," and addressing the matter of making himself over into Psyche's priest and celebrant, "singing her praises even while he keeps her secrets."[32] The decision to ordain himself is surely brought on by the dream or vision announced in the poem: "Surely I dreamt today; or did I see / The winged Psyche, with awaken'd eyes?" This is an arbitrary question, Di Piero says, one that serves mainly to engage the matter of meditation. But this self-investiture is also the result of that active reckoning with the world of circumstance and the soul's desire in the Vale of Soul-making. For it is clear that before composing the "Ode" he had discovered Psyche's true meaning for the world in his system of salvation.

Reading the account of the goddess in Lemprière's *Classical Dictionary*, and then Apuleius's *Golden Asse* during this whole time, Keats was struck by her many painful wanderings before

---

32. Di Piero, 149-150.

she became immortal and wedded to Cupid. His affirmation in the "Ode," "Yes, I will be thy priest and build a fane / In some untrodden region of my mind," is really a confirmation of his desire to find his own soul or salvation, and that of humankind, "in the highest terms for human nature." Indeed, revelatory of the new consciousness out of which Keats was writing, the "Ode to Psyche" aspires to Coleridge's ideal of poetry bringing the entire Soul of Mankind into activity. This aspiration appears particularly strong in the closing stanza, where Keats would make of the imaginative mind a nature to welcome the wedding of Soul and Love:

> A rosy sanctuary will I dress
> With the wreath'd trellis of a working brain;
> With buds and bells and stars without a mame;
> With all the gardner, fancy e'er could feign
> Who breeding flowers will never breed the same—
> And there shall be for thee all soft delight
> That shadowy thought can win;
> A bright torch, and a casement ope at night,
> To let the warm Love in—

This nature is one whose beauteous forms are assisted by the faculty of imagination or fancy, and as such it is true, "whether it existed before or not."[33] "Feigning" is making and invention, not the partial disillusion at the close of the "Ode to a Nightingale," but a marvelous process of renewal— like those "flowers [that] will never breed the same"—equal and identical to the vale of soul-making.

Although the "Ode to Psyche" is somewhat improvisatory, its ambition of an orderly, methodical preparation of mind was the result of Keats's system of spirit-creation and essential to all the later poems. And as Ian Jack reminds us, the "Ode" is

---

33. "Fancy" does not have for Keats the negative meaning given it by Coleridge in his distinction between "imagination" and "fancy" as formulated in *Biographia Literaria*. See *The Collected Works of Samuel Taylor Coleridge*, vol. 7:1, 304.

also the work of a man deeply in love with Fanny Brawne and with Love itself. Keats could not have written the "Ode" had he not discovered the true uses of the world in which Soul/Psyche and Love/Eros exist. The vale of soul-making proved the possibility of taking hold of identity forged out of all the mortal struggles and divine intimations of the past two years of his life. It also proved the possibilities of purifying the self in the search for definitiveness, allowing Keats to advance toward a fully internalized condition of self and object. Poetry and the character of the poet are the issue of an inwarding such as that which Keats had been concentrating on since the beginning of his poetic career. And now at the outset of his fully experiencing investigation of thought and feeling, the great odes began to appear, like destinations arrived at.

Love's Patient, Sleepless Eremite

These are the letters which Endymion wrote
  To one he loved in secret and apart,
  And now the brawlers of the auction-mart
Bargain and bid for each tear-blotted note,
Aye! for each separate pulse of passion quote
  The merchant's price! I think they love not art
  Who break the crystal of a poet's heart,
That small and sickly eyes may glare or gloat.

—Oscar Wilde
"On the Sale by Auction of
Keats's Love Letters"

In a Man's Letters, you know, Madam, his soul lies naked, his letters are only the mirrour of his breast, whatever passes within him is shown undisguised in its natural process.

—Dr. Johnson to Mrs. Thrale
October 27, 1777

Ah hertè mine!

—John Keats to Fanny Brawne
October 11, 1819

· VIII ·

MINUTE BIOGRAPHICAL investigation involving letters among other materials was already well established in the early nineteenth century as one of the consequences of success as an author. This development may owe something to the fact that the world knew so little of an author like William Shakespeare, a shadowy figure whose works of art, as Keats suggested, may be the best commentary on his life as an actual human being. It may also owe something to an unprecedented event in the history of English literature which contrasts strikingly with Shakespeare's extraordinary anonymity: the publication in 1616 of Ben Jonson's *Works.* This was the first time an English author had been so arrogant, so presumptuous, as to publish his collected works while still alive. At that time, moreover, the very title *Works* designated philosophy, which was queen of high literature in the Renaissance. Jonson's seriousness as a poet may have very well helped to solidify the already distinct and vital idea of the author developed by the classical tendencies of the Renaissance in England.

However it developed, the attention given to a famous author's life certainly helped to ensure that his or her letters, where such existed, were necessarily going to have readers. But what of the question of privacy? The intrusion of "small and sickly eyes" into matter that was always meant to be "secret and apart" is a kind of violence, one that shatters "the crystal of a poet's heart." The poet's heart may indeed be that fragile. Keats certainly knew that anyone's heart affections were "holy." Letters, no less than poems, are often like beads of that lifeblood which moves everything in life forward. The heart, with its ramifications and foliations, is ineluctably at the heart of Keats's life. And so his letters, like his poems, account for the experience he was always having of poetry and love, writing being a heart-felt, open occasion to an "audience" that was "home."

While I do not get the sense in reading Keats's letters that he expected anyone beside the original recipient to read them—they are totally spontaneous, focussed entirely on the topics at hand in relation to his reader, and contain things he would not want others to read and judge—Keats did expect to end up "among the English poets." The general fact that people saved letters, and the more specific fact that Keats's close friends (Charles Brown and Richard Woodhouse, for instance) went to a great deal of trouble to save his letters, would tend to support the idea that he knew they would be read by persons other than those they were intended for. But always the more important thing with Keats's letters is the words themselves. That is what anyone must attend to first, and by the terms of Keats's own recognitions. Whether written to Friend or Beloved, Keats's words invoke a creative time and presence which must be allowed its own order.

In my view the *Letters* have suffered less the violence of exploitation than the neglect of their crucial importance for comprehending the radical depth and prospect of Keats's poetics. As Wilde's sonnet shows, Keats became a very much beloved figure because of the romance attributed to his early death and because of those passionate, intense affections of both his poems and his letters. The real magnitude of his achievement in the *Letters*, however, hasn't been much considered outside circles of working poets, and seldom enough even among them. Even Keats's love letters must be granted a poetics which illumines the lore of love as much as do the poems. Just as the key in Negative Capability is love as *surrender*, so too in the letters to Fanny Brawne the thing that at once joins both persons together equally and possesses them is love as *relation*. Keats clings to love and works it as intensely as he can by way of all his faculties, because its center was a mystery annulling the "self"-centered reaching after fact and reason. He loved that *annihilation* of self. He was not afraid or repelled by his need to be there, at the center of devotion to an "other." It's where he was given his poetry. He is an inspiration, a hero whose courage allowed desire itself to descend all the way into the heart, with its realer points of "place."

Keats was writing some of his very best poems and letters when he met Fanny Brawne, the daughter of Samuel Brawne and Frances Ricketts. Some commentators believe that Keats met Fanny for the first time on the night of his return from Scotland (August 18, 1818), when he dropped by the Dilkes' home at Wentworth Place on his way to Well Walk. For that is where the Brawnes—Fanny, her widowed mother, and her sister and brother—were living at the time. Others maintain that most likely they met in September, or no later than the middle of November when Keats would go briefly to the Dilkes as a respite from nursing Tom. The Brawnes had since moved from Wentworth Place but still visited the Dilkes. It may very well have been on one of these visits that the two met. Whenever the precise date of their first meeting, they fell in love and at some point became secretly engaged.

Keats's love letters to Fanny begin in July 1819, though possibly earlier. They say many things about his personality as a lyric poet and as a man in love with a beautiful woman. The two are really twin sides of an intense yearning for human fulfillment on earth. At their first encounter, Keats declared himself Fanny's *donnoi* or love vassal: "The very first week I knew you I wrote myself your vassal; but burnt the Letter as the very next time I saw you I thought you manifested some dislike to me" (July 25, 1819). His remark invokes the tradition of Arthurian or troubadour romance in which the knight-lover and his chosen lady were extolled in poetry or musical homage. One wishes his declaration had survived the spell of self-effacement. For what is vital about Keats's expression of love is an essential quality of poetic consciousness. The letters to Fanny reveal a mind that moves among images to express fear, hope, pain, pleasure, jealousy, solicitude, and so on—a mind absorbed in all the possibilities of language whereof Keats's allegiance to a reality of beauty and truth might be embodied and preserved. This making in the letters to her—the life of the heart made tangible and holy—was the best sort of poetry Keats could write after a certain point, when his own death from consumption was close at hand. Yet it was not for his glory that he wrote what have become "classic" love letters. It was for the sake of a love that is as tragic and joyful at once as anything Shakespeare ever imagined.

Keats's love is both an ideal and a very particular earthly passion. He was quite painfully conscious, for example, of the admiration and demands he heaped upon Fanny, of the moods of hurtful suspicion his bitter illness elicited from him. On that score, one surmises that Fanny corrected him because Keats is sometimes seen deferring to her or repenting for his ill-feelings. But when love itself threatened to end his too narrowly conceived freedom as an artist (Keats's calling was extremely solitary and demanding in nature), he tried to force her from his life. His self-willed isolation had just this unfortunate consequence. However, Keats could not give up Fanny. Eventually he was willing to exchange "a fevrous life alone with Poetry" for a life of love with Fanny. For Keats could not sustain both the physical and psychic ardor of writing poetry and loving a woman at once. Toward the end of his life, he was afraid and felt himself "too weak" to live alone and bear "unhurt the shock of extreme thought and sensation" (August 24, 1819). His life was becoming a debilitating journey toward death. In a letter to Percy Shelley, for example, he wrote that he was going to Italy "as a soldier marches up to a battery" (August 16, 1820). By then he knew he had no strength to master poetry, marry Fanny, and understand the reasons for his dying, all at once. Yet in the beginning, Fanny was the inspiration for such great poems as "The Eve of St. Agnes," "La belle dame sans merci," *Lamia*, and "The Cap and Bells." In spite of the last several months of his life—months of bitterness and anguish and exhaustion—Keats had gone astonishingly far into both poetry and love, as his letters attest, and thus held true to the deepest core of his existence, even as he was losing life itself.

Although Fanny's letters to Keats do not exist (with her consent he destroyed the letters she had written to him on the eve of their farewell), it is clear from his letters that the attraction between them was strong. In a letter to his brother George, Keats had first described Fanny as "beautiful and elegant, graceful, silly, fashionable and strange" (December 16, 1818). For her part, Fanny observed a vital, sympathetic, and unconventional soul, one whom she never spoke to anyone about, even after his death, save Fanny Keats, as if to do so would be a profanation of his memory and love. By all accounts she was unsentimental, clear-sighted, frank, inquisitive, animated, kind, and invigorating. Her beauty resonated with the grace that comes of insight and deep abiding affection. She was seventeen when they met.

From the evidence of the letters and biographies, I believe their love was based on a mutual recognition of each other's life-force, a kind of religious identification.[1] Beauty is the basis of any truth for Keats, and beauty possesses a sacred if timeless nature whether it be human, natural, or man-made. Beauty "dost tease us out of thought," as with the Greek urn, into an immediacy of essential being. Immediacy is the point. Beauty informs us in all manner of ways and contents impossible or prevented before we are stirred by its existence. Like grief, it is part of a spiritual transformation wholly at the primary ground of the relation between oneself and an "other." Beauty or grief is a massively purposeful term of relation. It puts us in touch (a form of *intensity*) with another dimension of life than that spelled out by what Keats called "consequitive reasoning." This is what one finds eminently throughout the *Letters,* a vision of sacred life touched and savored by imagination.

---

1. For works that make clear the depth of Keats and Fanny's romantic love, see Joan Rees, *Bright Star* (London: Harrap, 1968) and Joanna Richardson, *Fanny Brawne* (New York: Vanguard Press, 1952).

The spiritual imagination in Keats's letters to Fanny restored him to the timelessness of invisible reality as did his art. Though the emotional tone of these letters ranges from infinite tenderness to abusiveness and despair, Keats's yearning for sacred knowledge is cast in images and symbols which absorb one in their reality. Writing of the spiritual symbolism in Shakespeare's "sacred art," Martin Lings explains:

> Every object of love is a symbol of the Divine Beauty of the Spirit and therefore has power to recall something of that Beauty. This explains why in all love worthy of the name there is always an element of worship. Love has always a double aspect: the beloved is loved for himself or herself and, beyond that, for the sake of the Reality in whose image man was created.[2]

Like his poems, which concentrate a sense not only of the beautiful but of the sacred as well, Keats's letters to Fanny are a realization of two worlds, suffering flesh and high romance. When he wrote the first version of his famous "Bright Star" sonnet to Fanny, his very vision of love had become part of that Reality in whose image Love appears:

> Bright star! would I were steadfast as thou art—
> Not in lone splendour hung amid the night
> Not watching, with eternal lids apart,
> Like nature's devout, sleepless eremite,
> The morning waters at their priestlike task
> Of pure ablution round earth's human shores,
> Or gazing on the new soft-fallen masque
> Of snow upon the mountains and the moors;
> No—yet still steadfast, still unchangeable,
> Cheek-pillow'd on my Love's white breast,
> To touch, for ever, its sink and swell,
> Awake for ever in a sweet unrest,

2. Lings, 85-86.

To hear, to feel her tender-taken breath,
Half passionless, and so swoon on to death.[3]

G. Wilson Knight defined the priestlike ceremonial nature of Keats's poetry in which the poet officiates, like the "eremite" of "Bright Star," over the domain of his love.[4] This office implies a dependence (hence "passivity" in some circles of Keats scholarship) on a mystery which is purely present in this poem. It's a mystery that fuses the ancient fact of the divinity of stars and the stirring sexual reality of love, and one that involves as well the poet living in and out of time. Keats does not want to feel caught between the "lone splendour" of the starry night sky and his "Love's white breast," lest he wind up caught in nets of sacrifice at love's altar. He chooses or takes both, no longer needing any ordinary prayers. The relation, Keats and Beloved, has its own order of creative presence and time: it is unchangeable yet forever beating like a heart in a "sweet unrest." In a consciousness that feels the convergence of beauty and truth, it is no wonder that the immediacy of lover and beloved is likewise sacred, at once physical and spiritual, sensuous and holy, as in the "warm" love of "Ode to Psyche."[5]

But is there no loss nor any proposal of loss in this divine-erotic context? What does "swoon to death" mean? Certainly the sense of ecstasy is associated with the swooning as we see it

3. See Stillinger, 638. This early version is from Charles Brown's MSS, turned over to Richard Monckton Milnes, who used them as the basis for the biographical narrative and a major portion of the texts of his 1848 edition of Keats's poetical works, where it is headed "Keats' Last Sonnet."

4. G. Wilson Knight, "The Priest-like Task: An Essay on Keats," *The Starlit Dome* (London: Methuen, 1964), 258-307.

5. The "Cold Pastoral!" exclamation of "Ode on a Grecian Urn" in no way calls into question the warmth and tenderness of Keats's sacred love. Nor does any dichotomy exist, either in the poem or in the poet's own thought, so far as love is concerned. For the urn itself is a "shape," an "attitude," a "silent form" that exists apart from the claims of human life, however well it images humanity's desire for beauty and truth. Moreover, the "love" that concerns this and other poems is not about fulfillment but about the soul's response, the bestowal or gift to the spirit by desire itself, which is "For ever warm" and "For ever panting."

in *Endymion.* In erotic mysticism Supreme Ecstasy (*raptus*) is an anticipation of death, the relation of Soul and Divine accomplished in the mystery of its fulfillment. Keats's destiny is fulfilled in the mystery of the Beloved, which is the experience of an exegesis of the soul anticipating the final ecstasy in the heaven of stars.

Keats's letters to Fanny are a faithful reflection of the spiritual reality of their love, and should be considered poetry because they achieve the nature and responsibility of poetry, which is an engagement with knowledge. We see this knowledge embodied in a moving, urgent quality in letters from July 1819 to August 1820. It's a knowledge that centers largely on the tragic contrast between the extreme perfection of love and the extreme imperfection of circumstance that it is set in. And yet Keats's love for Fanny is the most beautiful virtue of his life, so that the opposition between "the world" and "love" lends to the letters a deep and symbolic level of meaning. It reveals how one particular man participates in the allegory of his life, rising through a series of higher realities toward Absolute Reality, while at the same time dying into life. In the letters to Fanny one sees less the ceremonial aspect described by Knight, and more of the actual yearned-for consummation which the sacred sense implies.

In a letter to Fanny from Shanklin, where he had gone to write, Keats speaks directly of a consummation in terms of love and death. After referring to a part of her letter which he had lately received, a part "which hurt me" because it compared Keats and his friend Joseph Severn, he writes:

> My dear love, I cannot believe there ever was or ever could be any thing to admire in me especially as far as sight goes—I cannot be admired, I am not a thing to be admired. You are, I love you; all I can bring you is a swooning admiration of your Beauty. I hold that place among Men which snubnos'd brunettes with meeting eyebrows do among women—they are trash to me—unless I should find one among them with a fire in her heart like the one that burns in mine. You absorb me in spite of myself—you alone: for I look not forward with any pleasure to what is

> call'd being settled in the world; I tremble at domestic cares—yet for you I would meet them, though if it would leave you the happier I would rather die than do so. I have two luxuries to brood over in my walks, your Loveliness and the hour of my death. O that I could have possession of them both in the same minute. I hate the world: it batters too much the wings of my self-will, and would I could take a sweet poison from your lips to send me out of it. From no others would I take it. I am indeed astonish'd to find myself so careless of all cha[r]ms but yours—remembring as I do the time when even a bit of ribband was a matter of interest with me. What softer words can I find for you after this—what it is I will not read. Nor will I say more here, but in a Postscript answer any thing else you may have mentioned in your Letter in so many words—for I am distracted with a thousand thoughts. I will imagine you Venus tonight and pray, pray, pray to your star like a Hethen. (July 25, 1819)

It was Sunday night as Keats wrote these words, and night was the time, as he had explained to Fanny earlier, "when the lonely day has closed,...[and] my passion gets entirely the sway" (July 1, 1819). There are many passionate things in this letter, especially the final chant to Venus, which Robert Gittings believes led Keats to write the second version of his "Bright Star" sonnet at this time.[6] But of all these remarks, the one that perhaps upset Fanny the most was that of love and death. Here again Keats's desire for both at once implies a form of knowledge.

There is a sense that Keats would travel through the gates of death, but not for the sake of being united with the beloved in the next world, for Fanny is alive in this world. The chill one feels through the veil of his "luxury" here very likely has its source in the *contemptus mundi* Keats expresses. The wish to take "a sweet poison from your lips" suggests that Keats has in mind the power of contagion as it appears in Shakespeare's tragedy *Romeo and Juliet*. In the tomb scene at V.iii.162-166, Juliet says:

---

6. Gittings, 156–158.

What's here? A cup, closed in my true love's hand?
Poison, I see, hath been his timeless end.
O churl! drunk all, and left no friendly drop
To help me after? I will kiss thy lips.
Haply some poison yet doth hang on them
To make me die with a restorative.

The name of Juliet was often on his lips, if not always in his heart.[7] Yet whereas Juliet's poison is a "restorative" (bringing her back to Romeo in the land of the dead), Keats's poison is neither restorative nor opportune. The love between Romeo and Juliet has, Lings points out, "the strongest wings for the highest flights" as a symbol for love.[8] But one is not convinced that Keats is ripe for death, as were the lovers in Shakespeare's play. Indeed, Keats himself must have known that he was not. The wish for death seems a result of an extreme situation battering down the wings of both self-will and love. Like Romeo and Juliet, Keats and Fanny never knew any peace or security during their brief time together this side of the grave. To be sure, part of the reason involved Keats's avoidance of love; but that, it must be said, was partly due to being poor and ailing. No, it's the conditions of personal survival that appear to bring on a change associated with death.

Keats's expectations of the complete dissolution of his tie to Fanny begins after the summer of 1819. Throughout July and August he had worked simultaneously on *Lamia*, *The Fall of Hyperion*, and *Otho the Great*, his major attempt at drama, during which time he would alternately whip up Fanny's image and attempt to steel his heart against love. When he returned to London in September, he broke his "promise" made the month before "of seeing you in a short time." Over and over he

7. He wrote to the Reynolds sisters: "I feel such a yearning towards Juliet...that I would rather follow her into Pandemonium than Imogen into Paradize" (September 14, 1817). And when he was in Scotland, he had written to Reynolds that he yearned for his good friend's happiness in marriage "as much as I could myself after the lips of Juliet" (July 13, 1818).

8. Lings, 88.

repeated that he loved her "too much" to see her because visiting was "venturing into fire" (September 13, 1819). Keats tried to unencumber Fanny, even to the extent of offering her the chance to break off their engagement. She refused, and he refused to cease loving her. When he finally did see her on October 10, 1819, something definite changed. From here on, Keats's letters reflect his inability or refusal to avoid love any more. "The time is passed," he writes three days after their reunion, "when I had power to advise and warn you against the unpromising morning of my Life—My love has made me selfish. I cannot exist without you." It is in this same letter that he comes to a new realization. After trying to make a fair copy of some of his verse, he gives up the effort and begins writing to Fanny:

> I am forgetful of every thing but seeing you again—my Life seems to stop there—I see no further. You have absorb'd me. I have a sensation at the present moment as though I was dissolving—I should be exquisitely miserable without the hope of soon seeing you. I should be affraid to separate myself far from you. My sweet Fanny, will your heart never change? My love, will it? I have no limit now to my love—You note came in just here—I cannot be happier away from you—'T is richer than an Argosy of Pearles. Do no threaten me even in jest. I have been astonished that Men could die Martyrs for religion—I have shudder'd at it—I shudder no more—I could be martyr'd for my Religion—Love is my religion—I could die for that—I could die for you. My Creed is Love and you are its only tenet.
>
> (October 13, 1819)

In contrast to his feeling just a few months before, Keats's "luxury" now is happiness with Fanny, which is "richer than an Argosy of Pearles." Whereas before he was desirous of love and death in the same swooning instant, now he wants "to cast the die for Love or death" (October 19, 1819).

It was death that cast the die, however, nullifying Keats's lifelong desire for happiness here on earth. His health began to decline, and in February 1820 he suffered the first of three severe hemorrhages of the lungs. And yet for a man who was in league with death, albeit unwillingly, Keats was intensely occupied with perhaps the highest form of living: he was devoted to a center outside the self. While it is painfully obvious that illness makes of life a suffering thing, it certainly does not oblige the soul to forego, as Keats says, "its highest gust," love. The spirit breathes love around her who appears and is Love. This gust of life reminds one that Keats is not just *in* love, which is a state suffered or undergone. His words show how active his love could be, how decided were the conscious acts he took with respect to the present and the future. His is a love from the standpoint of the other, as much as from his own passionate being.

The ever present beginning in Keats's life and letters involves a journey to love. Only love and poetry are "creative of essential Beauty," that is, capable of renewing life here and now. This is the "reward" Keats intended when he spoke of that *repetition* coming on the spirit continually "with a fine suddenness" (November 22, 1817). Love and poetry for Keats are part of the same impulse that sent him on a voyage to bring back the lore of these two things. He went to Homer, Shakespeare, and Burns, among other poets, as he went naturally enough to every sweet, lushly sensual bodily excitement. Moreover, he acted on that voyage, explicitly and directly addressing the erotic-spiritual dimension of love in order to make it the terrain of his heart's habitation.

Love itself can be understood to have been so utterly degraded by conventional religion or morality that all of love which is not conventionally idealized expresses the human need of being in particular constellations of being. Keats's love is a discipline or practice, knowledge and love being identical to an illumination of the soul. Love is a discipline of a justice that keeps alive, concrete, and clear every discredited form of love whether "desire," "lust," or any other so-called deviation. Keats's "lustful" indulgence and "Cockney vulgarity" are really no more than expressions of his daring, in a brutish Anglo tradition, to yield to his desire, to all his faculties—intuition, emotion, imagination, instinct, felt-thought, and reason—which return the soul to the body.

The news delivered and taken by the physical senses, especially the erotic gifts, was vital to Keats and can be seen in his letter to George and Georgiana of October 14, 1818, a letter which records his meeting with another woman, Jane Cox, a relative of Jane and Mariane Reynolds. Upon his return from Scotland, he reports that he called on the Reynolds sisters who "were in a sort of taking or bustle about a Cousin of theirs":

> She is an east indian and ought to be her Grandfather's Heir. At the time I called Mrs R. was in conference with her up stairs and the young Ladies were warm in her praises down stairs calling her genteel, interresting and a thousand other pretty things to which I gave no heed, not being partial to 9 days wonder—Now all is completely changed—they hate her; and from what I hear she is not without faults—of a real kind: but she has othe[r]s which are more apt to make women of inferior charms hate her. She is not a Cleopatra; but she is at least a Charmian. She has a rich eastern look; she has fine eyes and fine manners. When she comes into a room she makes an impression the same as the Beauty of a Leopardess. She is too fine and too concious of her Self to repulse any Man who may address her—from habit she thinks that nothing *particular*. I always find myself more at ease with such a woman; the picture before me always gives me a life and animation which I cannot possibly feel with any thing inferiour—I am at such times too much occupied in admiring to be awkward or on a tremble. I forget myself entirely because I live in her. You will by this time think I am in love with her; so before I go any further I will tell you I am not—she kept me awake one Night as a tune of Mozart's might do—I speak of the thing as a passtime and an amuzement than which I can feel none deeper than a conversation with an imperial woman the very 'yes' and 'no' of whose Lips is to me a Banquet. I dont cry to take the moon home with me in my Pocket not do I fret to leave her behind me. I like her and her like because one has no *sensations* —what we both are is taken for granted—You will suppose I have by this had much talk with her—no such thing—there are the Miss Reynoldses on the look out—They think I dont admire her because I

> did not stare at her—They call her a flirt to me—What a want of knowledge? she walks across a room in such a manner that a Man is drawn towards her with a magnetic Power. This they call flirting! they do not know things. They do not know what a Woman is. I believe tho' she has faults—the same as Charmian and Cleopatra might have had—Yet she is a fine thing speaking in a worldly way: for there are two distinct tempers of mind in which we judge of things—the worldly, theatrical and pantomimical; and the unearthly, spiritual and etherial—in the former Buonaparte, Lord Byron and this Charmian hold the first place in our Minds; in the latter John Howard, Bishop Hooker rocking his child's cradle and you my dear Sister are the conquering feelings.
>
> (October 14, 1818)

"Charmian" of course is Shakespeare's attendant upon the Queen of Egypt in *Antony and Cleopatra*. She is all siren. Keats obviously admired Jane Cox, that is, her open display of flirting (being "particular"), her sexual charm. She was beautiful in a striking if unfortunate way, like a "leopardess." Keats's reaction to her was direct and masculine: "I should like her to ruin me." But he also contradicted himself by denying the obviously strong "sensations" Jane Cox created in him. Keats attempts to reconcile this difference by positing two distinct halves or "tempers" of mind, with Charmian on the "worldly" side and Georgiana on the "ethereal." One can only speculate that Keats, while drawn to Miss Cox, sensed in her an absence of capacity to love, as he decided there was an absence of generosity in the Reynolds sisters.

Fanny Brawne upset Keats's neat dichotomy, she being neither completely one "type" of woman nor another. Although she was adolescent when Keats first met her, interested in clothes and dances, "flying out in all directions," there was more to this vivacious woman of eighteen whom Keats called a "Minx," with her "very graceful" shape and quick, nervy intelligence. There was more desire, or more depth to Keats's desire, for Fanny than for Charmian or any other woman.[9] There

9. See Keats's remarks about Mrs. Isabella Jones in this same letter to George and Georgiana Keats.

was in fact a real not imaginary person whose beauty was in her life-force, her spirit. Keats had sworn in the same letter where he speaks of Charmian: "I shall never marry. Though the most beautiful Creature were waiting for me at the end of a Journey or a Walk." A year later, he had found on the journey of his life the most beautiful creature not only waiting but ready to share life with him. Keats's description of his Beautiful One is significant because in her person Fanny Brawne was identical with a paradise of the soul in love. That is the import of Keats's words to her on October 13, 1819, when he wrote, "Love is my religion—I could die for that—I could die for you. My Creed is Love and you are its only tenet."

Keats's realization that "Love is my religion" is shown most vividly in a letter to Fanny on March 1, 1820, after he had been confined to bed at Wentworth Place. In a brief message, he refers to a ring she had recently given him, a seal ring of agate or carnelian with both their names engraved on it. He also refers to Fanny herself as one of the *houri*, the beautiful maidens in Muslim belief who live with the blest in paradise. Here is Keats's letter in its entirety:

> My dearest Fanny,
>
> The power of your benediction is of not so weak a nature as to pass from the ring in four-and twenty hours—it is like a sacred Chalice once consecrated and ever consecrate. I shall kiss your name and mine where you Lips have been—Lips! why should a poor prisoner as I am talk about such things. Thank God, though I hold them the dearest pleasures in the universe, I have a consolation independent of them in the certainty of your affection. I could write a song in the style of Tom Moore's Pathetic about Memory if that would be any relief to me—No. it would not. I will be as obstinate as a Robin, I will not sing in a cage—Health is my expected heaven and you are the Houri—this word I believe is both singular and plural—if only plural, never mind—you are a thousand of them.

This imagery or mental vision is both beautiful and sacred, and not simply because Keats substitutes religious-ritual figures for factual reality. Such substitutions merely tend to promote impersonality, or worse, conventionally idealized love. When I try to understand what "Love is my religion" can possibly mean, I can only try to make some reciprocal spiritual response however incomplete and impure it must be.

As in his experience of Negative Capability, the form of Keats's love as worship here ought not to be arbitrarily restricted to the word "mystical," otherwise the quality of his figures will go overlooked. In sharp contrast to a mere prettifying, rationalist tendency, Keats's elevation proceeds from the reallife person occupying the center of his life. Fanny was visiting him daily since his attack in February. She was literally the center of his world. It's no wonder she should typify the paradise of the soul, the *houri,* bringing him benediction in the form of a consecrated chalice, namely the seal ring bearing and binding both their names. For the *houri* are "the most lovely forms" in paradise, perceived directly when a human achieves a knowledge of gnosis, when he is admitted to a mode of vision in which "the divine Emanation is perceived in each atom of the terrestrial and celestial world."[10] This sounds very much like Keats's system of salvation, in which he had already come to see how the "sparks of the divinity" and man's "atoms of perception" coalesced in the making of "Souls, Identical Souls of the sparks of [God's] own essence" (April 21, 1819). This kind of poetic guesswork is not unlike gnosis in that it yields a vision in which the Real and Actual coincide, individuated, binding life as a whole.

I do not see any reason to doubt that Keats had knowledge of this lore, no matter how complex Muslim gnosis is. His mind held no prejudices of spirituality. To say to Fanny, "you are the houri," certainly shows a purity of intent to image love in the midst of an increasingly spectral existence. But there are deep implications which register as well. After all, as gnostics have borne witness, it is the common human fact of love that gives rise to the essential or formal recognition of paradise, that is,

---

10. Corbin, *Temple and Contemplation,* 178.

love as union of self and other. Keats's love for Fanny led him to ascend, from level to level of being, to the soul of paradise. His illness, in fact, may have been one of the means by which the spirit ascended. Certainly in his response to illness the soul's salvation is evident. Throughout this period of his illness, Keats speaks of the "pleasant prison" which consciousness of Fanny's love makes of his confinement. Above all, love as a religion made it possible for paradise to be created in the person of Fanny Brawne. Like Adam awakening from his dream, Keats awoke to find love true. All this is more than rhetoric because love did make the "health" of romance equal to the "expected" heaven of religion in the here-and-now.

Like the poetic imagination, love encompasses extremes of experience: from simple yearning to ecstatic visions of paradise and everything in between. By the time he faced the real prospect of his death, Keats had traversed a path through the heart of love. When he writes to Fanny sometime in June 1820, "I see every thing over again eternally that I ever have seen," his statement has the ring of one of those axioms proved upon the pulse. This revision ("seeing again") may very well have been an act of suffering. But it was also, I think, a field of force wherein memory and imagination were freed from the tyranny of circumstance. That is one hint of "eternally."

Emily Dickinson's figures of love—the jewel, pearl, and treasure trove, owned and lost—bear a likeness to Keats's images. Her terms are part of an experience of pattern and order other than those we ordinarily know. But they all concern life, "*One Life*," as Dickinson writes, "of so much Consequence!":

> *One Pearl* —to me—so signal—
> That I would instant dive—
> Although—I *knew* —to *take* it—
> Would *cost* me—*just a life*![11]

11. Thomas H. Johnson, ed., *The Complete Poems of Emily Dickinson* (Boston: Little, Brown and Company, 1957), 123. From poem number 270, dated 1861, stanza two.

What is so "signal" here, as elsewhere in Dickinson's work, is the "*cost,*" in human terms, of something as brilliant as the pearl. Its brilliance or preciousness is precisely that consequence which the soul attributes to it. For the poet knows that it is "My Soul's *entire income* — / In ceaseless—salary" which she must pay in order to "*take*" the step or plunge and possess what is so singularly radiant in all the world. Whether poetry or love or both at once, *this* life is never more clearly seen than when desired or forced upon one by one's way of seeing things. Like Keats, Dickinson has an almost exclusive intensity on first axioms and fundamental questions in a life-long, death-long struggle. Indeed, she saw herself with Keats in death ("I died for Beauty"), a kinsman to a poet who "distills amazing sense / From ordinary Meanings" ("This was a Poet").

For Keats, the question of how to live in the knowledge of death and love—a knowledge that invests life's business with urgency—is taken up in his letters to Fanny throughout 1820 until their separation in September. Though few, the letters manifest Keats's excruciating consciousness of love and death. He tells of a "sweet vision" of Fanny in a "shepherdess dress," which brought tears convincing him that "a real Love is enough to occupy the widest heart" (May 1820). But increasingly the letters become torture boxes, spaces of great intensity and complexity of feeling, with seldom appearing tones of happiness. Sometime before his second hemorrhage he writes:

> Do nothing but love me—if I knew that for certain life and health will in such event be a heaven, and death itself will be less painful. I long to believe in immortality I shall never be able to bid you an entire farewell. If I am destined to be happy with you here—how short is the longest Life—I wish to believe in immortality—I wish to live with you for ever. . . . If I have been cruel and injust I swear my love has ever been greater than my cruelty which last[s] but a minute whereas my Love come what will shall last for ever If concessions to me has hurt your Pride, god knows I have had little pride in my heart when thinking of

> you. Your name never passes my Lips—do not let mine pass yours.... After reading my Letter you even then wish to see me. I am strong enough to walk over—but I dare not. I shall feel so much pain in parting with you again. My dearest love, I am afraid to see you, I am strong but not strong enough to see you. Will my arm be ever round you again. And if so shall I be obliged to leave you again. My sweet Love! I am happy whilst I believe your first Letter. Let me be but certain that you are mine heart and soul, and I could die more happily than I could otherwise live. If you think me cruel—if you think I have sleighted you—do muse it over again and see into my heart—My Love to you is "true as truth's simplicity and simpler than the infancy of truth" as I think I once said before How could I slight you? How threaten to leave you? not in the spirit of a Threat to you—no—but in the spirit of Wretchedness in myself. My fairest, my delicious, my angel Fanny! do not believe me such a vulgar fellow. I will be as patient in illness and as believing in Love as I am able—
>
> (June 1820)

Whereas Keats once took immortality for granted for the purpose of revealing the fact and system of soul-making, he now longs simply to believe in it, though one ought not to take his meaning in isolation. Immortality here means life with Fanny. Having become a soul, he longs to take the next step and unite his soul with Fanny forever. The creation of spirit may be one of the highest terms for human nature, but to have become a soul without having loved is somehow inadequate and undermines the interaction of life's materials which yields the sense of identity. The quote from Shakespeare's *Troilus and Cressida*, III.ii.161-162: "I am as true as truth's simplicity, / And simpler than the infancy of truth," constitutes Keats's plea for love over against "craft" (Charmian's artifice perhaps or anyone's empty rhetoric) in the matter of his relation with Fanny. It is his attempt to persuade her that he is indeed no "vulgar fellow." Moreover, Troilus's entire speech concerns constancy, the mind's self-renewing purity of faith in the beloved, and, above all, "true swains in love."

On June 22, 1820, Keats suffered his second hemorrhage, and what little strength he had was now gone. He had moved to Kentish Town weeks before this latest attack because Brown was going to tour Scotland again that summer and needed to rent his rooms in order to finance the trip. Keats's sitting room and bedroom at 2 Wesleyan Place were now dangerous to remain in alone. Leigh Hunt, who had helped him secure the rooms in Kentish Town, took him in after two eminent doctors recognized the severity of his illness. One of them was even convinced that Keats could not survive another winter in England. The plan to leave for Italy developed probably among the doctors and Hunt, who decided Keats's only chance for survival lay in the mild Mediterranean climate. His next to last letter to Fanny was written on July 5, 1820 from Hunt's home in Mortimer Terrace:

> I have been a walk this morning with a book in my hand, but as usual I have been occupied with nothing but you: I wish I could say in an agreeable manner. I am tormented day and night. They talk of my going to Italy. 'Tis certain I shall never recover if I am to be so long separate from you: yet with all this devotion to you I cannot persuade myself into any confidence of you. Past experience connected with the fact of my long separation from you gives me agonies which are scarcely to be talked of. When your mother comes I shall be very sudden and expert in asking her whether you have been to Mrs. Dilke's, for she might say no to make me easy. I am literally worn to death, which seems my only recourse. I cannot forget what has pass'd. What? nothing with a man of the world, but to me deathful. I will get rid of this as much as possible. When you were in the habit of flirting with Brown you would have left off, could your own heart have felt one half of one pang mine did. Brown is a good sort of Man—he did not know he was doing me to death by inches. I feel the effect of every one of those hours in my side now; and for that cause, though he has done me many services, though I know his love and friendship for me, though at this moment I should be without pence were it not for his assistance, I will never see or speak to him until we are both old men, if we

are to be. I *will* resent my heart having been made a football. You will call this madness.

It was a sort of madness since Keats had always been robust and bold in his mental and physical comportment. It was easy to go mad being confined and bedridden month after month. He was losing confidence daily in everything that mattered to him—family, friendship, poetry, and even love sometimes. But one must keep in mind that Keats's suspicions, mean and unjust as they were, also show how desperately he needed to hold onto Fanny, especially when he was destined for exile—an exile he did not freely undertake. As he wrote to her, "tis certain I shall never recover if I am to be so long separate from you." That, in effect, was as much a death sentence as the blood that had rushed to his lungs five months before. Keats continues his letter, imputing unfaithfulness and lack of seriousness to Fanny, and brooding on what he deems the brute facts of the world, past, present, and to come:

I have heard you say that it was not unpleasant to wait a few years—you have amusements—your mind is away—you have not brooded over one idea as I have, and how should you? You are to me an object intensely desirable—the air I breathe in a room empty of you is unhealthy. I am not the same to you—no—you can wait—you have a thousand activities—you can be happy without me. Any party any thing to fill up the day has been enough. How have you pass'd this month? Who have you smil'd with? All this may seem savage in me. You do not feel as I do—you do not know what it is to love—one day you may—your time is not come. Ask yourself how many unhappy hours Keats has caused you in Loneliness. For myself I have been a Martyr the whole time, and for this reason I speak; the confession is forc'd from me by the torture. I appeal to you by the blood of that Christ you believe in: Do not write to me if you have done anything this month which it would have pained me to have seen. You may have altered—if you have not—if you still behave in dancing rooms and other societies as I have seen you—I do not want to live—if you have done so I wish this coming

> night may be my last. I cannot live without you, and not only you but *chaste you; virtuous you.* The Sun rises and sets, the day passes, and you follow the bent of your inclination to a certain extent—you have no conception of the quantity of miserable feeling that passes through me in a day.—Be serious! Love is not a plaything—and again do not write unless you can do it with a crystal conscience. I would sooner die for want of you than—

Fanny must have been beyond indignation at this point, as Ward suggests. Though Keats complains bitterly of her behavior in society, it was no different than his own when he was well. She was in fact waiting faithfully for the chance to see him since he had forbade her to visit him at the Hunt's home. Her trips to town were seen by Keats as sinful or thoughtless binges of self-indulgence. In the most violent of his agonies, he demands: "Do not write to me if you have done anything this month which it would have pained me to have seen." "Be serious!" he cries, "I would sooner die for want of you than—" and is unable or unwilling to complete his last thought.

Like Achilles, Keats knows he is going to die. He can't do anything but suffer, and his suffering tips over into savagery when desire is utterly thwarted. He seems too pure for a world where his closest friend is unloyal, or more likely, unaware of how his actions affect Keats. Each thought and feeling traps him further in the constricted space of writing and living. The pain we feel in reading these letters is due to the knowledge that Keats and Fanny are doomed to part, while absorbed in the presentness of sickness, love, anger, and misunderstanding. And if we judge ourselves guilty witnesses of this moral life, then let it remain central in our imagination as the living substance of love rather than so many charged scenes.

Keats did not write to Fanny until a month later. She apparently wrote to him on August 10, having had no letters since July 5. Through an act of spitefulness on the part of the Hunts' maid, Keats was not given Fanny's letter until August 12. It had been opened and read. Keats supposedly wept for hours and then decided to leave Mortimer Terrace. Before doing so, he may have written his last letter to Fanny that day. The letter is undated, probably the next to last thing Keats ever wrote to his beloved:

My dearest Girl,

I wish I could invent some means to make me at all happy without you. Every hour I am more and more concentrated in you; every thing else tastes like chaff in my Mouth. I feel it almost impossible to go to Italy—the fact is I cannot leave you, and shall never taste one minute's content until it pleases chance to let me live with you for good. But I will not go on at this rate. A person in health as you are can have no conception of the horrors that nerves and a temper like mine go through. What Island do your friends propose retiring to? I should be happy to go with you there alone, but in company I should object to it; the backbitings and jealousies of new colonists who have nothing else to amuse them selves, is unbearable. Mr Dilke came to see me yesterday, and gave me a very great deal more pain than pleasure. I shall never be able any more to endure to society of any of those who used to meet at Elm Cottage and Wentworth Place. The last two years taste like brass upon my Palate. If I cannot live with you I will live alone. I do not think my health will improve much while I am separated from you. For all this I am averse to seeing you—I cannot bear flashes of light and return into my glooms again. I am not so unhappy now as I should be if I had seen you yesterday. To be happy with you seems such an impossibility! it requires a luckier Star than mine! it will never be. I enclose a passage from one of your Letters which I want you to alter a little—I want (if you will have it so) the matter express'd less coldly to me. If my health would bear it, I could write a Poem which I have in my head, which would be a consolation for people in such a situation as mine. I would show some one in Love as I am, with a person living in such Liberty as you do. Shakspeare always sums up matters in the most sovereign manner. Hamlet's heart was full of such Misery as mine is when he said to Ophelia "Go to a Nunnery, go, go!" Indeed I should like to give up the matter at once—I should like to die. I am sickened at the brute world which you are smiling with. I hate men and women more. I see nothing but thorns for the future—wherever I may be next winter in Italy or nowhere Brown will be living near you with his indecencies—I see no prospect of any rest. Suppose me in Rome—well, I should there see you as in a magic glass going to and from town at all hours,——I wish you could infuse a little confidence in human nature into my heart. I cannot muster any—the world is too brutal for me—I am glad there is such a thing as the grave—I am sure I shall never have any rest till I get there At any rate I will indulge myself by never seeing any more Dilke or Brown or any of their Friends. I wish I was either in your a[r]ms full of faith or that a Thunder bolt would strike me.

God bless you—J.K.—

It's almost incredible that Keats returns part of her letter with instructions to "alter" it, that is, express some matter "less coldly to me." Such was his state of mind and soul, especially if he had written this letter following the traumatic discovery of Fanny's opened letter. It is natural that Keats's dying soul should react against that which he believed to be killing it, but there can be no doubt that Fanny never betrayed him. She begged him, in fact, not to leave her. Keats perhaps did not know Fanny as well as he should have. But that is excusable—even his tendency to accuse her unjustly is excusable as the torment of illness and of not having poetry. When his rage of cruelty left him, it left him at the extreme of love, at the very edge of extinction and eternity: "I wish I was either in your arms full of faith or that a Thunder bolt would strike me."

Among several things that resonate in this letter is Keats's remark: "I cannot bear flashes of light and return into my glooms again." He is conscious of the eternal nature of light as hope or truth or love, which like a spirit haunts time, coming and going, a manifestation of the light that gave Dickinson her "heavenly hurt." Both Dickinson and Keats wrote in or from a state of grace, a visionary illumination. And for Keats, the transitory and occasional are all that more gloomy because they forbid pursuit of such things as love. Keats's absolutism, the authority with which he speaks his painful truth here, makes one cringe. Yet his unrelenting perception of the necessary sorrow of life—of what we can see will never be—makes possible, even at the tortured end of his life, a knowledge that is far from diminished.

When Keats left Mortimer Terrace, he may have begun walking directly toward Well Walk, where he and his brothers once lodged, but he ended up at the Brawnes' doorstep. He stayed with them for a month. Late in August, he had a third hemorrhage, which caused his publisher John Taylor to make arrangements to cancel all of Keats's debts to himself and his partner John Hessey. Copyrights of all three books (the *Lamia* volume had been out since July) were bought, advances from 1817 on deducted, and Keats was left with £30 plus £150 to be credited to him in Rome. William Haslam then approached Severn to accompany Keats to Rome. Severn agreed and in other ways helped to make preparations for the voyage. Keats said goodbye to the Brawnes on September 13 and spent the remaining four days in London at Taylor's home before boarding a ship for Italy.

On October 1, 1820 the *Maria Crowther* landed at Lulworth Cove or Holworth Bay off the Dorset coast before sailing out of the English Channel for the open sea the next day. Keats and Severn went ashore and, Severn writes, "For a moment he became like his former self. He was in a part that he already knew, and he showed me some of the splendid caverns and grottos with a poet's pride."[12] Returning to the ship, he wrote down on a blank page of Shakespeare's *Poems* the revised version of the "Bright Star" sonnet to Fanny, which Knight has called Keats's greatest poem "and perhaps the most marvellous short poem in our language":

> Bright star, would I were steadfast as thou art—
> Not in lone splendour hung aloft the night
> And watching, with eternal lids apart,
> Like nature's patient, sleepless eremite,

---

12. William Sharp, *The Life and Letters of Joseph Severn* (New York: Charles Scribner's Sons, 1892), 54.

The moving waters at their priestlike task
 Of pure ablution round earth's human shores,
Or gazing on the new soft-fallen mask
 Of snow upon the mountains and the moors—
No—yet still steadfast, still unchangeable,
 Pillowed upon my fair love's ripening breast,
To feel for ever its soft swell and fall,
 Awake for ever in a sweet unrest,
Still, still to hear her tender-taken breath,
And so live ever—or else swoon to death.[13]

His last words to Fanny were inscribed at the end of a letter to her mother on October 24, 1820: "Good bye Fanny! god bless you."

In the last few months of his life, Keats experienced a total agony of extinction while still in the flesh, a despair that we can still feel in his last letters. Writing to Brown on November 1, 1820, he urged him to come to Rome while speaking of his imminent death: "Oh Brown, I have coals of fire in my breast. It surprised me that the human heart is capable of containing and bearing so much misery. Was I born for this end?" Keats and Severn were in Naples where they had just been released on October 31 from ten days' quarantine about the *Maria Crowther*. During this whole time, the bad air and cramped confines of the cabin they occupied were worse than the entire month-long voyage from England to Italy. Although Keats was alert to the newness of things around him, his existence was more dreamlike than real. The persons he loved most walked in his imagination like ghosts: Tom, his sister, and his beloved Fanny. Fanny's farewell gifts—a traveling cup lined with silk, a paper knife, a lock of her hair, and an oval carnelian—all brought her presence near yet forced despair upon him constantly. He couldn't forget her. He cried to Brown: "I should have had her when I was in health, and I should have

13. Stillinger, 327-328.

remained in health. I can bear to die—I cannot bear to leave her."

On November 30, 1820 Keats wrote to Brown for the last time from his room on the Piazza di Spagna, Rome:

> 'Tis the most difficult thing in the world to me to write a letter. My stomach continues so bad, that I feel it worse on opening any book,—yet I am much better than I was in Quarantine. Then I am afraid to encounter the proing and conning of any thing interesting to me in England. I have an habitual feeling of my real life having past, and that I am leading a posthumous existence. God knows how it would have been—but it appears to me—however, I will not speak of that subject. I must have been at Bedhampton nearly at the time you were writing to me from Chichester—how unfortunate—and to pass on the river too! There was my star predominant! I cannot answer any thing in your letter, which followed me from Naples to Rome, because I am afraid to look it over again. I am so weak (in mind) that I cannot bear the sight of any hand writing of a friend I love so much as I do you. Yet I ride the little horse,—and, at my worst, even in Quarantine, summoned up more puns, in a sort of desperation, in one week than in any year of my life. There is one thought enough to kill me—I have been well, healthy, alert &c, walking with her—and now—the knowledge of contrast, feeling for light and shade, all that information (primitive sense) necessary for a poem are great enemies to the recovery of the stomach. There, you rogue, I put you to the torture,—but you must bring your philosophy to bear—as I do mine, really—or how should I be able to live?

There is more pain than one wants to imagine in his comment about "leading a posthumous existence." But the becalmed dignity of his suffering has a richness of feeling that is seldom found anywhere in literature or life. His remark, "Yet I ride the little horse"—what can it mean but Keats's ambition or desire as a poet? Though it may seem that poetry is an "enemy" to his condition, it never failed or abandoned him. For his letter to Brown has that quality of response, a depth of heart and soul, which is identical to poetry. A poetry of wisdom and spiritual wholeness. I cannot imagine anyone who brought his "philosophy" to bear if Keats did not.

Were it not for the intensity of his love and the vitality of his imagination, even the "one thought enough to kill"—of being "well, healthy, alert &c, walking with her"—would be merely horrible and sad. But Keats's last two years with Fanny changed his life as much as anything before her. Indeed, Fanny changed everything. His letters to her are tense with rearrangements of the world his mind needed to compose. And if they do not invite us, emotionally they do not exclude us either. From first to last, these letters are vital to a full appreciation of a remarkable poet. And as Brown wrote to Fanny, eight years after Keats's death: "His love for you formed so great a part of him [that] we may be doing him an injustice in being silent on it."[14]

---

14. See Jack Stillinger, ed., *The Letters of Charles Armitage Brown* (Cambridge: Harvard University Press, 1966), 296. Letter from Brown to Fanny Brawne, December 17, 1829.

CONCLUSION

Will and Beauty

A life in the poem, or for it, is precisely as one has read it in the lives of others for centuries. But this life for most poets is as difficult to accept as one's own death might be. While the poet supposes it to have been elective, it becomes altogether clear as time passes that if it was in fact a choice, then it was the most unconsidered choice he or she could make, an infinitely extensible error from which he or she can never be free. I do not believe that choice has anything to do with the poet's work: he or she is elected somehow by something as absolute as fate. Hence the practically mystical premium, in the imagination thereafter, on choice of any degree, in any situation—and the anguish of choice thereafter, since one knows in the bones that choice is a chimaera. For the poet, consciousness of this fact is more acute than that of any other because it is wedded to thought itself and to language itself. No other art is so intimate to the self, though now and then one encounters the sort of artist who has the equal depth of recognition. Life comes to one last fact for certain poets: the only possible way to meet that which is so endlessly tragic to know is by writing into it. Writing becomes the only hope or means for a poet. A work of art, a thing which is able to be conceived and liberated by one's own hand, such a thing really is an absolute, whether a poem or a letter. It asks and needs the deeper flow of heart, and *its* recognitions, to make it the thing it is.

Keats's *Letters* constitute that heartflow in the form of a poetics which took shape over the course of a few tragic yet brilliant years. What continually impresses me in reading them is not some image or picture of "the real John Keats," but the meaning and usefulness of his poetics. I would like to close this study (I dare say that Keats can never end for me) by returning to my original question: Do Keats's *Letters,* read as a poetics, help us go beyond the poems? First of all, the *Letters* do contain a great poetics of life, in the broadest possible sense, which developed from Keats's early poetry where beauty and truth are a paramount concern. Out of this twofold unity, Keats apprehended a formal recognition, Negative Capability, relating to the soul's desire in the world. From that point on, his "speculations" yielded not a program but an impetus of life for the labyrinthine ways among which any human being must necessarily proceed. The poetics in the *Letters* —revealing simultaneously how we are here, in the actual world, and also in the real world that shines behind any physical disclosure—is the same poetics that is in the poems.

The liberty of mind, the spaciousness and engagement of thought that I originally proposed as being more available in the letters than in the composition of the poems, seems to me a phenomenon related to the form of the letter. Life often seeks some particular form for its particular needs, whether it be going away to the Isle of Wight for meditation and writing, or gaining insight out of the unexpected experience in the Highlands of Scotland. The poem offers its form too. But the letter for Keats releases a flow that no other form can contain, and such a flow is not by any means simply an emotional torrent. It is an actual fusion of argument and style more often found in the letters than in the poems.

The circumstances of composition in the *Letters* differs from that in the poems very particularly, although in general the poetry in Keats's spirit seems perfectly wedded to his intellectual and emotional resources in either prose or verse. Often when Keats composed a poem he was compelled to go back to it with a new urgency, having in the interim labored on other things that in turn led to quite a different approach and result. *Hyperion,* for example, gave rise to *The Fall of Hyperion* only after the crucial work on the odes. In the *Letters,* one sees these kinds of links vividly on a daily basis. But Keats does not so much return to earlier material as he continues to advance and push beyond the boundaries of a certain preoccupation that is of a piece with and usually forward of the poems. Each letter is a step further in the making of a system. This, it seems to me, is supremely characteristic of the ordered progress M.R. Ridley expounded on nearly sixty years ago.

Throughout his poetic career, Keats had a storehouse of images and concerns that grew richer, deeper, as he labored and selected and distilled them all into a poetry of great beauty and power. In the best of the *Letters,* as in the best of the poems, this poetry expresses his new knowledge of the world always gleaned from his own bittersweet experience. At times, as in the Chamber of Maiden Thought and the Vale of Soul-making letters, the poetry is equal to such high works as the odes and the two *Hyperion* poems. One can never say with any certainty that mysticism characterizes the *Letters* while craftsmanship distinguishes the poems. Both elements are transparent and unflecked in the beauty of all that Keats wrote. One can say from the evidence that the *Letters* are the place where everything converges, though never in some willy-nilly fashion. For Keats shows an amazing discipline. What he disciplines is a function of intellect, whereby imagination renders unto life its own special actions and meanings, and makes of that life something absolute. All this is centered in the creation of a form-language (the poet's music) out of the raw, undeveloped resources of language. In both poems and letters, the discipline of the word interprets the given of life and invokes a devotion to that life, once rightly interpreted and understood.

It may seem that in giving so much attention to the spiritual and imaginative dimensions of Keats's *Letters* I have given short shrift to the social and political. But I've tried to balance my study by detailing, wherever possible, the origin of feelings and the conflicts of one individual writer in whom society's conflicts are present. The letters from Scotland certainly show how society worked on Keats's affections. Moreover, throughout the *Letters,* a constant interweaving occurs between the inner searching world of self and the outer harsh world of circumstance. Indeed, Keats's poetic statements can be seen as attempts to give strength to humanity and "lift the thoughts of men," as he proposed in *Endymion,* so that they might see life more clearly and adopt a fuller attitude toward it. This is at once a social and a cosmological process. My belief is that Keats's ideas are neither wholly the product of historical conditions nor of some reality wholly independent of history. The crucial achievement of the *Letters* is the fusion of the world and self, resulting in freshness, possibility, and grace.

Douglas Bush said of Keats that there was no one better able among his close circle of distinguished friends to give advice, encouragement, and consolation than the young, so-called uneducated, five-foot Cockney lad who knew how to live in the body and know the world by direct intercourse and sympathy. Keats's poetics expresses a concern for any human being to learn how to relate to himself, to others, and to the world. His propositions, so seldom taken in their pedagogical emphases, are generous if rigorous ways of teaching, giving pleasure, and consoling. In our estimation of the *Letters,* we ought not fail to consider that Keats believed ardently in his imaginative action. He not only envisioned a poetic career modeled after Milton, a learned poet who worked from lyric to epic, who had something to say, and who was not limited to his personal disposition. He also showed the intensity of a career in its care and attention to things in the universe, in its risk, knowing, and selection of things which concern a union of will and beauty. Few careers have managed so much in so little time.

The Book of the Heart, Keats's *Letters,* is always open for me. I would like to say finally, and as briefly as possible, how Keats's example works as a ferment in the life of one born a hundred and fifty years later, in the midwestern United States, to a Mexican American background. I know from Keats that the intensity and form of identity is intrinsic, that is, essential to life, beyond one's origin in any particular class or race, and it is absolutely tied to vocation. Yet all the details of life (Cockney English, Mexican American, working class, and so on) are also what anyone has to work with, and one must not despair that there is ultimately no comprehensive expression of identity, because there is. It's what a very wise friend of mine calls *"el son entero."* An inner music or spiritual song. Identity is so enormous, in time and space and spirit, that a Keats or a Blake or an Olson, finally, can merely suggest it or point at it. I happen to believe that the question of identity is hemispheric, even global. But this is only what I believe. Nevertheless, everything that has happened to me, everything I've done, everything happening to me now, is *the* work. One must always be working on life, and whether we call such work soul-making or something else it remains a work necessary to existence. Although existence sometimes feels like a box, all that is in that box is all one needs and all one ever wanted. It only needs to be worked, and as it is worked the world opens into something so big one would need a thousand lifetimes to learn the least bit of it. We are all fooled by the tangle of identity as if we were wandering in a Spenserian forest of error. But error is not anything else but what we do, except when we are not doing it. It seems to me that one must permit an arrogance of the fact of this work of identity in order to learn anything at all. For there is always something that can be intensely complicated right in front of oneself, like every single day and night. And none of it is to hate, deny, or be embarrassed about. It is all who we are.

Keats tried to make a world out of all he had to work with, out of all he needed to know, and without embarrassment. He needed to know the limit. And he was absolutely fearless in his pursuit of this course. For seeing the limit matters. It is like seeing the proverbial light, which then elevates everything into a dimension upon which to build. What I love about Keats is that everything in the poems and in the letters is *inside* of him. He is much like Shakespeare, whom he loved, in that respect.

What Keats teaches us, in the late twentieth century, is that all we really have or possess is what is inside ourselves, especially a faith that must be commensurate to all that is and has been and will be outside ourselves. Such a faith can seem desperate, given harsh circumstance or the sheer difficulty of penetrating the depths or many masks of identity. How long it often seems to take for identity to find its own simple form! But until one really gives oneself over to one's faith, one scarcely realizes what one knows. This is not a matter of individual greatness, though Keats was undoubtedly a great artist and human being. It is a question of anyone interpreting both the inner and outer cosmos.

In the Chamber of Maiden Thought letter, Keats said that there really is a grand progression of the intellect. But intellect for Keats was not divorced from the soul. From our vantage point in time, what we have seen is the continual separation of the two, resulting in more monstrous versions of what Keats had perceived and named "the Man of Power." Such men today cover the earth, influencing others to follow in their steps. That way is one of destruction, with all the problems of nationalism and imperialism and racism, and now with threats to existence inconceivable in Keats's time. So reading Keats's letters has more significance now than ever before. They are timely—evidence of genuine spiritual work of the kind humanity is sorely lacking. Indeed, *soul-making*, like *civility*, is currently not in our lexicon.

It is a *time* we are all living in. A *world* is only the real thing when it is like what we find in Keats or Homer or García Márquez. Keats felt he was living in a barbaric time. It seems to me we still are. But time is the same thing as the heart when it is understood to have or yield love as its mathematic. The real sympathesis, the true healing among us, is love, which is the presence of the Whole Heart. Heart is everything.

SELECTED BIBLIOGRAPHY

I. Texts: Letters and Poems

Barnard, John, ed. *John Keats: The Complete Poems*. New York: Penguin, 1973.

Colvin, Sidney, ed. *Letters of John Keats to His Family and Friends*. London: Macmillan, 1891.

De Selincourt, Ernest, ed. *The Poems of John Keats*. 5th edition. London: Methuen, 1926.

Edgcrumbe, Fred, ed. *Letters of Fanny Brawne to Fanny Keats 1820-1824*. New York: Oxford University Press, 1937.

Forman, Harry Buxton, ed. *The Letters of John Keats*. 2nd edition. New York: Oxford University Press, 1935.

——. *The Poetical Works and Other Writings of John Keats*. [Hampstead edition] 8 vols. New York: Charles Scribner's Sons, 1938-1939.

Forman, Maurice Buxton, ed. *The Letters of John Keats*. 4th edition. London: Oxford University Press, 1952.

Garrod, H.W., ed. *The Poetical Works of John Keats*. London: Oxford University Press, 1976.

Gittings, Robert. *The Letters of John Keats*. London: Oxford University Press, 1970.

Rollins, Hyder E., ed. *The Keats Circle: Letters and Papers 1816-1878*. 2 vols. Cambridge: Harvard University Press, 1948.

——. *The Letters of John Keats 1814-1821*. 2 vols. Cambridge: Harvard University Press, 1958.

——. *More Letters and Poems of the Keats Circle*. Cambridge: Harvard University Press, 1955.

Sharp, William, ed. *The Life and Letters of Joseph Severn*. New York: Charles Scribner's Sons, 1892.

Stillinger, Jack, ed. *John Keats: Poetry Manuscripts at Harvard, A Facsimile Edition*. With an Essay on the Manuscripts by Helen Vendler. Cambridge: The Belknap Press, 1990.

——. *The Letters of Charles Armitage Brown*. Cambridge: Harvard University Press, 1966.

——. *The Poems of John Keats*. Cambridge: The Belknap Press, 1978.

——. *The Texts of Keats's Poems*. Cambridge: Harvard University Press, 1974.

II. Other Epistolary Texts

Burns, Robert. *The Letters of Robert Burns.* Edited from the original manuscripts by J. De Lancey Ferguson. 2 vols. Oxford: The Clarendon Press, 1931.

Byron, George Gordon. *Letters and Journals.* Edited by Leslie A. Marchand. 12 vols. Cambridge: The Belknap Press, 1976-1982.

Dickinson, Emily. *The Letters of Emily Dickinson.* Edited by Thomas H. Johnson. 3 vols. Cambridge: The Belknap Press, 1958.

García Lorca, Federico. *Selected Letters.* Edited and translated by David Gershator. New York: New Directions, 1983.

Gramsci, Antonio. *Letters from Prison.* Selected, translated, and introduced by Lynne Lawner. New York: Harper and Row, 1973.

Hopkins, Gerard Manley. *Further Letters of Gerard Manley Hopkins.* Edited by Claude Colleer Abbott. London: Oxford University Press, 1956.

Johnson, Samuel. *The Letters of Samuel Johnson.* Edited by R.W. Chapman. 3 vols. Oxford: The Clarendon Press, 1952.

Lawrence, D.H. *Selected Letters.* Edited with an introduction by Diana Trilling. New York: Farrar, Straus, and Cudahy [1958].

Olson, Charles. *Mayan Letters.* Preface by Robert Creeley. Mallorca: The Divers Press, 1953.

Pound, Ezra. *The Selected Letters of Ezra Pound 1907-1941.* Edited by D.D. Paige. New York: New Directions, 1971.

Williams, William Carlos. *Selected Letters of William Carlos Williams.* Edited with an introduction by John C. Thirwall. New York: McDowell, Obolensky, 1957.

Wordsworth, William. *The Love Letters of William and Mary Wordsworth.* Edited by Beth Darlington. Ithaca: Cornell University Press, 1981.

III. Secondary Sources

Abrams, M.H. *The Mirror and the Lamp: Romantic Theory and the Critical Tradition.* London: Oxford University Press, 1953.

Alighieri, Dante. *The Divine Comedy.* Translated by John D. Sinclair. New York: Oxford University Press, 1939.

Apuleius, Lucius. *The Golden Ass.* Translated by Robert Graves. New York: Farrar, Straus and Giroux, 1951.

Aristotle. "Poetica (Poetics)." *Introduction to Aristotle.* Edited, with a general introduction and introductions to the particular works, by Richard McKeon. New York: The Modern Library, 1947.

Baker, Jeffrey. *John Keats and Symbolism.* Sussex: Harvester Press; New York: St. Martin's Press, 1986.

Barnard, John. *John Keats.* Cambridge: Cambridge University Press, 1986.

Barthes, Roland. *A Lover's Discourse: Fragments.* Translated by Richard Howard. New York: Hill and Wang, 1978.

Selected Bibliography

Bate, W.J. *John Keats.* Cambridge: Harvard University Press, 1963.

Benjamin, Walter. *Illuminations: Essays and Reflections.* Edited with an introduction by Hannah Arendt. New York: Schocken Books, 1969.

Berger, Harry, Jr. *Second World and Green World: Studies in Renaissance Fiction-Making.* Berkeley: University of California Press, 1988.

Blake, William. *The Complete Poetry and Prose of William Blake.* Edited by David V. Erdman. Los Angeles: University of California Press, 1982.

Bloom, Harold. *Romanticism and Consciousness.* New York: W.W. Norton, 1970.

——.*Visionary Company: A Reading of English Romantic Poetry.* Garden City, N.Y.: Doubleday, 1961.

Buber, Martin. *I and Thou.* Translated by Walter Kaufmann. New York: Charles Scribner's Sons, 1970.

Burke, Kenneth. *A Grammar of Motives.* Los Angeles: University of California Press, 1969.

——. *Language as Symbolic Action: Essays on Life, Literature, and Method.* Los Angeles: University of California Press, 1966.

Bush, Douglas. *John Keats: His Life and Writings.* New York: Macmillan, 1966.

Caldwell, James R. *John Keats' Fancy: The Effect on Keats of the Psychology of His Day.* New York: Octagon Books, 1972.

Clarke, John. *From Feathers To Iron: A Concourse of World Poetics.* San Francisco: Tombouctou/Convivio, 1987.

Coleridge, Samuel Taylor. *The Collected Works of Samuel Taylor Coleridge.* General editor, Kathleen Coburn. 14 vols. Princeton: Princeton University Press, 1968-1981.

Corbin, Henry. *Avicenna and the Visionary Recital.* Translated by Ralph Manheim. Princeton: Princeton University Press, 1960.

——. *Creative Imagination in the Sufism of Ibn 'Arabi.* Translated by Ralph Manheim. Princeton: Princeton University Press, 1969.

——. *Temple and Contemplation.* Translated by Philip Sherrard. London: Islamic Publications, 1986.

Crossan, John Dominic. *The Dark Interval: Towards a Theology of Story.* Allen, Tex.: Argus Communications, 1975.

D'Avanzo, Mario. *Keats's Metaphors for the Poetic Imagination.* Durham: Duke University Press, 1967.

De Man, Paul. "The Negative Road." *John Keats: Modern Critical Views.* Edited by Harold Bloom. New York: Chelsea House, 1985.

——. *The Rhetoric of Romanticism.* New York: Columbia University Press, 1984.

De Santillana, Giorgio and Hertha von Dechend. *Hamlet's Mill: An Essay on Myth and the Frame of Time.* Boston: Gambit, 1969.

Di Piero, W.S. *Memory and Enthusiasm: Essays 1975-1985.* Princeton: Princeton University Press, 1989.

——. *Out of Eden: Essays on Modern Art.* Berkeley: University of California Press, 1991.

Dickinson, Emily. *The Complete Poems of Emily Dickinson.* Edited by Thomas H. Johnson. Boston: Little, Brown and Company, 1957.

Dickstein, Morris. *Keats and His Poetry: A Study of Development.* Chicago: University of Chicago Press, 1971.

Duncan, Robert. "Why 'Poetics'?" *Program in Poetics* (college catalog). San Francisco: New College of California, 1982.

Eliot, T.S. *The Use of Poetry and the Use of Criticism.* London: Faber and Faber, 1933.

Emerson, Ralph Waldo. *The Complete Works of Ralph Waldo Emerson.* Edited by Edward Waldo Emerson. 12 vols. Boston: Houghton Mifflin, 1903-1904.

Finney, Claude Lee. *The Evolution of Keats's Poetry.* 2 vols. Cambridge: Harvard University Press, 1936.

Fleming, Ray. *Keats, Leopardi, and Hölderlin: The Poet as Priest of the Absolute.* New York: Garland Publishing, Inc., 1987.

Frye, Northrop. *A Study of English Romanticism.* Chicago: University of Chicago Press, 1968.

García Lorca, Federico. *Deep Song and Other Prose.* Edited and translated by Christopher Maurer. New York: New Directions, 1980.

Gittings, Robert. *The Keats Inheritance.* New York: Barnes and Noble, 1965.

——. *John Keats: The Living Year, 21 September 1818 to 21 September 1819.* Cambridge: Harvard University Press, 1954.

——. *The Mask of Keats.* Cambridge: Harvard University Press, 1956.

Graves, Robert. *The White Goddess: A Historical Grammar of Poetic Myth.* New York: The Noonday Press, 1948.

Harrington, Michael. *The Other America: Poverty in the United States.* New York: Macmillan, 1963.

Hartman, Geoffrey H. *The Unremarkable Wordsworth.* Foreword by Donald G. Marshall. Minneapolis: University of Minnesota Press, 1987.

Heaney, Seamus. *Preoccupations: Selected Prose 1968-1978.* New York: Farrar, Straus, Giroux, 1980.

The Holy Bible. King James Version 1611. New York: Amerian Bible Society, 1984.

Homer. *The Iliad.* Translated by Richmond Lattimore. Chicago: University of Chicago Press, 1951.

——. *The Odyssey.* Translated by Richmond Lattimore. Chicago: University of Chicago Press, 1967.

Hyde, Lewis. *The Gift: Imagination and the Erotic Life of Property.* New York: Vintage Books, 1979.

Jack, Ian. *Keats and the Mirror of Art.* Oxford: The Clarendon Press, 1967.

James, William. *The Varieties of Religious Experience.* New York: The Modern Library, 1936.

Johnson, W.R. *The Idea of Lyric: Lyric Modes in Ancient and Modern Poetry.* Berkeley: University of California Press, 1982.

Jones, John. *The Egotistical Sublime: A History of Wordsworth's Imagination.* London: Chatto and Windus, 1960.

——. *John Keats' Dream of Truth*. London: Chatto and Windus, 1969.

Kazin, Alfred. "Rome: A Meditation." *Contemporaries: From the 19th Century to the Present*. New York: Horizon Press, 1982.

Kerényi, Karoli. *Dionysos: Archetypal Image of Indestructible Life*. Translated by Ralph Manheim. Princeton: Princeton University Press, 1976.

Knight, G. Wilson. *The Starlit Dome: Studies in the Poetry of Vision*. London: Methuen, 1964.

Kucich, Greg. "The Poetry of Mind in Keats's Letters." *Style* 21, 1 (Spring 1987), 76-94.

Leopardi, Giacomo. *Pensieri*. Translated by W.S. Di Piero. New York: Oxford University Press, 1984.

Levinson, Marjorie. *The Origins of Keats's Style: A Life of Allegory*. London: Basil Blackwell, 1988.

Lings, Martin. *The Secret of Shakespeare*. New York: Inner Traditions International [1984].

Lovell, Ernest J. and John Clubbe. "Keats the Humanist." *The Kentucky Review* 3, 2 (1982), 3-18.

Lucretius, Titus Carus. *On the Nature of the Universe*. Translated and introduced by R.E. Latham. New York: Viking Penguin, 1951.

McGann, Jerome. "Keats and the Historical Method in Literary Criticism." *MLN* 94 (1979), 988-1032.

——. *The Romantic Ideology: A Critical Investigation*. Chicago: University of Chicago Press, 1981.

McLeod, Randall. "Editing Shakespeare." *Sub-Stance* 33/34 (1982), 26-55.

McNaughton, Duncan. "Love Triumphant: Meditations on Shakespeare's *Sonnets*." Dissertation. State University of New York at Buffalo, 1973.

Maurer, Margaret. "The Poetical Familiarity of John Donne's Letters." *Genre* 15, 2-3 (Spring-Summer 1982), 183-202.

Mayhead, Robin. *John Keats*. Cambridge: Cambridge University Press, 1967.

Mellor, Anne K. "Chapter 3: Keats and the Vale of Soul-Making." *English Romantic Irony*. Cambridge: Harvard University Press, 1980.

Milton, John. *The Complete Poems and Major Prose of John Milton*. Edited by Merritt Y. Hughes. Indianapolis: The Odyssey Press, 1957.

Neumann, Erich. *Amor and Psyche: The Psychic Development of the Feminine*. Translated by Ralph Manheim. Princeton: Princeton University Press, 1960.

Nietzsche, Friedrich. *The Birth of Tragedy*. Translated, with commentary, by Walter Kaufmann. New York: Vintage Books, 1967.

——. *The Genealogy of Morals*. Translated, edited, with commentary, by Walter Kaufmann. New York: Vintage Books, 1967.

Olson, Charles. *Charles Olson at Mansfield: Last Lectures*. Transcribed and edited by John Cech et al. Boston: Northeastern University Press, 1978.

——. *Poetry and Truth: The Beloit Lectures and Poems*. Transcribed and edited by George F. Butterick. San Francisco: Four Seasons Foundation, 1971.

——. *The Special View of History*. Edited with an introduction by Anne Charters. Berkeley: Oyez, 1970.

Pack, Robert. "Keats's Letters: Laughter as Autobiography." *New England Review and Bread Loaf Quarterly* 7, 2 (Winter 1984), 175-191.

Pagels, Elaine. *Adam, Eve, and the Serpent*. New York: Vintage Books, 1989.

Patrides, C.A. "The Epistolary Art of the Renaissance: The Biblical Premises." *Philological Quarterly* 60, 3 (Summer 1981), 357-367.

Perkins, David. *The Quest for Permanence: The Symbolism of Wordsworth, Shelley and Keats*. Cambridge: Cambridge University Press, 1959.

Plato. *The Dialogues of Plato*. Translated into English with Analyses and Introductions by B. Jowett. 5 vols. London: Oxford University Press, 1931.

Prynne, J.H. "English Poetry and Emphatical Language." *Proceedings of the British Academy* LXXIV (1988), 135-169.

Redford, Bruce. *The Converse of the Pen: Acts of Intimacy in the Eighteenth-Century Familiar Letter*. Chicago: University of Chicago Press, 1986.

Rees, Joan. *Bright Star: The Story of John Keats and Fanny Brawne*. London: Harrap, 1968.

Richardson, Joanna. *Fanny Brawne: A Biography*. New York: Vanguard Press, 1952.

Ridley, M.R. *Keats' Craftsmanship: A Study in Poetic Development*. Oxford: The Clarendon Press, 1933.

The Romantics Reviewed: Contemporary Reviews of British Romantic Writers. Part C: Shelley, Keats, and London Radical Writers. 2 vols. Edited, with introductions, by Donald H. Reiman. New York: Garland Publishing Company, 1972.

Rueckert, William S. "Literary Criticism and History: The Endless Dialectic." *NHL* 6 (1974-1975), 491-512.

Ryan, Robert M. *Keats: The Religious Sense*. Princeton: Princeton University Press, 1976.

Schein, Seth L. *The Mortal Hero: An Introduction to Homer's Iliad*. Berkeley: University of California Press, 1984.

Seznac, Jean. *The Survival of the Pagan Gods*. Translated by Barbara F. Sessions. Princeton: Princeton University Press, 1953.

Shakespeare, William. *The Arden Shakespeare*. General Editors, Harold F. Brooks, Harold Jenkins and Brian Morris. London: Methuen, 1960.

Shelley, Percy Bysshe. *Shelley's Poetry and Prose*. Edited by Donald H. Reiman and Sharon B. Powers. New York: W.W. Norton, 1977.

Sperry, Stuart. *Keats the Poet*. Princeton: Princeton University Press, 1970.

Stillinger, Jack. *The Hoodwinking of Madelein and Other Essays on Keats' Poems*. Urbana: University of Illinois Press, 1971.

Storm, Hyemeyohsts. *Seven Arrows*. New York: Harper and Row, 1972.

Thoreau, Henry David. *Walden and Civil Disobedience*. Edited by Owen Thomas. New York: W.W. Norton, 1966.

Thorpe, Clarence. *The Mind of John Keats*. New York: Russell and Russell, 1964.

Trilling, Lionel. "The Poet as Hero: Keats in His Letters." *The Opposing Self: Nine Essays in Criticism.* New York: Harcourt, Brace, Jovanovich, 1979.

——. *Sincerity and Authenticity.* Cambridge: Harvard University Press, 1972.

Vendler, Helen. "Keats and the Use of Poetry." *The Music of What Happens.* Cambridge: Harvard University Press, 1988.

——. "The Living Hand of Keats." *John Keats: Poetry Manuscripts at Harvard, A Facsimile.* Edited by Jack Stillinger. Cambridge: The Belknap Press, 1990.

-----. *The Odes of John Keats.* Cambridge: The Belknap Press, 1983.

Vergilius, Publius Maro. *The Aeneid.* Translated by Robert Fitzgerald. New York: Vintage Books, 1984.

Vogler, Thomas A. "Keats: In the Interim." *Prelude to Vision: The Epic Venture in Blake, Wordsworth, Keats, and Hart Crane.* Berkeley: University of California Press, 1971.

Ward, Aileen. *John Keats: The Making of a Poet.* Revised edition. New York: Farrar, Straus, Giroux, 1986.

Wasserman, Earl R. *The Finer Tone: Keats' Major Poems.* Baltimore: Johns Hopkins University Press, 1953.

Whigham, Frank. "The Rhetoric of Elizabethan Suitors' Letters." *PMLA* 96, 5 (October 1981), 864-882.

Williams, William Carlos. *I Wanted to Write a Poem.* Reported and edited by Edith Heal. New York: New Directions, 1978.

-----. *Selected Essays of William Carlos Williams.* New York: New Directions, 1969.

Wilson, Katherine M. *The Nightingale and the Hawk: A Psychological Study of Keats' Ode.* New York: Barnes and Noble, 1964.

Wolfson, Susan J. "Keats the Letter-Writer: Epistolary Poetics." *Romanticism Past and Present* 6, 2 (1982), 43-61.

——. *The Questioning Presence: Wordsworth, Keats, and the Interrogative Mode in Romantic Poetry.* Ithaca: Cornell University Press, 1986.

Wordsworth, William. *The Poetical Works of William Wordsworth.* Edited by Ernest de Selincourt. 5 vols. Oxford: The Clarendon Press, 1940-1949.

Wright, Susan. "Private Language Made Public: The Language of Letters as Literature." *Poetics* 18, 6 (December 1989), 549-578.

Yeats, W.B. *Autobiographies: Reveries of Childhood and The Trembling of the Veil.* New York: Macmillan, 1927.

——. *The Collected Poems of W.B. Yeats.* New York: Macmillan, 1933.

Zillman, Lawrence John. *John Keats and the Sonnet Tradition: A Critical and Comparative Study.* New York: Octagon Books, 1970.

INDEX